'A book of positively encyclopaedic range. Before her lie the great prairies of feminine experience between 1500 and 1760, and she chugs across these expanses like a combine harvester, leaving each topic – sex, life-expectancy, marriage, children, labour, religion, crime – neatly bundled and stacked in her wake. Literacy and lesbians, nuns and needlework: they are all treated here. Ambitious in scope, and refreshingly undoctrinaire in tone, *Women in England* is the best general introduction to the subject yet to appear, and deserves to be widely read.' John Adamson, *Sunday Telegraph*

'A rich and varied picture of the experiences which women were allowed within the confines of their social positions. And it is in the wealth of anecdotal and incidental detail which underpins and illuminates the book that is perhaps its greatest appeal.' Greg Walker, *History Today*

'To her eternal credit, Anne Laurence has broken the moulds of both "victim" and "heroine" history, and presented us with a marvellously rich and fresh survey of English women from the reformation to the dawn of the industrial revolution ... She offers us far more than a history of women: sections on crime, custom, popular culture, the family and so forth provide a broad and balanced portrait of pre-industrial England at large ... *Women in England* affords a panorama of society, showing women young and old, at work and prayer, engaged in production and reproduction.' Roy Porter, *Sunday Times*

'This is social history at its best, not the ideal world reflected in the law, in admonitory guidebooks and ... in contemporary literature ... a readable and humane text ... she writes about our women ancestors as they themselves spoke, in plain English.' Professor Joyce Ewings, *Social History Society Bulletin*

ANNE LAURENCE studied history at the Universities of York and Oxford. She has worked at the Open University since 1976, where she is a Senior Lecturer in History. Her earliest research was on the English Civil War. She has worked on Anglo-Irish relations and on women in Scotland, Ireland and Wales in the seventeenth century, on which she has broadcast and written articles and reviews. She is currently working on a comparative study of women in the British Isles and on a book on women and building in seventeenth century England. She recently completed an Open University course and TV series on France and the British Isles in the seventeenth century.

WOMEN IN ENGLAND

1500–1760

A Social History

Anne Laurence

A PHOENIX GIANT PAPERBACK

First published in Great Britain
by Weidenfeld & Nicolson in 1994
This paperback edition published in 1996
by Phoenix, a division of Orion Books Ltd,
Orion House, 5 Upper St Martin's Lane,
London WC2H 9EA

A CIP catalogue record for this book
is available from the British Library.

ISBN 1 85799 734 4

Printed and bound in Great Britain by
Butler & Tanner Ltd, Frome and London

Contents

v

Contents

Part III. Women's Material Worlds

Contents

Contents

Part V. Women and Men's Worlds

Illustrations

Teresia Lady Shirley (*National Trust Photographic Library/J. Whitaker*)

Pocahontas (*British Library, London*)

Jane Ebbrell, spider brusher at Erdigg (*National Trust Photographic Library*)

Mrs Mary Honeywood (*Lincoln Cathedral Library*)

Harvesters at Dixton, Gloucestershire (*Cheltenham Art Gallery*)

Dairymaids at Charlton Park (*Cheltenham Art Gallery*)

Weston Park, Shropshire

Elizabeth Wilbraham

The Countess of Arundel (*National Portrait Gallery, London*)

Mary Beale (*National Portrait Gallery, London*)

The Duchess of Portland's collection (*British Library, London*)

Flower painting by Mrs Delany (*British Museum, London*)

Mary Ward (*The Bar Convent Museum, York*)

Preface

This book is an attempt to look at the experience of women and at the variety in their lives in early modern England. It is not representative: childbirth, something which millions of women experienced in the period, does not rate proportionately more space than nuns and religious vocations, an experience which only a few thousand women underwent. What I have tried to do is to give some idea of the kinds of life which women from a variety of different circumstances might have had and the ways in which their expectations might have changed between 1500 and 1760. Much of the material is about women who have no names, but this does not make it less valuable.

This book is also concerned with the debates between social and economic historians which bear upon the history of women and which have shaped the kinds of research done on the circumstances in which women in early modern England lived. Scholars in other disciplines, notably literature, have been concerned with attitudes towards women and women's own attitudes, but their work concentrates upon literate people. In all this my guiding principle has been to try to answer the question: in what ways and for what reasons did women's lives change between 1500 and 1760? Women's experience (and not just the gynaecological and obstetrical) was fundamentally different from men's, and it is this consideration which has shaped the book.

Of course, there were great differences between the lives and experiences of individual women: their class, whether they were married, where they lived and their religion all determined the kinds of life they led. So the book is about variety and difference in women's lives, as well as shared and common experiences. It is also about men's experiences in relation to women. There was equally little escape for men and women from an unhappy marriage, though the double standard of sexual conduct and the lack of contraception meant that women were much less free to engage in extra-marital sexual liaisons than men. Illness took men and women indiscriminately, though the risks of accidental death and occupational illness were generally greater for men, while women suffered the problems of repeated child-bearing.

Wherever possible I have tried to illustrate my remarks with examples, but I cannot pretend that the women who appear on these pages are necessarily typical. The mere fact that they have entered the record may make them untypical. However, it is becoming increasingly clear that while women in, for example, public office were very unusual, there were many areas of life, such as the lower-level church and magistrate's courts, where women appeared as a matter of course.

What then was unique about women's lives, apart from their strictly reproductive functions? Their restriction to the household (and the restriction of the household itself) was perhaps the most important because it limited their social contacts, confined their economic activities to a circle dictated by men, and gave them all the problems associated with work to which there is no particular beginning and no particular end. The development of the household in which women did little but control the domestic arrangements gave them the opportunity to shine at being good housewives and managers, but deprived them of the opportunity to do anything else.

This study deals with a period covered by many works of social history: the Reformation to the industrial revolution. Historians of women are increasingly aware that accepted schemes of periodization do not necessarily fit the changes which took place over the long term in women's lives. Processes and events which advanced men's development may well have had different or even contrary effects on women. Liberation for men from anciently established constraints did not necessarily have the same consequence for women.

Did the Reformation and the industrial revolution actually introduce into women's lives the kinds of discontinuity which they produced in men's? Did the Reformation and the industrial revolution change women's lives, and if so, did either of them do so for the better? Is this even an apt time-span for considering the history of women, or were there other, more important turning points which mean that we should be looking at women according to a different timetable? I think we probably should, but it is a much longer time-span than that into which even social history is conventionally divided. The history of women is a rather more seamless garment than many other people's history.

This book may strike the reader as being parochial in its restriction to England. It is a work of synthesis and there is a large literature on the social history of England which has no equivalent for Scotland, Wales or Ireland. The literature on women in early modern England grows apace, certainly at a vastly greater speed that that for Scotland, Wales and Ireland. In the early modern period Scotland and Ireland were more separate culturally, legally and politically than they were to become in the nineteenth century. There were also marked differences within England and in countries and regions like Wales, the Isle of Man and the Channel Islands. I have tried to examine some of the differences to be found within England both between regions and between the English and other groups to be found living in England.

The book is organized in thematic sections. The first part sets the history of women in its present-day context and looks at the position of women in the population of early modern England. The second looks at women's relationships with other people. The third considers women's physical and material circumstances: their health, their working lives and the things they used, made and bought. The fourth part is concerned with women's mental worlds, and the fifth with the absence and presence of women in those aspects of life concerned with public power relations and dominated by men: politics and the law.

Some chapters (such as Chapters 3 and 15) or parts of chapters deal with technical or statistical subjects. These may be omitted by general readers.

Acknowledgements

In the writing of this book many people have been extremely helpful, sometimes unwittingly. I would like to thank the following: Gerald Aylmer, Rosalin Barker, Dianne Barr, Tim Benton, Michael Bennett, Trish Crawford, Valeria Taylor (Drake), John Gingell, Helen C. Gladstone, Sister Gregory of the IBVM, Ena Halmos, Maggie Hanbury, Lorna Hardwick, Joanna Innes, Henrietta Leyser, Catherine King, D. R. Laurence, Peter Laslett, Sara Heller Mendelson, Susan O'Brien, Margaret Pelling, Thea Randall, Robert Philip, Marie Rowlands, the Revd A. T. J. Salter and Paul Slack.

I am particularly grateful to Cicely Palser Havely, Arthur Marwick, Mary Prior and Frank Thackray for encouragement as well as advice.

I am grateful for permission to quote from the following material: the Bradford papers in the Staffordshire County Record Office; the State Papers in the Public Record Office; and manuscripts in the National Library of Scotland and the British Library.

A Note on Dates and Prices

In the text the following periods and reigns are referred to:

Early modern period, early sixteenth century to late eighteenth century.

Henry VII reigned 1485–1509, married to Elizabeth of York who died 1503.

Henry VIII reigned 1509–47, married to Catherine of Aragon, divorced 1533, she died 1536; Anne Boleyn, executed 1536; Jane Seymour, died 1537; Anne of Cleves, divorced 1540, she died 1557; Catherine Howard, executed 1542; Catherine Parr, she died 1548.

Reformation, 1530s and early 1540s.

Edward VI reigned 1547–53.

Mary Tudor reigned 1553–8, married to Philip II of Spain who died 1598.

Elizabeth reigned 1558–1603.

James VI and I reigned over England 1603–25, married to Anne of Denmark who died 1619.

Charles I reigned 1625–49, married to Henrietta Maria of France who died 1669.

Civil War, 1642–8

Interregnum, 1649–60

Restoration, 1660

Charles II reigned 1660–85, married to Catherine of Braganza who died 1705.

James II reigned 1685–8, died 1701, married to Anne Hyde who died 1671; Mary of Modena who died 1718.

Glorious Revolution, 1688

William III and Mary of Orange 1688–1702 (Mary died 1694).

Anne 1702–14, married to Prince George of Denmark who died 1708.

George I reigned 1714–27, married Sophia Dorothea of Brunswick, divorced 1694, she died 1726.

George II reigned 1727–60, married to Caroline of Anspach who died 1737.

George III reigned 1760–1820, married Charlotte of Mecklenburg who died 1818.

Industrial revolution, 1760s to 1830s.

Dates

The year is taken as beginning on 1 January, though until 1751 it began on 25 March.

Money

Prices are given in the currency of the time (though in the earlier part of the period there were also various other denominations in use, like the mark). I have not attempted to give modern equivalents because it is difficult to compare modern prices with those in a pre-industrial economy, especially as wage rates have a rather different meaning when payment may be partly in kind or in the form of board and lodging.

£1 = 100p = 20 shillings = 240d. (old pennies)
5p = 1 shilling = 12d. (old pennies)
1p = 2.4d. (old pennies)
1 mark = 13s. 4d. = 67p.

PART ONE

Women in History

CHAPTER ONE

Introduction: Women and the Historians

Some historians have neglected women entirely; others have sought to demonstrate with missionary zeal that feminism has always existed and that the purpose of history is to tell the story of women's continuing oppression. Most historical disciplines now consider it necessary to include women, and women have formed the subject of a number of recent historical debates. This chapter looks at how women have fared at the hands of historians.

Hidden from History

The term 'hidden from history' is used when the history of a hitherto neglected group begins to appear: as, for example, in the case of black history, women's history, lesbian and gay history and, most recently, the history of gypsies and travelling people.[1] The phrase is not simply used to describe the group's emergence into mainstream history: it also has an explicit message that these groups have lacked a history because society has been unwilling to see them as a separate group with particular rights. If a group does not exist, it can have no rights; equally, it can have no past and no history. Historians often accept these judgements, especially when they depend upon written sources generated by the rich, the powerful and the literate. Groups hidden from history are hidden for three reasons. They are hidden because of prejudices against the group in the past; because of modern prejudices; and because of the absence of records.

[1] Sheila Rowbotham, *Hidden from History: 300 Years of Women's Oppression and the Fight against It*, Pluto Press, 1973; Martin Bauml Duberman, Martha Vicinus and George Chauncey, Jr (eds), *Hidden from History: Reclaiming the Gay and Lesbian Past*, Penguin, 1991.

Women have been concealed from view by historical prejudices which excluded them from exercising power in public; from participating in public arenas; and from gaining access to education and the church, both of which provided men with a powerful voice. The modern prejudice which has done much to conceal women is the taking of a view of the past which gives greatest weight to people exercising power and doing things, and to forces of dynamism and change in society. Some historians do not consider ordinary life to be a proper subject for historical study. They also neglect 'unsuccessful' developments, movements and groups, despite the fact these may provide great insight into the societies in which they did not succeed. In this kind of history men's experience is considered to be universal and representative of the human condition in the past: women's experience is merely measured against it. History books are shaped by the passage of men's lives: women are the 'other'. Men's lives are dynamic and women's are passive. As for the absence of sources, once women are included in the scheme of things, it becomes evident that there is not such a paucity of sources as at first appears.

Historians who work to uncover the history of previously hidden groups have concerns which are shaped by contemporary issues. The historians who brought women out into the open in the 1970s were concerned with women's rights, and their work was shaped to a large extent by the search for the origins of feminism. They concentrated upon the nineteenth and twentieth centuries, particularly upon the origins of the feminist movement in general and demands for female suffrage in particular. They formulated the issues which it was felt the history of women should address: patriarchy; nature and perceptions of nature; women's work and the reliance of women on wage labour; and the exploitation of women by manufacturing industry – concerns central to the study of women in a modern industrialized society.

These concerns assume a different significance in the early modern period. Early modern English society was highly patriarchal. From the monarch to the father of the humblest family, culture and institutions upheld the dominant position of men. But men's dominance is not synonymous with the oppression of women and there were checks upon men's actions. The most important of these was what may be described as the sense of community, a sense which was increasingly eroded between 1500 and 1760. Ancient institutions which had flourished in the Middle Ages and survived through to the seventeenth century promoted a sense of common good rather than the primacy of the individual's profit. This sense of a common good worked to women's advantage. Early medieval gilds, for example, allowed full membership to some women, normally the widows of freemen, but with the hard times of the mid-sixteenth century and greater competition for trade, women were increasingly excluded.

In early modern England, human nature was believed to be shaped by God and tainted by the fall of Adam and Eve. A secular idea of human nature really came into common currency only at the end of the eighteenth century, and even then, as one may see in the nineteenth-century debate about evolution, most people retained some notion of the divine origins of the human race. The natural world was believed to have been provided by God for the use of the human race: not to use God's bounty properly was to fail him. The nineteenth-century Romantic view of the natural world would have been utterly alien to anyone in the seventeenth century.

The idea of 'natural' qualities or characteristics did have a currency in early modern England. Sometimes this was forced on people. It was 'natural' for children to be breast-fed because there was no other form of nourishment for the newborn. It was not necessarily 'natural' for women to feed their own babies. Women were believed to have various moral characteristics which distinguished them from men. They were 'naturally' sexually voracious. It was 'unnatural' for them not to bear children. In these ideas of what constituted nature, there were similarities with ideas to be found in the nineteenth and twentieth centuries, but the ideological context was very different.

Historians' ideas about women's work in the nineteenth century are dominated by the idea of waged labour, and often concentrate upon factory work even though the major source of employment for women throughout the nineteenth century was paid domestic work. Capitalist labour relations certainly existed in early modern England, and to some extent they exploited women, but there was no choice between a career and staying at home, since home was where most wage-earning activities took place. In the early modern period, domestic work was also the principal form of employment open to women. Other forms of work for women existed and, like domestic work, took place in the household or, as with farm work, were associated with it. Many forms of manufacturing took place in workshops that were part of a household and where the measurement and regulation of what was made were much less clearly set out than they were to become with the factory system; likewise there were often no wages, especially for family members.

The move to factory production, which took place from the late eighteenth century and which integrated more women into the economy, led to two schools of historical thought. There was the school which, broadly following Alice Clark, said that women's lives deteriorated with the introduction of factory work by reducing the variety of work they did, giving them more uncongenial working conditions, and paying them so little that they were trapped in a cycle of poverty and deprivation.[1] The other school, following Ivy Pinchbeck, argued that factory work released women from the domination of their families. It gave them the free disposal of their own lives and incomes, and freedom to associate with people outside their own family and community.[2]

The concern with women's rights which has dominated the nineteenth- and twentieth-century history of women plays a different part in the history of women in the early modern period. Much important history was written by women concerned with the suffrage movement, and it sought to show that women in earlier periods had had rights of which they were later stripped.[3] But the search for the origins of modern feminism in early modern England has provided little satisfaction. However radical the demands of such groups as the Levellers and Diggers in the mid-seventeenth century, there is no evidence that they sought political rights for women; nor is there any evidence of women demanding such rights for themselves. There is evidence of women intervening in subjects of direct personal concern to themselves, as when they campaigned for widows' pensions, but, with the exception of the wives and mistresses of a few powerful men and of the occasional political hostess, there is little sign of women taking any initiative in broader political issues. It was not until the second half of the eighteenth century that it became possible to think of women as having a position as autonomous beings in the world outside the household.

Women and the Disciplines of History

Probably the greatest contribution to the history of women has come from social history. Keith Wrightson begins his *English Society*

---

[1] Alice Clark, *The Working Life of Women in the Seventeenth Century*, George Routledge, 1919, republished Routledge and Kegan Paul, 1982.

[2] Ivy Pinchbeck, *Working Women and the Industrial Revolution 1750–1850*, George Routledge, 1930, republished Virago, 1981.

[3] For example, Charlotte Carmichael Stopes, *British Freewomen: Their Historical Privilege*, Swan Sonnenschein, 1907; Rose Graham, 'The civic position of women at common law before 1800', 1917, reprinted in *English Ecclesastical Studies*, SPCK, 1929.

1580–1680 with an account of the 'faceless and passive' people who, until recently, 'stood . . . in the penumbra of historical conscious-ness, while matters of significance were left to the consideration of a narrow circle of their betters'. The new social history has done much to rediscover these people, especially women. But the social history of the early modern period is much less well developed than it is for later periods, though the amount of published work is increasing and the techniques of social anthropology and eth-nography are providing new insights. Women feature little in the more traditional specializations of political, military and intellectual history. There is a good deal of work on women in ecclesiastical history, in literary history and theory, in the history of medicine and of education, and in local, agrarian and urban history. There is also a serious concern for gender issues in the history of regions and counties.

Economic historians have relied upon records generated by official bodies concerning taxation, accounts, court proceedings, apprenticeship and so on. But official records seriously under-record economic activity, and the kinds of activity which appear least are those in which women were most active: the unofficial, the small-scale and the domestic. Economic historians' definition of work as necessarily involving the payment of wages fails to take account of the fact that many people, especially women and children, worked but were not being formally remunerated for it.

Historical demography – the study of populations in the past – deserves singling out from other historical disciplines because it professes to consider women equally with men. Many demographers would argue that, unlike historians in other disci-plines, they have always considered the differences between men and women, and ages of marriage and death and life expectancy figures are given for both sexes. But it is in the application of their work that historical demographers are less neutral and have been slow to respond to the issues posed by the consideration of gender. It is, for example, almost impossible to find out about female migration except in the most recent work. Olwen Hufton has criticized recent historical demography on the grounds that it under-represents the social phenomena which affect women's lives.[1] We know very little about sex differences in demographic trends. Even in as recent a social history as J. A. Sharpe's we learn nothing about the historical demography of women as distinct from

---

[1] Olwen Hufton, 'Women in history: early modern Europe', *Past and Present*, 101, 1983, pp. 129–30.

the population at large, except in relation to their age at marriage.[1] Was their life expectancy different from that of men? Did they experience different demographic peaks and troughs from men? Did they respond to larger demographic crises in a different way from men? Bubonic plague, typhus and smallpox, often combined with food shortages, could have a catastrophic effect upon the population. Did they affect women at a different time or in a different way from men?

The study of the material world, through archaeology and architectural history, is starting to enlarge our knowledge of women in early modern society, and it will certainly contribute much more in the near future. The study of the detritus of everyday life, and the buildings and objects used by illiterate people, allows the material world of unnamed people to be reconstructed, particularly in relation to the objects they used in households and workshops. The study of the functions and local contexts of buildings reveals how they were adapted to meet changing needs, and it unites social and architectural history. England is fortunate in having many buildings surviving from the sixteenth, seventeenth and eighteenth centuries, as well as older buildings which were in use in the early modern period. These are an enormously important reservoir of evidence of how people lived in past times.

Public and Private: the Role of the Household

The public/private dichotomy is invoked in studies of women both in the past and in the present. But a number of historians have suggested that this is not an appropriate device for looking at pre-industrial England. To be sure, women were excluded from public political life, but then so were many men. The household was the locus of many men's lives as well as of women's, and it was here that much economic activity took place: the dichotomy between the family at home and its members at work outside did not really exist.

The relationship between the household and the family is a highly complex one, not least because the term 'family' might be used of members of a household, regardless of whether or not they were related to the householder. Lady Anne Clifford, a northern aristocrat who ran her estates on feudal lines; Nehemiah Wallington, a London master-craftsman; and Samuel Pepys, the

---

[1] J. A. Sharpe, *Early Modern England: A Social History 1550–1760*, Edward Arnold, 1987.

government official; all referred to their households, including servants and apprentices, as family. Many households contained people who were unrelated by blood or marriage, such as servants, apprentices and lodgers. They also contained people related in different ways: step-parents and half-brothers and -sisters for example. Complex households might be produced by remarriage or by poverty, especially life-cycle poverty: that is to say, poverty associated specifically with a particular stage of life when the capacity for wage-earning was reduced. A family with young children and a wife unable to work for wages might, for example, take lodgers. Newly married couples seem to have quite often had their first home in the house of the parents of one or other, and single women sometimes set up house together.

The household economy is usually defined by the occupation of the economically active male member. Yet if we consider the household as an economic unit, especially as one in which both agriculture and manufacture coexist, it is evident that economic activity is not primarily male. Many households operated as cottage economies, occupying a couple of acres of land where a fairly high proportion of the household's needs were met by its own production. In such circumstances it is almost impossible to differentiate between the male and the female contribution to the domestic economy. However, by the sixteenth century households could not operate without some cash, and that need increased through the seventeenth and eighteenth centuries. Many of the household's financial transactions were conducted by men, and these were the most visible part of its economic life.

Although the household was important, it was not necessarily autonomous: people were both employers and employees, though these relationships were blurred. We know that the proportion of men who were employees rather than employers increased progressively between the sixteenth and the eighteenth centuries. In 1520 about 25 per cent of men were wage labourers and 75 per cent employers (chiefly of servants and apprentices rather than adult men and women). By 1851 the figures were almost reversed with 80 per cent of men labourers and 20 per cent employers. The proportion of women living in households which were primarily reliant upon wages for their maintenance increased progressively between the sixteenth and the eighteenth centuries, but we cannot deduce anything about the relative proportions of female employers and employees from these figures.

Much work was the product of a family economy, but there was work which was done in the household by women independently.

9

Lace-making is a good example: this was work which did not depend upon the man's occupation and where the woman acted as an autonomous producer, an independent wage earner in her own right. The lace-making community of Colyton in Devon, where Honiton lace was made between about 1600 and 1740, had a preponderance of women in the population and a later than average age of marriage. Lace-makers' earnings were high, probably higher than those of wool spinners. Women may even have migrated to Colyton seeking better-paid work.

The private, hidden nature of women's lives has been offered as a reason for historians' lack of attention to women. But it is clear that the notions of public and private do not really fit the organization of the economy and family based on the household. The household economy was part of public life itself. Equally, even the most private relations are influenced by the public sexual politics of male domination and women's oppression. Feminism and the lesbian and gay movements have enlarged the definition of politics to include personal relationships, and have emphasized the need to study such relationships to understand the nature of power in society. Other developments in contemporary England, notably the creation of a national history syllabus for schools in England and Wales, have shown that history is a much more political subject than many English people would have cared to acknowledge. (Other European countries from Ireland to Russia have never been in any doubt on the point.) What was previously considered to be private has been brought into the public domain, but how did it become private in the first place?

Later medieval England was a more communally minded society than that of early modern England, where the old concept of community was giving way to a greater emphasis on the individual and (his) achievements. This diminished the significance of the household which was the focus of a communal economy; and it increased the importance of the efforts of individuals acting on their own behalf. This may well have liberated men from the constraints of a hierarchical society, but it almost certainly restricted women. The free market, for the individual, serves the strong better than the weak.

Patriarchy, Proto-industrialization and the Development of Individualism

It is impossible to consider the history of women in early modern

England without at some point touching upon three important historical debates. The first concerns the nature of the family and whether the patriarchal family gave way to the affective family. The second is the extent to which women's lives were affected in ways different from men's by the changing work patterns embraced by the terms 'the proletarianization of labour' and 'proto-industrialization'. The third is how far the development of individualism affected women, and this brings together both the debate about changes in family structure and relationships, and the debate about economic change.

Lawrence Stone's work on the nature of the family has been important both for the history of the family and for the study of women. Not only has he written extensively on these subjects, but he has expressed strong views upon them. In 1985 he set down ten commandments for the writing of women's history, the most significant of which for our purposes is 'Thou shalt not assume the ubiquity in the past of modern emotional patterns – neither premarital love, nor conjugal affection, nor maternal devotion to children.'[1] Among other commandments he has set down are that 'Thou shalt be clear about what constitutes real change in the experience and treatment of women' and 'Thou shalt not omit to analyze with care the structural constraints on women created by values, religion, customs, laws, and the nature of the economy.'

Stone's work is important for the fact that the debates which he initiated have shaped much subsequent research on the family and on the history of women's place in the family. Historians who disagree with Stone's findings themselves have added greatly to our knowledge of the early modern family. His thesis that during the early modern period the family ceased to be patriarchal and became affective has been challenged by many historians. By a patriarchal family he meant one governed by the husband or father conducting himself according to precepts drawn from the Bible, in which duty and obligation featured prominently. By an affective family he meant one where marriages were made for affection between the partners, rather than for economic or dynastic reasons, and where parents developed a real sense of affection for their children.

The terms 'proletarianization of labour' and 'proto-industrialization' have been coined by historians who, interested in

---

[1] Lawrence Stone, 'Only women', *New York Review of Books*, 11 April 1985, p. 21. Professor Stone has expressed these views elsewhere, notably in *The Family, Sex and Marriage in England 1500–1800*. They influence his approach to women in other works like *An Open Elite?* and *The Road to Divorce*.

the industrial revolution, have looked at the period leading up to it for signs of what was to come. Proletarianization of labour refers to the process by which craft and trade regulation after 1660 declined and was replaced by a freer labour market. In this process both agricultural and manufacturing jobs were reorganized so that there were fewer employers, more employees and a greater division of labour, which required fewer people with specialized skills. In 1550 most of the working population consisted of people who were, if not their own bosses, part of a farm or workshop where they were associated with all the processes carried out there. By 1760 the majority of the workforce consisted of people who were working in unskilled jobs for wages.

In certain kinds of manufacturing, notably cloth production, the division of labour took the form of putting out different processes in the manufacture to different households, so that one would spin, another would weave, and another would dye. This division of labour is regarded by some historians as little different from factory work in that workers did not own the materials they worked on, often did not own their tools or equipment, and were paid wages. Putting-out took place in some areas from the early eighteenth century, and it has been described as proto-industrialization. Historians have argued that both the proletarianization of labour and proto-industrialization worked to women's disadvantage by excluding them from many areas of work, and by devaluing those areas in which they did continue to participate.

The notion that English society was becoming more individualistic in the early modern period has existed for a long time. In the early twentieth century, Max Weber was one of the most influential exponents of the idea that the Reformation was fundamental to the ideological shift which allowed people to consider themselves as individuals in relation to both God and the world, instead of in terms of a hierarchical community which placed family and collective interests before the individual. Since Weber, many historians have examined English society in the light of a shift towards more individualistic values. Alan Macfarlane's work, based partly upon insights gained from social anthropology, has made an important and a much discussed contribution to this debate.[1] He dates the origins of individualism in England to the early Middle Ages, both in the economic sense of private ownership and a free market in land and labour, and in the social sense of a society based not on kinship ties and arranged marriages but

---

[1] Alan Macfarlane, *The Origins of English Individualism*, Basil Blackwell, 1978.

upon freely entered-into relationships in business as well as marriage.

The debates about the patriarchal and affective family, proto-industrialization and individualism have provided academics with employment for decades. They have also influenced the way in which the study of women in the early modern period has been directed. Books and articles using new historical sources have been written about all of them and have expanded our knowledge of women in the past. Studies of the patriarchal and affective family have enlarged our knowledge of family structures; studies of the proletarianization of labour and proto-industrialization have increased what we know about the employment of women, the kinds of work they did and their part in the industrial economy of the country; studies of the development of a more individualistic society show how this worked to women's disadvantage.

CHAPTER TWO

Gender, Class and Race

Gender, class, race and age are fundamental divisions of the human race. They determine how people are treated and what they are permitted to do. Many legal, social and economic restrictions are applied in terms of gender, class, race or age. Much human activity is made possible or prevented by membership of one gender, class, race or age group rather than another. We shall consider age in chapter 3. The word 'gender' is more useful than the word 'sex' in this context because we are considering not simply biological differences, but all the features embraced by the notion of socially constructed roles.

Everybody has a gender, a class and a race, and the disabilities or advantages conferred by one might mitigate or accentuate those conferred by one of the others. The privileges to which upper-class women had access could do a very great deal to mitigate the disabilities conferred by gender, especially when class carried associations with both power and responsibility.

Historians have often debated the relative importance of gender, class and race. Two historians of women in Europe have written recently that 'While differences of historical era, class, and nationality have significance for women, they are outweighed by the similarities decreed by gender.'[1] Other historians remain convinced that differences of class transcend those of gender in the effect that they have on people's lives. Race has featured less in historians' discussions about early modern England, since it is clear that many English people then never came across anyone of another race; nor did any consciousness of supposed differences between races have a significant bearing upon their daily lives. Nevertheless, England became between the sixteenth and the

---

[1] Bonnie S. Anderson and Judith P. Zinsser, *A History of their Own*, Penguin, 1989, I, xv.

eighteenth centuries an increasingly cosmopolitan and racially mixed society.

In early modern England there were debates about the restrictions imposed by social status, and there was some discussion of race in the context of whether people who were slaves in America or the Caribbean remained slaves on English shores. But it was not until the very end of the period that there was any discussion of women's role as autonomous beings rather than in relation to men. Why, then, discuss these subjects here if they were not part of the public consciousness of early modern England? Historians' questions are shaped by subjects of concern to us now. We are constantly measuring what we know in the present against what we can discover about the past, and by these means trying to uncover more about what people thought, about mentalities in the past rather than events alone.

Class and Wealth

Modern concepts of class, social divisions characterized by consciousness of one's own class, and antagonism between classes, have influenced historians looking at early modern England. Many historians avoid the term 'class' on the grounds that it was not used at the time; it describes a system of social relations not applicable to that society; and it is associated with the study of economic and social structures after the industrial revolution. Early modern society was, however, highly stratified: status was measured by ancestry, land ownership, royal favour and the disposal of patronage. Barriers to social advancement, which prevented people from entering the political elite, were increasingly under attack, especially by men who had made money and wanted to match it with power. The events of the Civil War and the Interregnum show that by the mid-seventeenth century there was no single conception of the social order, and that there was a good deal of social mobility. But how far did this affect women's lives?

Women might acquire and benefit from some of the formal attributes of status, but they were excluded from the power which accompanied men's possession of status. Ancestry was important, and it gave women a powerful sense of their own place in the world. The law allowed women to own land in their own right by inheritance or purchase, but placed many restrictions on their use of it. Peeresses in their own right (of which there were always a few) were not summoned to sit in the House of Lords. Women officeholders were normally expected to appoint a male proxy. Women might acquire royal favour as members of the queen's court or as the king's mistress, but they were rarely in a position to act as patrons themselves. They were also excluded from formal political processes. So, it might be said, were most men: a woman who mixed with the political nation had much more opportunity to exercise influence, even though it was not formally recognized, than any man from the labouring or artisanal classes. But in many important ways the lives of the richest and most privileged women in early modern England more closely resembled those of the poorest and least privileged women than they resembled the lives of men.

I am using the term 'women' in its normal twentieth-century sense, to denote females of all statuses. The social status of women in early modern England was determined by their father's or husband's status and their own matrimonial status. Thus they were women, ladies, gentlewomen or noblewomen, and maids, spinsters, married women or widows. These distinctions were considered to be very important. A woman was the lowest category of adult female. The term 'lady' implied the female head of a household (usually in partnership with a man), having people under her direction. Merchants' wives might be described as ladies. Gentlewomen were generally the wives or daughters of men entitled to bear a coat of arms and thus of higher status, though not necessarily of greater wealth. Noblewomen were the wives and daughters of men possessed of hereditary titles, occasionally with titles in their own right. But these catagories were not exclusive and there was, for example, a good deal of blurring at the edges between ladies and gentlewomen and between gentlewomen and noblewomen.[1] Women in the early modern period were virtually never identified by their own occupations, though they were often referred to by their husbands'. Certain kinds of status were more important than the husband's occupation. Thus it is common to see a woman referred to as 'citizen's wife', indicating that her husband was a freeman of the city, a master of his craft and a person of some standing in the community.

Social historians have long debated the extent to which it was possible for people to change their social status in early modern England. By this they mean how much upward social mobility was there for men; or, more specifically, how easy was it for a man who

---

[1] There is a helpful discussion of male social status in J. A. Sharpe, *Early Modern England: A Social History 1550–1760*, Edward Arnold, 1987, chapters 6–8.

had made money to enter the ranks of the gentry or aristocracy? Not much attention has been devoted to downward social mobility, except in considering the fluctuating numbers of the poor. Women were transmitters of status by marriage, and they might enhance or confirm a man's standing and acceptance; but whether they could actually advance a man's social aspirations, rather than halt his social decline, is doubtful. Very occasionally a woman might rise in society on her own account by becoming the mistress of a wealthy or important man as did Jane Bickerton (*c.*1644–93) daughter of the king's cellarman, who eventually married the Duke of Norfolk, but it cannot be said that the career opportunities offered by this course were ever open to many women, even in the reign of Charles II.

The most obvious way in which a woman might aid her husband's social aspirations was by being an heiress, but dynastic alliances to support political ambitions, or to consolidate land holdings, also took place. The rise of William Feilding, Earl of Denbigh in the court of Charles I was undoubtedly aided by his marriage to the sister of the royal favourite, the Duke of Buckingham. Lawrence Stone has suggested that opportunities for men to rise into the landed elite increased after the Reformation when daughters who might previously have become nuns had to be found husbands. He sees these opportunities for upward mobility declining from the late seventeenth century because of a change in social values. Heirs were more likely to choose a wife for love rather than to preserve the dynasty.[1] Nunneries by the early sixteenth century recruited their novices chiefly from higher-status families, however the overall numbers recruited were small and declining.

Although most women had little chance of advancing themselves socially, those of the highest status might pursue their own dynastic ambitions. Elizabeth Countess of Shrewsbury (1518–1608) is said to have chosen her husbands with an eye to consolidating her estates in Derbyshire. She was accused by the family of her third husband, Sir William St Loe, of excluding them from their inheritance. One of the conditions she set for marrying her fourth husband, George Earl of Shrewsbury, was the satisfactory negotiation of marriages between one of her daughters and one of his sons and between one of her sons and one of his daughters. Lady Anne Clifford (1590–1676), however, refused to allow a dynastic match between her daughter and the son of her second

---

[1] Lawrence Stone and Jeanne C. Fawtier Stone, *An Open Elite?*, Oxford University Press, 1986, p. 279.

husband, Philip Herbert, Earl of Pembroke, because her daughter was, in Lady Anne's words, 'extremely averse' to it.

We know little about mobility lower down the social scale, but in the sixteenth century, when the gild system still operated effectively, the widow of a craftsman could inherit her husband's right to take on apprentices; and if she remarried, she could confer the status of freeman on her new husband, or at least hasten his acceptance as a member of her late husband's gild or company. Greater social advancement might be achieved by a young woman considered to be pretty. The Earl of Egmont in 1745 noted that

> This has been a lucky season for low people's marrying, for I am told that since the Duke of Chandos's marriage with the innkeeper's maid near Slough, the Duke of Ancaster has married his kept mistress and the Duke of Rutland will own his wife his kept mistress, the Earl of Salisbury has married his steward's niece – Miss Keate, daughter to a barber and shower of the tombs in Canterbury, and the Earl of Bristol his late wife's maid, and the Duke of Buckingham his tutor's niece.[1]

Recent studies of servants by Ann Kussmaul and D. A. Kent suggest that they were socially and geographically mobile to a degree unusual in other occupations. Indeed, especially in the earlier part of the period, to spend time as a servant was not necessarily a sign of low social status; it was part of the education of young people rather than just something to fill in the time. Servants' social status changed as they passed successively from childhood into service (in which few of them remained after the age of twenty-five or so) and then into adult occupations, with more responsibility for men, and marriage for women. Servants were socially mobile more because they came from a wide variety of backgrounds than because service itself afforded opportunities for social advancement. Job mobility was very high: the population of farm servants in a parish could change by anything from 50 to 100 per cent in a two-year period. Farm service was an informal form of apprenticeship, and one of the reasons for the high rate of mobility was to secure experience of different kinds of farm work. Most farm work was skill- and age-specific, though the number of skilled farm jobs declined in the eighteenth century. Domestic service was also associated with the period between childhood and marriage for both men and women.

Wealth was an important ingredient in social status. The number of servants and dependants, and the standard of hospitality and

---

[1] Historical Manuscripts Commission, Egmont MSS, Diary of the 1st Earl of Egmont, III, 307–8.

dress were all important indicators of status, and they required money to sustain them. Wealth alone, however, was not enough to ensure an entrance into the social and political elite. Women were important transmitters of wealth between families in the higher social groups, but they were also more vulnerable than men to poverty. For those at the bottom of the social hierarchy there was little opportunity for upward mobility. Women made up a high proportion of the settled poor (people, not being vagrants, who received parish poor relief), sometimes outnumbering men by as many as two to one, and heading a disproportionately large number of households as widows or deserted wives. In the 1570 Norwich census of the poor, 62 per cent of the total number of adults over sixteen were women. Advancing age increased a woman's prospects of poverty, and 68 per cent of those over sixty-one years of age were classed as poor. Moreover, women may well have made up more of the mobile poor than figures suggest, because they were less likely than men to appear in court.

Women in early modern England were defined firstly by their sex, secondly by their relationship to a man, and thirdly by their class, or, rather, the status they assumed from their fathers or husbands. Differences in status also defined relations between women. High status women expected deference from low status women and, to a large extent, received it. There might, however, be close relations between women of different standing, especially between mistresses and servants.

Race

In early modern England there were a variety of people who might be considered outsiders from the point of view of the political elite: religious dissidents, outlaws, vagrants, people from other countries, and people of other races. Religious dissidents were persecuted under a variety of laws which became progressively less restrictive from 1689 on. Outlaws had been deliberately excluded from society, and vagrants, by their unsettled lives, seemed to threaten the values of the ruling elite.

Immigrants were familiar to the inhabitants of cities and ports. In late sixteenth century London about 5 per cent of the population of 40,000 was from outside England: Scots, Irish, Welsh, French, Dutch and a scattering of people from other places, including some Jews and a small number of blacks. Jews, even if born in England, were not permitted to acquire full English nationality. Differences of language and religion sometimes caused tension, but xeno-phobia was most prevalent when competition for jobs was fiercest. It was an element in popular unrest in London, where in 1517 resentment at the supposedly unfair competition from alien craftsmen and merchants sparked off serious riots and resulted in several executions; foreigners were attacked and their shops looted. A hundred and fifty years later, London merchants petitioned Charles II to repeal Cromwell's readmission of the Jews on the grounds of unfair competition.

But what determined English people's attitudes to those they regarded as foreigners? A large and flourishing travel literature informed the literate about foreign races; and the arrival of visitors from the lands newly discovered by Europeans excited much curiosity. Most such visitors were men. Seamen of various races were to be seen at ports. Black slaves were sometimes brought over by plantation owners. The first black Africans came to England in the 1550s as merchants. By the early seventeenth century there were black servants in royal and noble households. There were two, a man and a woman, in the Sackville household at Knole in the early seventeenth century. Dedery Jaquoah, the twenty-year-old son of a king in Guinea, was baptised at St Mildred Poultry, London, in 1611. A few black women (described as negras) came as maids. Samuel Pepys employed a black cooking maid and *The Daily Ledger* of 1761 advertised 'A healthy Negro girl aged about 15 years, speaks English, works at her needle, washes well, does household work, and has had the smallpox.' Those black women who were not household servants tended to be theatrical performers, appearing as acrobats and dancers. Black women on the stage, dressed either in the latest fashions or in little at all, intrigued English audiences.

With the expansion of the slave trade in the late seventeenth and early eighteenth centuries, blacks were to be seen more commonly, though they came from across the Atlantic rather than from Africa. It was estimated that there were about 15,000 blacks living in England by the mid-eighteenth century: sailors; servants and slaves who had been brought to England from the plantations; and the descendants of blacks who had come to England earlier.

The question of the status of blacks perplexed the authorities. Many blacks had come from places where they were slaves, while others had been born in England. It was a matter of much controversy and learned discussion whether people who came as slaves remained slaves on reaching English shores. In the late seventeenth century it was believed that slaves who were converted to Christianity were entitled to their freedom in England, and so slave owners took steps to prevent their slaves being converted:

> A gentlewoman, who commending a certain Negro wench that she had, for her towardliness and other good qualities, in the hearing of a minister; he demanded of her, Why she made her not a Christian? Whereat, casting her eyes strangely on him, and greatly wondering, she replied, That she thought he would have given her better counsel.[1]

The gentlewoman plainly thought that the minister was naïve not to know that her slave would be lost if she were converted to Christianity.

The black immigrant population was predominantly male, and it was alleged that black men had a preference for lower-class white women. Since these were the women with whom they had most contact, this was scarcely surprising. Unions between black men and upper-class white women were regarded as scandalous. The infatuation of the Duchess of Queensberry (d.1777) for her black manservant, Soubise, was widely reported. He was eventually deported in 1777 for allegedly raping a servant girl. The duchess died shortly afterwards from a surfeit of cherries. It is unclear whether it was the man's colour or his class which caused the greatest offence to her friends. Elizabeth Chudleigh, Duchess of Kingston (1720–88), who was tried for bigamy, used to take her black servant, Sambo, to the theatre with her. Black women were less the subject of scandal. The only black woman to achieve comparable fame was Phyllis Wheatley (c.1753–84) from Boston, Massachusetts, who visited England in 1773 having published a collection of poems.

Attitudes to marriages between the races were complicated, but social class could do much to mitigate prejudices. In 1607 Sir Robert Shirley, envoy in the service of the Shah of Persia, married a Circassian woman, whom he brought to England. They spent much of their married life travelling on diplomatic missions, and after his death in 1628, Lady Shirley (d.1668), whose portrait was painted by Van Dyck, retired to Rome to live.

The Irish occupied a kind of twilight world: they were neither foreigners nor natives. Observers noted that English settlers in Ireland, especially those who migrated before the Reformation, when both the English and the Irish were Catholic, and who married Irish men and women, became assimilated into Irish

---

[1] Quoted in Folarin Shyllon, *Black People in Britain 1555–1833*, Institute of Race Relations and Oxford University Press, 1977, p. 18.

society and lost their 'Englishness'. Edmund Campion wrote in 1571 that 'the very English of birth conversant with the brutish sort of that people [i.e. the Irish] become degenerate in short space', and the suggestion of degeneration runs through the English writing on Ireland until the mid-eighteenth century.[1]

Contact with indigenous Americans provoked mixed reactions: there were anxieties about marriage between English men and Indian women on the grounds of the women's religion; that such marriages would give Indians an undue influence over the English; and that American Indians were widely infected with syphilis. However, these objections were believed to be surmountable if it were possible to convert the Indians to Christianity. Indian rulers were in their own way as exploitative of their own women as the English. Powhatan, ruler of the Powhatan Indians who lived in the area settled as Virginia, was keen for political reasons to cement his treaty with the English in 1608 with marriages between his women and the English men. The Spanish ambassador at the court of James I reported to his master in 1612 that about forty or fifty English colonists had married Virginia Indians and that 'other Englishmen after being put among them have become savages', though he is not a very reliable witness because of the hostile relations between England and Spain. The most celebrated marriage was that between Pocahontas (1595–1617) and John Rolfe in 1614, which led to peace between the Indians and the settlers.

Pocahontas was one of Powhatan's daughters and was converted to Christianity in about 1613, when she adopted the name Rebecca. In 1616 Pocahontas, her husband, child and Indian attendants came to England where they excited much curiosity and were entertained at court. She was reluctant to return to America but was unhappy in England and died in 1617, during the preparations for her return home. Though this marriage was much celebrated as a sign that Indians might be 'civilized', the English settlers thought the Indians' own customs of little account, for it was reported that Pocahontas had an Indian husband at the time of her marriage to Rolfe.

This illustrates an attitude which occurred frequently in the English treatment of other races: their disregard for any established social order and its customs which they could not recognize as being comparable to their own. The absence of Christian marriage was seen as a licence by English men to behave as they wished with

---

[1] Edmund Campion, *Two Bokes of the Histories of Ireland (1571)*, ed. A. F. Vossen, Assen, Netherlands, 1963, p. 20.

women of other races. The supposed sexual insatiability of women was also used to justify men's behaviour, and Rolfe was accused by the 'vulgar sort' of settlers of 'wanting to gorge [himself] with incontinency' in his marriage to Pocahontas. Formal marriages between the Indians of Virginia and the English settlers virtually ceased after the rising of 1622, but unofficial unions with Indian women continued. Some English men, unable to provide for themselves, used unions with Indian women as a way of obtaining food and shelter in the harsh circumstances of the early colonies. But these unions became less common with the arrival of English women and of black women slaves.

After Pocahontas other native Americans came to England, though they were usually men. A party came over in Queen Anne's time, and in 1734 the Earl of Egmont brought over a group of Yamacree Indians from Georgia, eight men and one woman, the men exciting more interest than the woman. Lord Egmont described the appearance and character of Chief Toma-chiki in some detail, but all he could find to say of the woman, the chief's wife, was that she was an ugly old creature who prepared the men's food. Perhaps if she had been young, she might have been regarded with rather more curiosity.

Foreigners

During the seventeenth century two groups of foreigners arrived in England, and settled there for a mixture of economic and religious reasons. Greatest in number were the immigrants from France. Many French Protestants came to England in 1685 following the revocation by Louis XIV of the Edict of Nantes, which deprived them of the limited religious freedom they had had until then. French workers had been coming to England for a long time before that. Whole families migrated from France to the Wealden iron works in Kent in the early sixteenth century, because of the decay of the iron industry in certain regions of France. The term 'Huguenot' is usually associated with Protestants, but it was used of all French immigrants regardless of their religion.

The numbers arriving from France increased from the late sixteenth century, when the persecution of Protestants began there in earnest. Many of the French Protestants were cloth workers. In 1593 there were in London 631 French families, two-thirds of whom had children. Relations between the native population and the French immigrants were not always harmonious, but even so the

newcomers were assimilated quickly, often within two generations, and by the 1650s nearly half of the officers of the principal
French church at Threadneedle Street, London, had been born in
England. Many of the mid-seventeenth-century immigrants were
from the Spanish Netherlands (modern Belgium), and tended to
ally themselves with Dutch settlers. They set up their own
congregations in Norwich, Canterbury and Southampton.

A group which had a considerable impact upon English urban
society, out of proportion to their numbers, was the Jews. In the
sixteenth and seventeenth centuries there was a considerable
movement of Jews in Europe, especially into Holland. Those who,
in the early 1650s, were looking for asylum were chiefly Marranos,
Spanish Jews who kept up the outward forms of Christianity, and
Dutch Sephardic Jews who had, in the 1630s, established a colony
in Brazil which was dissolved in 1654 with the collapse of the Dutch
colony there. Until 1655 most English Jews worshipped as
Catholics in the Spanish embassy because of their language and
connections with Spain. In 1656 Oliver Cromwell, in response to
approaches from Holland, authorized the readmission of Jews to
England; they had been expelled by Edward I, though small
numbers were to be found living surreptitiously in London, most of
them from Spain and Portugal whence they had been expelled.
Cromwell's motives were partly economic and partly religious.
Jews were responsible for various commercial ventures in which
English merchants were interested, and there was a belief among
millenarians that the conversion of the Jews was a necessary
prelude to the second coming of Christ. Following Cromwell's
measure it was possible for Jews to live openly in England, and they
established a synagogue and a cemetery in London. They were not,
however, allowed to become naturalized or treated without
prejudice.

At the time of the Restoration there were thirty-five Jewish heads
of household in London (probably between 100 and 200
individuals). The City of London campaigned against their remaining in England, on the grounds of commercial competition; but
Charles II rejected this appeal and in 1664 unequivocally gave Jews
permission to remain in England. Their numbers increased considerably and by 1663 there were ninety-two households (perhaps
400 people), chiefly in London. Catherine of Braganza had several
Marranos in her train. Persecution was renewed in the 1680s, but
with the accession of William and Mary it diminished and immigra-
tion from Amsterdam increased, so that in 1695, when a census was
taken, there were over 700 Jews in London. By the late seventeenth

century there were Jewish communities in the Caribbean, in Dublin and in London, where there was a voluntary welfare organization and synagogue. These Jews were very different from their English neighbours: they spoke Ladino, a dialect of Spanish, and worked predominantly as merchants in precious metals and stones.

Until abut 1700 the majority of Jews in England were Sephardim from Spain and from North Africa, sometimes having come via Amsterdam. At about this time large numbers of poor Ashkenazi Jews from Germany and Poland, who had little except religious ceremony in common with the already settled Sephardim, began to arrive in England. Sephardic Jews were respected for their learning and especially for their expertise as physicians. The Ashkenazi Jews of central and eastern Europe were poorer, spoke German or Yiddish and were generally less integrated into western European culture. They had intermarried much less than had Iberian Jews. The existence of two different Jewish communities in England led to greater integration because their common language was English, and by the mid-eighteenth century a substantial proportion of Jews spoke English as their mother-tongue.

The names of the male heads of household are known, but virtually nothing is known of the lives of Jewish women living in England in this period, still less of their relations with other women. The civil disabilities under which Jews of both sexes lived were similar to those of most women in England: they were not allowed to own land and they were unable to become freemen of cities, and thus were unable to participate in urban government or trade regulation. The Jewish community had its own regulatory mechanisms; disputes were settled within the community rather than by resort to state institutions, so there was little contact between Jews and officials. There is little information about the few Jewish women who appear on censuses and official lists beyond their marital status. Only two women on a census of Jews of 1803 are not described as spinster, wife, widow or pensioner. Both of them had come to England as young women: one was a watch-string maker who had come to England in 1768 from Leghorn, though she had been born in Marseilles; and the other, an old clothes dealer, had come to England in 1781 from Amsterdam.

Exiled communities are always difficult to research because exiles often avoid creating documents which might incriminate them, and in times of political uncertainty it was safer not to become too settled. There is much still to be discovered about the communities which settled in England and in particular about their women. There has been a tendency for historians to concentrate upon the public face of these communities and their relations with their hosts, both predominantly male preserves. But the study of the internal workings of the communities will show us more of the lives of the women in them and, most tantalizing of all, their informal links with the indigenous population. Women immigrants to England and women members of religious and racial minorities in the early modern period are new candidates for recruitment to the category of those 'hidden from history'.

In this chapter I have looked at the experience of women in early modern England in relation to the divisions imposed by class, gender and race, subjects of great concern in the twentieth century, but also important to our understanding of the mentalities of early modern society. I have also indicated some of the ways in which class and race affected women's lives in early modern England, though their relative importance will continue to be debated by historians.

CHAPTER THREE

Women in the Population

Counting People

In the last twenty years, historical demographers have enormously enlarged our knowledge of the nature of the population of early modern England. Until this work was done, estimates were highly speculative because there were no censuses until 1801 and contemporary estimates were unreliable. Demographers working on early modern society use the household as their basic unit. Population size and composition are estimated by means of the process of family reconstitution, in which communities are reconstructed from a variety of population sources, like parish registers, taxation returns and churchwardens' accounts. Another technique, pioneered by E. A. Wrigley and R. S. Schofield, is back-projection, by which population totals and age structures for earlier times are estimated by means of the study of known later populations.

We now have a much better idea of how the population was composed and what expectations of life, marriage and children people had, but only in very general terms. We can say what life expectancy at birth was for the population as a whole, but we can say little about the variations from this which might result from living in one region rather than another, or from being richer or poorer. Historical demographers' findings have been criticized for their lack of attention to deviations from the average, which give much insight into real human experience. We can observe that the average age of marriage for women fell during the eighteenth century, but we have little idea of what real impact this had upon people's lives.

The English population grew rapidly between about 1500 and 1640, possibly doubling in size and certainly replacing the losses by disease of the later Middle Ages. A probable figure for the size of the population of England and Wales in 1640 is between five and six million. From the 1650s until 1690 the population remained static or even declined, partly because of the effects of plague, but also because of a lower birth rate. In 1700 the population was smaller than it had been in 1640, though it probably did not fall below five million. Then, from 1690 to the 1740s, it grew slowly, and from the 1740s onwards it increased rapidly. In 1740 it was perhaps five and a half million, and in 1800 eight million. This pattern of growth, for which numerous different explanations have been advanced, was reproduced in several western European countries.

Life Expectancy

Women tended to live longer than men. The overall life expectancy at birth for men and women together ranged between thirty-two and forty, whereas in the 1990s it is seventy-eight for women and seventy-two for men. But the periods of their lives when women were most likely to die were different from those of men. They were four times more likely to die in the first ten years of marriage than were men (i.e. between the ages of twenty-six and thirty-six), and twice as likely in the second ten years (between the ages of thirty-six and forty-six). Thereafter they were more likely to survive than men. It is fair to say that, if a woman survived her first pregnancy and pregnancy in her late thirties or early forties, she had a reasonable expectation of living to at least sixty. However, there were changes over time, and there was a discernible increase in maternal mortality between the late sixteenth century and the late seventeenth century, and a decline in the eighteenth century.

The effect of differential mortality between men and women on the age and sex structure of the population was almost certainly less than the effect of extensive migration, except in very unusual communities. The death rate was not only different between the sexes, but it was uneven over time. Mortality crises (periods of greatly increased incidence of death) were a significant feature of the earlier part of the period. These crises were probably caused by a combination of food shortages and epidemic disease. By the late seventeenth century plague had more or less disappeared, and the effect of harvest failures was much diminished.

It is easy to think that, because the average life expectancy at birth was so low, people's lives were somehow accelerated and that they acquired the qualities of old age faster than people do nowadays. A poor diet accentuates the effects of age and many people must have lost their teeth when quite young, so that they looked older than their years. But people were not considered to be unusually old if they had reached the age of sixty. The Norwich census of the poor of 1570 gives two men and five women aged between ninety-one and a hundred out of a total of 1,400 people; and a similar survey in Salisbury in 1625 produced in one parish a woman of a hundred, another of ninety-nine, five women in their eighties, a married couple consisting of a man of ninety-nine and his fifty-year-old wife, and seven men over eighty. These examples are from a group, the poor, which might be expected to have a lower expectation of reaching old age than the rich. It is difficult to know how literally to take the ages which people claimed to be, because of the lack of detailed registrations of births, but it is clear that there certainly were old people – not in as great numbers as today, but in considerable numbers – and that some of them attained what even now are regarded as very great ages.

The size of the aged population varied considerably from place to place. In the population overall in the late sixteenth century, 22 per cent were aged fifty or over, and about 7 per cent were aged over sixty. In Norwich in 1570 about 30 per cent of the poor population were over fifty, and about 15 per cent were over sixty. Older women exceeded older men in numbers: the ratio was about 60:40; though in Norwich in 1570 it was more like 68:32. In the countryside the proportion of older people seems to have been smaller than in the town, possibly because of the lack of facilities for those who could not support themselves. In Micheldever, Hampshire, in the early eighteenth century only 6 per cent of the population were over seventy (5 per cent men, 7.5 per cent women), and this was lower than the national average. Contrast this with the 17 per cent of over-seventies in a modern Oxford-shire village.

The age composition of the population underwent a number of changes during the period 1500–1760. In the sixteenth century the population was relatively young with over a third (39 per cent) under the age of fifteen; about 18 per cent young adults; about a third adults; and only about 7 per cent over the age of sixty. During the seventeenth century the population became relatively older as it ceased to grow. The greatest decline in size was in the youngest age group (29 per cent in 1676) and the greatest increase in size was in the oldest (10 per cent in 1676). Thereafter the average age of the population began to fall until at the beginning of the nineteenth century it had reached a similar level to that of the seventeenth century.

It is tempting to liken the age structure of early modern England to that of the developing world today, where the proportion of under-sixteens may be as high as 40 per cent, compared with the developed world where it is about 28 per cent. Overall life expectancy was low for both sexes, and levels of mortality, especially female mortality, are comparable with the developing world. But there are some important differences. The impact of birth control and medical intervention is difficult to calculate and may well be slight, but cultural factors regarding fertility and the treatment of children of different sexes are likely to have an impact on the population of the developing world different from that in early modern England.[1]

Slightly more male children were baptised than female (105 males to 100 females), but male children normally have a higher mortality in infancy than female, so the numbers of older female and male children were roughly equal. Illegitimate children, who made up a small proportion of the total number of births, were not always baptised and may have been more vulnerable to early death by reason of the circumstances of their birth. Levels of infant mortality started to rise in the late seventeenth century. They reached their highest in the first half of the eighteenth century and remained constant until the end of the eighteenth century.

In this general increase in infant mortality, female infant mortality rose faster than male, but the higher the overall mortality rate, the less significant was the difference between male and female deaths. London had much the highest mortality, and also the least difference between the death rates of male and female children. Market towns had lower mortality, but when infant mortality rose it rose higher among female children. Isolated rural communities had the lowest infant mortality, but the most marked rise in female deaths when infant mortality rose. This suggests that epidemics of infectious disease were an important cause of rising

---

[1] For example, the 1990 census for China found that there were 111.3 boys for every 100 girls under the age of one, and the figures recorded in the censuses for 1987 and 1989 are similar. Nowhere in early modern England were differences of this order recorded.

infant mortality, because a number of diseases, such as whooping cough, are more often fatal for girls than for boys. There is also some evidence that female deaths increased in families with more than five children. There is no evidence of any generalized feeling that boys should be privileged over girls in times of illness and food shortage, but it may nevertheless be that when food and medical attention were in short supply, boys were favoured. Lack of food and warmth might be critical in surviving an acute illness. However, more significant than gender in determining infant mortality were wealth – mortality increased with poverty – and the type of settlement in which the family lived – infant mortality was highest in London, then in market towns and lowest in dispersed settlements.

While deaths of children from disease may have been influenced by social factors, accidental deaths certainly were. Coroners' records show that among slightly older children the accidental deaths of girls were most often the result of burns and scalds (in the home), while boys were most likely to drown (outside the home). Social factors might also determine the likelihood of children being born. The tendency of aristocratic and gentry families to seek out heiresses for their sons to marry reduced the likelihood of male heirs since heiresses were usually the product of relatively infertile families or families with a high incidence of childhood death.

Marriage and Children

The characteristics of marriage in England in the sixteenth and seventeenth centuries conform to the 'western European marriage pattern'. These are identified as late age of marriage; a small difference in age between the partners; a high rate of people never marrying; and a relatively low birth rate. Young unmarried women might earn their own livings, often saving up to get married. This pattern was not repeated all over Europe: in early modern Ireland, for example, marriage seems to have taken place younger and there were few unmarried people.

The mean age of marriage for women in early modern England was at least twenty-six. (In Britain in the 1990s it is 23.9 for women and 25.8 for men.) Only 15 per cent of married women were under twenty-four and in rural communities it was common to find no one below that age married. The age of marriage in towns was lower than that in the countryside: in Alcester, Gainsborough,

Banbury and London, for example, the mean age of marriage was 23.1 years, compared with 25.6 for a group of rural parishes.[1] But one of the most striking developments over the period was how the mean age of marriage fell, and with this fall, the age difference between the sexes diminished.[2]

Although the mean age of marriage for men is greater than that for women, the age difference rarely exceeded three years. The decline in the age difference may well be explained by a higher rate of people marrying in their twenties and a smaller proportion of men marrying or remarrying when they were older. There might be considerable individual differences, often accounted for by re-marriage, as examples from Salisbury in the 1620s show. Dorothy, wife of William Hall, was twelve years younger than her husband; Katherine, wife of Henry Senyer, was twenty-two years younger than hers; and Anne Buckett was forty-seven years younger than her 87-year-old husband. But these differences were partly compensated for by the 20–25 per cent of couples where the wife was older than the husband, like the 52-year-old blind Austin Belly whose wife Katherine was sixty, and Joan Curtis, aged eighty, who was twenty years older than her husband. Local factors might affect the age of marriage, if, for example, there was a marked preponderance of one sex over the other, or a high level of poverty (which before the eighteenth century tended to result in deferred marriage).

Age of marriage has a very direct effect upon the birth rate in a society with no easy means of contraception: the younger the age of

---

[1] Bridget Hill has criticized the figures relating to the mean age of marriage for their lack of sensitivity to regional variation in social behaviour, particularly in relation to women. See Bridget Hill, 'The marriage age of women and the demographers', *History Workshop*, 28, 1989.

[2] Mean age at first marriage

	1600–49	1650–99	1700–49	1750–99
Female	26.0	26.5 (+0.5)	26.2 (–0.3)	24.9 (–1.3)
Male	28.0	27.8 (–0.2)	27.5 (–0.3)	26.4 (–1.1)

Source: E. A. Wrigley and R. S. Schofield, *The Population History of England 1541–1871*, Edward Arnold, 1981, Cambridge University Press, 1989, p. 255.

Age difference between partners

1600–49	1650–99	1700–49	1750–99
2.0	1.3	1.3	1.5

marriage, the larger the number of births to a couple. Population levels may also be influenced by the rate of remarriage, and something like a third of marriages were second or subsequent marriages for one partner. Remarriage was so common because of the large number of marriages terminated by the early death of one partner. The incidence of remarriage began to decline in the eighteenth century for cultural rather than demographic reasons, the ideal of a single, life-long union acquiring greater currency.

A significant proportion of the population did not marry at all. Women who had not been married by the time they were thirty found it progressively more difficult to find a husband, and those unmarried at forty might expect to remain unmarried. There is some evidence that the life expectancy of spinsters was less than that of married women.

Proportions of married, widowed and single people in the population, 1574–1821

	Married	Widowed	Single
Whole population	33.4%	6.2%	60.4%
Women	32.1%	8.7%	59.2%
Men	34.8%	3.5%	61.7%

Source: P. Laslett, 'Mean household size in England since the sixteenth century', in P. Laslett and R. Wall (eds), *Household and Family in Past Time*, Cambridge University Press, 1972, p. 145.

The proportion of women never marrying increased from the beginning of the seventeenth century, and reached a peak in the 1690s, when 16–18 per cent of people of marriageable age did not marry, by comparison with 5–7 per cent in the late eighteenth century. Changes in the proportion of people not marrying occurred at the same time as changes in the mean age of marriage: when one fell so did the other.

Very few unmarried women lived independently. Unmarried women under forty-five were more likely to live with their parents than to live in someone else's house as a servant. Only about 10 per cent of households were headed by women, but these were more often widows than spinsters. The proportion of households headed by women rose in the eighteenth century, but given that the numbers of women not marrying declined, this was probably because fewer widows remarried. The figures for Romford in 1562 are fairly typical: of 175 households, 144 (82 per cent) were headed by a husband and wife, 10 (6 per cent) by men alone, and 21 (12 per cent) by women alone. Fourteen (two-thirds) of the households headed by women alone were headed by widows.

Women might expect to have between six and seven live births during their lives, though it was not uncommon for only two children to reach adulthood. The first child was commonly born less than nine months after marriage, though this became less usual during the sixteenth century, and was most unusual in the late seventeenth century, when the age of marriage was at its highest and the illegitimacy rate at its lowest. The number of pregnant brides increased in the eighteenth century with the fall in the age at first marriage and the rise in the illegitimacy rate.

Teenage pregnancies were very uncommon for much of the period, as were illegitimate births. The illegitimacy rate may be more closely associated with impediments to marriage than with increased sexual activity, given that sexual activity seems to have been an accepted part of courtship. There were regional variations, and also fluctuations over time between the mid-sixteenth century and the mid-eighteenth century. The rate of illegitimate births was particularly low in the 1650s and rose steadily in the eighteenth century.[1] These figures are somewhat deceptive, because we cannot know what proportion of children were born to people living in stable partnerships who were not married to each other. In 1990, 28 per cent of all births took place outside marriages, and we still do not know what proportion of them took place within stable partnerships. It is also likely that fewer illegitimate than legitimate children were baptised (baptisms being the only record of birth), so illegitimate children were probably under-recorded.

[1]

Long-term trends in illegitimacy in England
(as a percentage of baptisms)

1580s	1590s	1600s	1610s	1620s	1630s	1640s	1650s	1660s	1670s
2.84	3.08	3.20	2.61	2.54	2.06	1.70	0.94	1.48	1.30

1680s	1690s	1700s	1710s	1720s	1730s	1740s	1750s	1760s
1.52	1.82	1.80	2.12	2.24	2.69	2.85	3.35	4.17

Source: P. Laslett, *Family Life and Illicit Love*, Cambridge University Press, 1977, p. 125.

Family Composition

Further characteristics of the western European marriage pattern are that households rarely contained more than two generations of the same family; rarely contained relations other than parents and children; but often contained other adults. The combination of a low age of life expectancy and late marriage meant that it was common for there to be only two generations in families. Over 70 per cent of households in the period 1754–1821 contained only two generations of relatives. Only 5.8 per cent of households contained three generations and virtually none four. It was perfectly possible for there to be three generations alive and living in fairly close proximity to one another, though the migration figures suggest that this may not have been very common.

In the mid-eighteenth century, before a younger age of marriage had become widespread, the average woman had had her last child by the age of thirty-nine and could expect to die twelve years before the birth of her last grandchild. A third of female children were dead by the age of five; one in seven of those who survived to the age of five did not survive to the age of twenty-five; and more than half of those who reached twenty-five had died before the age of sixty-five. The figures were worse for males: two-fifths died before the age of five and three-fifths of those who reached twenty-five did not survive to sixty-five. These figures are significant not simply for the overall population, but for the composition of the family and of the household.

Household size varied surprisingly little over the period, there being a mean household size of four to five people throughout. Many children had left home by the age of twelve, the usual age at which children started in domestic or farm service, or parish apprenticeships. In Romford in 1562, out of 175 households only thirty (17 per cent) had resident children over the age of twelve. Most families were nuclear rather than extended, but they might be complex. There were rarely relations other than parents and children living in the household, but the high rate of death among young adults meant that both men and women with children might remarry and have second or third families. Households might, therefore, consist of people who were related to each other in a variety of different ways: step- and half-brothers and -sisters. Deaths of the parents of young children might also result in them going to live with uncles and aunts. Perhaps 15 per cent of households were complex ones. The decline in the rate of widows remarrying in the eighteenth century must have reduced the complexity of family groups. There are some interesting regional variations. London townswomen in the sixteenth and seventeenth centuries were likely to marry younger, and were more likely to remarry if widowed, than women in other parts of the country.

There were often other people in the household not related to the family. Some of these were servants: 28.5 per cent of households had one or more servants, and throughout the period 13.4 per cent of the population (chiefly young adults) were in service. Young people in the household who were not the children of the householder might be servants or apprentices: 40 per cent of all children became servants for a time, and 20 per cent of all children grew up in households where there were resident adults other than their parents. Although well over 80 per cent of gentry households had resident servants, most servants worked in less socially exalted households. Households with the largest numbers of servants, apart from noble households, were those of landowners, who had farm servants; and of traders who sold food and drink or ran inns. Noble households might contain not just servants, but the children of other noble families sent to live with another family for educational purposes.

The concepts of family and service have different connotations in the twentieth century from those which they had in early modern England. We have seen how householders might refer to their servants as 'family'. It is evident that servants might regard their employers as being on a par with their own relations. The wills of women servants in Leeds and Hull in the sixteenth and early seventeenth centuries show many bequests by servants to their employers, their employers' families and other members of the household, as well as bequests to their own relations. Equally, employers normally made bequests to their servants.

Settlement and Migration

A small proportion of people lived in towns – perhaps only a quarter of the population in the sixteenth century, and mortality there was generally higher than in the countryside.[1] Infant

[1]   Approximate populations of the principal towns in England

	c.1520	c.1603	c.1695
London	60,000	200,000	575,000
Norwich	12,000	15,000	29,000
Bristol	10,000	12,000	19,000
York	8,000	11,000	12,000 (c.1670)

Source: adapted from, P. Clark and P. Slack, *English Towns in Transition 1500–1700*, Oxford University Press, 1976, p. 83.

mortality in towns was high, at about 200 per 1,000 live births, but there was a good deal of variation both within and between towns. Life in towns was unhealthy, and increases in the size of towns were usually the consequence of migration from the country rather than a rising birth rate, though different towns grew at rather different rates. The population of London barely replaced itself, yet the number of inhabitants more than doubled between the beginning and the end of the seventeenth century, while the population of Salisbury declined over the same period. London was the largest English town, and its nearest rivals, Norwich, Bristol and York, were several times smaller. Though there were some changes in the hierarchy of towns, the most dramatic change – the rise of the new manufacturing towns – did not take place until after 1760.

Migration was an important factor in the maintenance or growth of urban populations, and this had an impact upon the population structure of towns. Population movement was largely generated by economic circumstances, both those of age (young unmarried men and women looking for work) and of economic difficulty (as in the 1590s). The authorities accepted migration where it led to a stable place of residence, but where it led to people drifting about, with no fixed abode, they regarded it as a threat to public order.

The mobile poor, especially those who were the subject of the Elizabethan vagrancy laws, are often assumed to be mainly men, but William Harrison, writing in the 1570s, estimated their numbers 'of one sex and another, to amount unto above ten thousand persons', suggesting that women were a significant proportion of the whole. In late-sixteenth-century London women made up about 30 per cent of the vagrant poor, and in the provinces about 50 per cent. Some of these women were on their travels in search of an errant husband. Others were unmarried servant girls with young children. The number of women vagrants seems to have risen and fallen with the number of vagrants in general, being most numerous in the late sixteenth and early seventeenth centuries.

Regardless of whether migrants had somewhere to go to, migration was an important feature of early modern England, and in the late seventeenth and early eighteenth centuries many English people, men and women, town and country dwellers, migrated at some time in their lives. The proportion of migrants in London may have been as high as 70 per cent by the early eighteenth century. Many were young and single, and in some towns, especially those which were resorts, the numbers of women exceeded those of men by about 15 per cent. This was the result of the employment opportunities for women in domestic service and in urban trades. Ludlow, a market town and social centre, had a ratio of about seven men to ten women because of the large numbers of domestic servants and women working in such trades as glovemaking and victualling in the eighteenth century. Poor single women with children tended also to gravitate to towns. Young women immigrants to London tended to have travelled further than men, but male farm servants travelled greater distances than female farm servants. There were also age differences: women tended to migrate to towns in their twenties, while men were more likely to go in their teens. The long-distance migration of the early eighteenth century was replaced later in the century by more migration over smaller distances. Regional variations in migration reflected local economic circumstances, proximity to a city and, increasingly important as the eighteenth century progressed, opportunities for emigration abroad.

Although young single people formed the largest group of migrants, families also migrated. In two Midlands villages a third of the migrants were found to be families, and emigration abroad largely consisted of families rather than single people. Migrants were not simply the poor and dispossessed, though owning land made migration less likely. Moving about the country was a normal part of many people's lives, especially for young adults, women as well as men. Many women, when married, had already been away from their parents' homes for ten years or more, having left their childhood village and had experience of life somewhere else – not necessarily very far away, but certainly outside their immediate community.

This chapter has suggested in bald terms what expectations a woman in early modern England might have of her life. Later chapters are concerned with the effects of these statistics upon real lives. The story that the statistics tell is of a general change in the mid- to late eighteenth century when the age of marriage declined, fewer people remained unmarried and the population began to increase. This population increase has been exhaustively examined, but no one has come up with a single explanation for it. The rise in the birth rate, due both to the lower age of marriage and to more people marrying, was partly responsible, but no one knows what relative weight to give to these two factors. There was also a decline in the death rate, possibly because of a reduction in the effects of starvation and epidemic disease.

PART TWO

Marriage, Sex and the Family

CHAPTER FOUR

Marriage

Marriage was crucial to a woman's identity. Nevertheless, at any one time, only a third of women were actually married, so marriage had a symbolic importance separate from its incidence in the population. Recent work on marriage by historians concentrates on two aspects: on the arrangements for making a marriage (courtship, dowries, portions, settlements, inheritance) on the one hand, and on relationships within marriage (particularly the conjugal relationship, but also relations between parents and children) on the other.

Marriage is a form of legal contract. It also describes a relationship between a woman and a man which has both a public and a private aspect. We know most about the legal and public aspects from the large literature produced by lawyers, moralists and theologians. We know the colourful stories of noble matches: the divorce of Frances Howard (1593?–1632) from the Earl of Essex in 1613; and the arranged marriage of Mary Wroth (1587–c.1652) and her lifelong love for William Herbert, Earl of Pembroke, which resulted in the birth during her widowhood after 1614 of two of Pembroke's children. The private relationship is much more difficult to penetrate, because it produces little evidence accessible to historians. It is also the aspect of marriage in which our own preconceptions are most evident.

What was Marriage?

The purpose of marriage was set out in the Book of Common Prayer, the form of marriage officially used by everyone from the sixteenth century until 1645 and from 1660 until 1689. It was first, for the procreation of children; second, for a remedy against sin and to avoid fornication; and third, for the mutual society, help and comfort of the partners.

Most people seem to have agreed that these were the primary purposes. Childlessness was regarded as an affliction, even though, with the combination of high infant mortality and adult infertility, a quarter of all married couples had no children. The effects of this upon a marriage can be seen in eighteenth-century London, where many of the marriages in which one partner deserted the other were childless. Fornication (sex between unmarried people or between an unmarried woman and a married man) and adultery (sex between a man and a married woman) were punished by the church courts, though not very effectively; and when the church courts were in abeyance, adultery was prosecuted in the secular courts. As for the mutual society, help and comfort of the partners, the notion of companionship in marriage seems to have become more widespread.

There were detailed instructions concerning the conduct of church weddings: forbidden days of the week and seasons (Lent, for example), and the publication of banns announcing the forthcoming marriage. A public church marriage was necessary to ensure the inheritance of property. Nevertheless, marriages which failed to comply with the canon law might still be legally binding. Clandestine marriages, as these marriages were known, might take place before witnesses, but they were much more private affairs than the usual church wedding. During the sixteenth and seventeenth centuries, church marriages became more popular, but this was not the only means of marrying. All that was necessary under canon law was a public declaration (a spousal or marriage contract) made in the present tense before witnesses that a man and woman considered themselves married. A couple might also state in the future tense that they intended subsequently to get married, but this was not irrevocable unless they had sexual intercourse.

The two most celebrated campaigners for the reform of the law governing marriage were Henry VIII and John Milton, both of them wishing, for different reasons, to be separated from an unsatisfactory partner. Some reforms were proposed during the sixteenth century, but these chiefly concerned the proper fulfilment of the canonical requirements, and allowing marriages between stepbrothers and -sisters and with deceased wives' sisters.

During the Civil War and Interregnum, reforms were enacted of which the most far-reaching was the 1653 Act which instituted civil marriage before a justice of the peace. Church weddings, or rather weddings performed solely by a clergyman, were prohibited. The civil ceremony was so unpopular that couples often had both a civil and a church marriage. In 1653 Dorothy Osborne (1627–95) wrote to her fiancé of the new marriage service, 'In conscience, I believe the old one is better; and for my part I am resolved to stay till that comes in fashion again'; and another woman, married before a justice, wrote that 'if it had not been more solemnly done afterwards by a minister, I should not have believed it lawfully done.[1] Civil marriage satisfied no one and by 1658 marriages before clergymen had resumed. The proliferation of religious sects produced a variety of different forms of religious service. At the Restoration pre-war practices were reinstated, but marriages contracted before justices in the 1650s were recognized.

The greatest change in the law relating to marriage came in 1753 when a new Marriage Act was passed. From 1754 the only legally valid form of marriage was one conducted in church according to the ecclesiastical canons, and recorded in the parish register. Pre-contracts (promises to marry someone in the future) and oral spousals ceased to have any force, and the consent of parents or guardians was required for anyone under twenty-one. Contraventions of the Act were dealt with in the secular courts and not in the church courts. Until 1754 there had been a considerable overlap between the ecclesiastical and secular jurisdictions. One of the effects of the Act was to reduce the number of instances when a husband or wife might claim that the marriage was invalid because of some defect in procedure.

We have little idea of how much the laws about the making of a marriage actually impinged upon ordinary people's lives. Both men and women from most social classes brought cases to the church courts about the validity of spousals. Between the mid-sixteenth century and the mid-seventeenth century the number of spousal actions in the church courts declined markedly, partly because of the increasing belief that the only proper form of marriage was one solemnized in a church. The approval of family and friends was also very important, which made marriage a very public affair. A good many church court actions originated in marriages where there was a conflict between the partners on the one hand and the family and friends on the other as to the suitability of the match, and where the opposing family withheld financial support for the couple.

These actions did not allow the award of damages, and during the later seventeenth century actions by seduced maidens and their fathers began to appear in the secular courts, the first recognizable

---

[1] Quoted in C. Durston, ' "Unhallowed wedlocks": the regulation of marriage during the English Revolution', *Historical Journal*, 31, 1988 pp. 56–7.

breach of promise case being heard in 1763. After the Marriage Act of 1753 ecclesiastical courts lost their power to compel marriage on grounds of pre-contract and the only remedy for disappointed expectation of marriage was to be had in the secular courts. Here the father could allege aggravated trespass, or that he had been deprived of his daughter's labour, for both of which damages might be payable. This might seem to be a blatant case of woman as property, but it was generally recognized that these devices were legal fictions since it was a principle of the law that no one might claim redress for a wrong to which they had consented.

For those who wished to be spared some of the publicity of banns and a church ceremony, the clandestine marriage, with no banns, in a parish away from home and conducted by a strange and possibly unbeneficed clergyman, had much to recommend it. After the introduction of a tax on marriages in the 1690s, it also provided a form of tax evasion. Clandestine marriages increased in number during the later seventeenth century as more people sought cheaper and more private ways of getting married. They were not in themselves illegal, but they were difficult to prove if there was any doubt about validity. In 1617, for example, Nicholas Caiford of Warminster, Wiltshire sought a clandestine marriage with Amy Parrett to avoid publicity for, though she was willing, her friends were much opposed to the match.

Getting Married

Popular courtship customs varied greatly and often allowed a good deal of licence between young couples. Ballads with titles like 'A Merry Ballad of a Rich Maid that had Eighteen Several Suitors of Several Counties' (*c*.1625) and 'The Northern Lad: or, the Fair Maid's Choice, who Refused all for a Ploughman' (*c*.1672), suggest that young people had considerable freedom of choice. Chapbooks like *Cupid's Soliciter of Love* even advised bashful swains on how to approach young women. The consent of both partners to the marriage was expected, but family and friends might be influential in approving of or objecting to a marriage. Family disapproval was likely to cause considerable trouble and sometimes litigation. One of the commonest reasons for objecting to a match was a marked difference in the social status of the couple. Arranged marriages were generally restricted to those who had major dynastic or economic considerations; they were regarded in the popular press as a poor way to start out on adult life. Samuel Pepys helped to negotiate the marriage between the daughter of his patron, Lord Sandwich, and Sir George Carteret's son in 1665. Even in great noble families the proposed partners seem to have had the right of veto, and the custom of arranging dynastic matches between children became increasingly unusual.

The timing of marriage was determined by the stage of people's lives, the season of the year and the church calendar. Men of the artisan class would marry when they were established as masters, with their own workshops, apprentices and journeymen. Apprentices were not allowed to marry and journeymen were generally too poor to do so. For women of a similar class marriage usually followed a period when they had worked for a living (often away from their parental home). In the late sixteenth century, rural marriages were most numerous between April and July. By the late seventeenth century, marriages were more evenly distributed between early summer and autumn. This shift occurred because there was a greater disregard for the church calendar (people ignored the prohibition on marriage in Advent and, to a lesser extent, Lent), and because of greater regional specialization in agriculture. Autumn marriages were most popular in arable regions, following the harvest; and spring marriages were most popular in pastoral regions, following lambing and calving. The timing of marriages was related to hiring fairs, which, in turn, followed the busiest time of the year. There was least seasonality in urban marriages.

The earliest age at which marriage was recognized under canon law was twelve for a girl and fourteen for a boy, though marriages at such a young age were extremely uncommon and were confined to royalty and the upper nobility, contracting complicated dynastic unions to secure titles and property. The seventeenth-century couple from Myddle, Shropshire, who fell in love at school and married when their combined ages were scarcely thirty, were the subject of comment because there was no parental involvement. The usual age for both men and women was their mid-twenties, the age declining as the eighteenth century progressed. With the likelihood of the death as a young adult of one or other partner in a marriage, the average length of the marriages of the poor was between seventeen and nineteen years, rising to twenty-two in the later eighteenth century. Only a fifth to a quarter lasted for more than thirty-five years. These periods were longer by a couple of years for the gentry. Compare this with modern Britain, where in 1988 the average duration was thirty years with 63 per cent of marriages ending with the death of one partner. In early modern

England there was little likelihood of a couple surviving until all their children reached adulthood.

Given that many marriages lasted for a relatively short period, it is not surprising that about a third of all marriages were remarriages for one of the partners (a similar statistic to that of the 1980s), though the rate of remarriage declined in the eighteenth century. As we saw in chapter 3, there was sometimes a very considerable age difference between the partners, especially in men's second or subsequent marriages. Older women were less likely to remarry and were less likely to be married to anyone markedly different from them in age. Of women over fifty, about 60 per cent had no husband, though this figure includes those who had been deserted, and those who had never married.

Widows in London were more likely to remarry than were widows in the provinces: in the early seventeenth century between a third and a half of the brides in some London parishes were widows, often remarrying less than a year after the death of a husband. Various explanations have been offered for the decline in the rate of widows remarrying from the later seventeenth century: changed sensibilities or better employment opportunities for women, for example. Much of the evidence for the rate of remarriage is based on London, where men outnumbered women for much of the sixteenth and seventeenth centuries. From the later seventeenth century women began to outnumber men, partly because of the increase in jobs both in domestic service and in new luxury industries like silk spinning and weaving. The prospects for a widow's remarriage diminished sharply when there were plenty of unmarried women to choose from. Also the prosperity and gild membership which a citizen's widow might bring with her became of less worth with the decline of gild regulation from the later seventeenth century.

Funerary monuments provide evidence for a change in sensibility. It was not unusual in the later Middle Ages and even in the early seventeenth century for a man who had been married more than once to commemorate himself, his wives and their children all on the same monument. The man is often depicted on a brass between both his wives or in an effigy between or above them. In the period from about 1480 to 1640 in three counties (Gloucestershire, Northamptonshire and Hertfordshire) there are at least twenty-four monuments depicting a man and two wives, two monuments to a man and three wives, and one to a man and four wives. The only example of a monument to a woman with more than one husband is that of 1718 in Cirencester, to Rebecca Powell, who was a wealthy woman and who founded a school there. After the middle of the seventeenth century it is very unusual to find men's monuments commemorating more than one wife. One of the latest examples is a brass inscription of 1674 at Long Itchington, Warwickshire, to John Bosworth and his two wives. By the later seventeenth century, monuments were becoming less representational, and it had become very unfashionable to commemorate multiple marriages on the same monument. This suggests the greater prevalence of the ideal of the single, lifelong union.

Adultery and Fornication, Incest and Bigamy

After the Reformation the church courts ceased to be able to administer corporal punishment. Churchmen and moralists considered their penalties for adultery, incest and fornication were insufficiently severe. One of the Puritans' strongest objections to the established church was its inability to punish sexual crimes with the severity which they believed was warranted, and they supported the idea that such offences should be dealt with by the secular courts. Very loosely, church courts dealt with transgressions of morality and the secular courts with matters regarding public order and property, though the definition of property came to include seduction.

In fact, the common law courts had been active against sex offenders since the early sixteenth century, usually for breaches of the peace. Urban magistrates sentenced adulterers, fornicators and whoremongers to the stocks, to whipping or even to prison or a house of correction. Women might, in addition, have their hair cut off. The extension to magistrates of the power to order maintenance payments for bastards also gave them power over the parents. Women were commonly whipped; men were not. Not only were punishments more readily meted out on women, but in general parents who were able to support their illegitimate children did not come before the courts because there was no need to arrange their maintenance. Thus the poor were more likely to be punished for their sexual lapses than the rich, and women more likely than men.

Prosecutions for adultery in the church courts were often of people living together as man and wife as well as of more casual encounters. Proof of an intention to marry might mitigate the charge. Cases at the Durham High Commission in the 1620s included one against Richard Hopper of Coundon. The fact that he used often to offer to cut Isabel Little's hay and other such courtesies, which he performed for no one else, was given as circumstantial evidence of adultery. Elizabeth Dixon, spinster, was accused of notorious incontinency with Christopher Atty, gentleman, by whom she had borne two children in the last two years. The couple were to perform a corporal penance in Durham cathedral for three Sundays, and she was to live in the custody of William Strother until ordered otherwise.

During the Interregnum reforms were enacted, since the church courts were no longer sitting except for proving wills. In 1650 an Act was passed for suppressing incest, adultery and fornication. Incest and adultery were declared felonies punishable by death; fornication by three months in gaol and a year's being bound over for good behaviour. These attempts to use the civil power to enforce sexual morality were of limited success because the sentences were so draconian that they were rarely carried out. Simply proving that the crime had been committed was technically difficult. What is very striking about the 1650s is that the bastardy rate fell to an unprecedented low, even given defects in the registrations of births. Here is one example of Puritan morality apparently having a real effect on human behaviour.

In the late sixteenth and early seventeenth centuries, the severity of punishment appropriate for an adulterer was much debated. At one extreme were those who wished to apply the penalties prescribed in the Old Testament book of Deuteronomy: the death of both parties in the case of adultery by a married woman. Others cited Christ's mercy to the woman taken in adultery: 'He that is without sin among you, let him first cast a stone at her.' The application of the Mosaic law had many attractions for reformers, and indeed had a good deal of cross-party support in the unsettled political situation of the 1650s. The basis of the debate was that adultery constituted the theft of a wife from her husband. That the same arguments continued to be put in the morally laxer atmosphere of the Restoration may have been because of an increasingly idealized view of both marriage and the family, emphasizing new values of conjugal companionship and domestic felicity, but continuing to be concerned with the public consequences of adultery. The moral reform movements of the late seventeenth century, especially the societies for the reformation of manners, continued the pressure for severer penalties for adultery, and further attempts at stiffening the law were made in the eighteenth century.

Incest was defined by the church courts as a sexual act or marriage between anyone related within the prohibited degrees of matrimony (including first cousins). Cases which came to court most often involved a man and his wife's sister or his step-mother, or a relationship of that kind, rather than parents and children or brothers and sisters, though these would have been very much harder to detect. Nuns who were dispensed from their vow of chastity, and then had the dispensation revoked in 1539, were divorced by their husbands on grounds of incest, a matter of legal technicality. Cases involving children of incestuous unions rarely came to court, and the offence itself does not seem to have featured very largely in people's minds. It is impossible to know how large the dark figure of undeclared cases might be, but it is unlikely that it was widespread and tolerated. Certainly shortage of possible partners is not a likely explanation given the high level of migration and the large numbers of young people who lived and worked away from home. Most communities were relatively exogamous.

Bigamy was probably uncommon, happening through genuine mistakes arising from clandestine marriages, lack of records, migration and poor communication. That it was regarded as a problem is evidenced by the fact that in 1604, when the ecclesiastical canons were revised, bigamy was made a felony in the secular courts (and therefore punishable by death). A Wiltshire man was hanged for the crime in 1617. Many of those who were prosecuted for bigamy were poor people who had lost touch with a previous spouse. Other cases like that of Bridget Gowee were the result of genuine mistakes. She sought a pardon for her conviction for bigamy in 1646. She had been married to a Dr Nevill who went abroad and was imprisoned by 'Jesuitical papists', who informed her of her husband's death. She then married James Gowee, whereupon Dr Nevill returned home and Mr Gowee, wanting to marry someone else, indicted her with bigamy. Occasionally there was a scandalous case, like that of Richard Cleaton, of Myddle in Shropshire, who, against the wishes of both sets of parents, married Annie Tyller. The parents, to show their displeasure, gave them no money to live on, and Richard deserted Annie when she was pregnant. He took another wife near Bridgnorth and had several children by her. Annie finally caught up with him and 'indicted him at an Assizes at Bridgnorth upon the statute of polygamy'. Richard was acquitted because Annie could not prove that he was married to the second wife, and the second wife asserted that they were not married.

The church courts were the official custodians of the proprieties of marriage, but what about those people who were not members of the Church of England? Although nonconformity was not officially permitted until the Toleration Act of 1689, nonconformist congregations regarded the discipline of members as a serious matter even during the period of persecution of 1660–89. The surviving records of several denominations show how marriage was one of the subjects which they considered fell within their jurisdiction. The Buckinghamshire Quakers, for example, expressed their fear of 'unlawful affection' between a man and a women who were first cousins and lived together. Elizabeth Wood of Great Missenden was admonished on more than one occasion for her 'loose and disorderly conversation' and in 1673 was reported to have been married 'by a priest to a man of the world', i.e. by an Anglican minister to a man who was not a Quaker. The Friends in High Wycombe resolved to visit her 'and lay the evil and weight thereof upon her'.

Domestic violence appears a good deal in the chapbook and almanac literature, often in the misogynistic guise of the wife beating the husband. When this did actually take place it was sometimes marked by one of the popular demonstrations known as skimmingtons. There was a level of tolerance for men beating their wives on the grounds that it was a wife's duty to be obedient to her husband, and that he was justified in taking corrective measures if she was disobedient. However, where this intruded into the community, it was not tolerated. A husband in Myddle in Shropshire was notorious in the village for having overstepped the mark and put out one of his wife's eyes.

Unofficial Unions

Evidence for the very poor suggests that many of them never actually contracted a legally recognized marriage and were thus free to change common law partners at will. It is not possible to know how many people took this course of action since it leaves no records, and in any case it took place among the most geographically mobile section of the population. The Norwich census of the poor of 1570, and similar listings for Salisbury in the early seventeenth century, suggest that there were a good many men and women cohabiting. Many of the Salisbury cases refer to women as alleged wives or otherwise cast doubt upon the validity of marriages. For example, Morgan Percyvall, 'one Rebecca to whom he says he was married' and their daughter were sent back to Oxford from Salisbury in 1599. In the same year Thomas Wheler, a wandering vagrant, was sent back to Romsey, Hampshire, from

Salisbury with Elizabeth Carpenter, 'a lewd woman, whom he alleges to be his wife'; and Humphrey Pearce and Margaret Hooper, 'living lewdly together and not married', were sent back to Southampton. In 1631 James Groce, wandering with Anne Wooddes, affirmed that she was his wife (which on examination proved not to be the case), that they had had one child who had died, and that she was pregnant.

Cohabitation was a matter for the church courts. William Whiting and Marie Gillet of Charlbury, Oxfordshire, were cited in 1584 for 'keeping together in one house'. Anyone who permitted cohabitation to take place might also find himself or herself in trouble, as did the unnamed wife of Giles de Wickington for suffering Ralph Wattes and Margaret Giles her daughter 'to keep together' in her house at Wigginton, Oxfordshire, in the late sixteenth century. The matter was complicated by the discovery that Margaret had a husband still living. From the late seventeenth century, unmarried people living together were usually only reported by the church-wardens if there was a child involved. What was at issue was less the morality of a couple cohabiting than the possibility of the care of a child or unmarried mother becoming a cost to the parish.

The Breakdown of Marriage

We have seen that the average duration of marriage was less than twenty years. Virtually all marriages ended in the death of one of the partners because the Church of England did not recognize divorce. (Only a divorce or an annulment allowed the parties to remarry. Separation, a procedure recognized by the Church of England, permitted the parties to live apart but not to remarry, and entailed considerable penalties for a wife.) Like other reformed churches the Church of England had ceased to regard marriage as a sacrament, but alone along them, it adhered to the Roman Catholic belief in the indissolubility of marriage during the lifetime of both partners. Annulment and separation were lengthy and expensive procedures, and divorce was impossible for all but those who could afford a private Act of Parliament. Between 1539 and 1857 there were 317 divorces by the latter means. In 1542 the Marquis of Northampton secured a canon law divorce from his wife on the grounds of her adultery, but had to go to Parliament for a private bill to allow him to remarry, which was forbidden under canon law. This was granted under Edward vi's parliament of 1552, but revoked by Queen Mary's parliament. The Marquis had in fact remarried in 1547.

The recent publication of two large books on divorce by Roderick Phillips (1988) and Lawrence Stone (1990) is indicative of the preoccupations of the late twentieth century rather than of the historical importance of divorce.[1] Roderick Phillips very properly couples his discussion of divorce with marital breakdown, pointing out that it is only with a relaxation of the divorce laws that the two might become more congruent, and that, if divorce is virtually impossible, people will find other ways out of an intolerable marriage.

During the sixteenth and seventeenth centuries one of the questions frequently asked in the visitations of ecclesiastical officials was whether there were any married people who, being not legally separated, were living apart. Elizabeth Bradbury of St Mary's parish, Oxford, was cited in the archdeacon's court in 1584 for not living with her husband. The case was dismissed when she explained that

her husband John Bradbury is a man that useth to go of messages for gentlemen, and being a tailor and not free of the town [i.e. not a freeman] is driven to be most abroad for their living and no other cause.[2]

William Fuller and his wife Mary, of Swanborne, Buckinghamshire, were cited in 1662 for living apart, and Anne Hannah of Ravenston, Buckinghamshire, was reported to have a husband living in the same county. He had left her seven years earlier and wandered around without a fixed abode. In the meantime she had married a second husband who died within a month.

Presentments for living apart became progressively less common after 1660, and by the eighteenth century this kind of supervision was much less vigilantly maintained, the chief consideration apparently being the question of poor relief. There does seem to have been a rise in the number of separations, though whether this was the result of a change in attitude to marriage or to separated people, or of there being more opportunities for people to escape from their partners, is not clear. The recruitment of soldiers and sailors for the foreign wars of the eighteenth century provided men with an opportunity for leaving, and in London desertions increased in war years.

Separation was unusual in country districts in the sixteenth

---

[1] Roderick Phillips, *Putting Asunder: A History of Divorce in Western Society*, Cambridge University Press, 1988; and Lawrence Stone, *The Road to Divorce: England 1530–1987*, Oxford University Press, 1990.
[2] E. R. C. Brinkworth (ed.), *The Archdeacon's Court: Liber Actorum, 1584*, Oxfordshire Record Society, 23–4, 1941–2, p. 131.

and seventeenth centuries, and when it did happen it was most often the desertion of the woman by the man, and usually when the wife was in her thirties. The Norwich census of the poor shows that in 1570 deserted women were 8 per cent of all women surveyed between the ages of thirty-one and forty. Separation as the resolution of an intolerable marriage was a desperate measure, of considerable disadvantage to both partners. Vagrant women were often searching for errant husbands, like the Lincolnshire woman who, in 1582, was seized by the authorities in Warwick. She tracked her husband all over the Midlands until she ran him to ground at a fair, where, having promised to meet her at an alehouse, he took her cloak and absconded again. In 1633 Elizabeth Warner was apprehended in Norwich. She had been born in Shrewsbury, the daughter of a tanner, and there met and married her husband. They had moved to London, then to Kings Lynn, and then to Wisbech, where he had left her some ten days earlier. She was looking for him in Norwich and intended to go to London, where he had friends, and thence to Shrewsbury to her parents' and to claim poor relief for herself and her child.

Other kinds of separation occurred. At the beginning of the eighteenth century Elinor Hussey had

upbraided her husband in such opprobrious terms that, not being able to live in peace with her, he left her. . . . He gave his wife her £100 portion, and she went to Little Drayton, where she kept an alehouse, and William Tyler [with whom she was on terms of some familiarity before her husband left her] went often to visit her and at last had a child by her whom they called Nell Hussey.[1]

Separation occurred often enough for patterns to be observable, though differing between country and town. Most studies concentrate upon the eighteenth century, using evidence from settlement examinations. Separated families in the country were more likely to have children, and had more of them, than did the average couple. Typically, couples were illiterate and had usually married younger and were more geographically mobile than the population at large. Husbands were most likely to depart in September and the marriages had rarely lasted as long as ten years at the time of desertion. Desertion was about three times commoner in the town than in the country. In eighteenth-century Colyton, Devon, a town with an unusually high population of single women who worked as lace-makers, 10 per cent of marriages ended in desertion; the usual rural rate was about 5 per cent. Evidence for the London parish of St

---

[1] Richard Gough, *The History of Myddle*, Penguin, 1981, p. 125.

Martin-in-the-Fields suggests too that the rate of desertion fluctuated more in the town than in the country, ranging between 7 and
15 per cent. In some urban families it happened when the family
was at its poorest, with several dependent children; in others
childlessness seems to have been significant. The numbers of
desertions rose in the eighteenth century with the rising population
and a lower age of marriage.

Poverty and opportunity were the main causes of desertion.
Husbands were most likely to desert when there were dependent
children and the family was poorest. Opportunities for enlistment
in the army and navy (a way of avoiding both an unsatisfactory
marriage and financial problems) increased the likelihood of
desertion; the number of abandoned families rose in war-time.
Apart from soldiers and sailors, alehouse keepers, ex-prisoners and
servants of the aristocracy who stayed on in service were the most
likely to desert their wives. Some desertions were clearly the
equivalent of a divorce, leaving one family in order to set up
another household, something which became easier in the
eighteenth century with the reduced likelihood of being presented
in the church courts.

Women might be separated from their husbands for reasons
other than desertion. Husbands might be working abroad as
soldiers, sailors or merchants; or they might be in prison. Separation might also take place because of poverty or old age. Overseers
of the poor seem to have regarded the separation of married
couples, in order to provide them with accommodation, as an
acceptable expedient, and almshouses might require men and
women, even when married, to live separately.

A curiosity rather than a numerically significant phenomenon
was wife sales. These were a popular subject for almanacs and
chapbooks, but in real life they were very unusual and hardly ever
happened before the eighteenth century; they usually took place
among people who may well not have actually contracted legal
marriages. Only sixteen recorded sales took place before 1760 in
England. One of the better-known instances was the supposed
purchase by Godfrey Kneller, the painter, during the 1670s or
1680s, of Mrs Vos, the wife of a Quaker. The purchaser was often
known to both the husband and the wife and the sale was probably
a public ritual denoting an agreed change of partner rather than a
financial transaction. The sums involved were very small, shillings
rather than pounds, or were goods like a leg of mutton or a quantity
of ale. There is no evidence in the period 1500–1760 of husband
sales.

Women without Husbands

Although women expected to marry, two-thirds were on their own, either widowed or having never been married. Poverty was a serious problem for them. Widows and deserted wives often had young families to provide for, and wage rates were often insufficient for women to be able to support themselves alone. Domestic service was fine for the younger women; it was no answer for the woman with children or for the older unmarried woman.

Apart from the material hardship, the loss of a husband was devastating in other ways. Mrs Hannah Allen (fl. 1650–66) wrote of how, when she received the news of the death of her husband, 'I began to fall into a deep melancholy, and no sooner did this black humour begin to darken my soul, but the devil set on with his former temptations.'[1] Religion might provide the means to treat death with resignation, but many women found it difficult to find comfort. A late-seventeenth-century woman whose husband died suddenly of a fever wrote, 'I was in such a case as it was not possible to express my grief, nor could I come at the least degree of submission to a final parting with him.'[2] Widowhood could also last a long time, as an inscription in Redgrave church, Suffolk, to Mrs Anne Butts who died in 1609 testifies:

> The weaker sex's strongest precedent
> Lies here below, seven fair years she spent
> In wedlock sage; and since that merry age
> Sixty-one years she lived a widow sage.

The proportion of unmarried people in the population as a whole fluctuated between 5 and 18 per cent. Nunneries were chiefly resorted to by women from noble and gentry families, but there were only 2,000 nuns in 1500, and the number of vocations was falling. The dissolution of the nunneries in 1536–9 must have had only a limited impact upon the number of unmarried women. This number was at its highest in the late seventeenth century when Mary Astell's *A Serious Proposal to the Ladies* (1694) addressed itself to a possible solution – a secular college or nunnery for women. But these were proposals for women of higher social status. What became of lower-class spinsters? Their numbers declined with a lowering of the age of marriage. The majority of unmarried women lived with their parents, and about 30–40 per cent were in service. Groups of unmarried women sometimes set up house together, a

---

1 Mrs Hannah Allen, *A Narrative of God's Gracious Dealings*, London, 1683, p. 7.
2 National Library of Scotland, MS 1037, f. 10.

response to the low level of women's wages. It was common to find large numbers of unmarried women in towns, chiefly working in service and in trades connected with service. Spa towns had especially large numbers because of the opportunities for work in millinery and dressmaking and other trades connected with consumption and entertainment, as well as domestic service. The most invisible women of all are the older unmarried women, with no family and less opportunity for employment in domestic service. Their disadvantaged status is emphasized by their high rate of early death.

Between 9 and 14 per cent of households were headed by women, more commonly by widows than by spinsters. The number rose in the eighteenth century, possibly because of the low rate of marriage in the 1690s, but also because of the smaller numbers of widows remarrying. A third of women heading households lived alone, but those who had servants were likely to have a higher proportion of female servants than a household headed by a man. Single and widowed men were less likely to head households than their female equivalents, suggesting that men on their own were more likely to become dependent upon another household than women in the same position.

The Experience of Marriage

Marriage was an unalterable fact of life, and people rarely wrote about it even in their private diaries. We also know relatively little about women's expectations of marriage. It is clear from surviving correspondence that some husbands and wives were very close and missed their spouses greatly when they were parted. There are also heart-rending accounts of unhappy marriages. However, virtually all the accounts we have are produced by literate and articulate people. It was only when a plebeian marriage got into difficulties that it entered the record, by means of depositions in the church or secular courts, or by neighbours' reports.

Marriage is, however, one of those universal subjects which produces folk-songs and legends. It was a subject of never-failing interest to the theatre-going public and the purchasers of popular ballads and chap books. These publications suggest that to a great extent the stresses and strains of marriage were regarded as regrettable, but not without their comic aspects, and that companionship was not merely an ideal, but was widely experienced. Titles such as 'The Cruel Shrew' were balanced by 'The Married Woman's Case'.

It is plain that it was not simply love, but fierce passion which bound some marriages together, though these feelings were most often expressed when one of the partners died. An anonymous woman regretted in the 1650s that 'The Lord discovered to me that I had too much loved my husband in a fleshly love, making an idol of him.' Such passions are more often celebrated in poetry than, as here, in the words of the women seeking admission to an Independent church.[1] The plainest evidence for the depth of love which might exist between a wife and her husband can be found in a widow's lamentations:

> When it pleased God to call my husband from me . . . I was for a time exceedingly cast down, and troubled, as I think any poor creature could be; in which I was so overwhelmed that I did not know which way to turn myself, nor what to do. . . . I had lost a good estate, had nobody to look after my business, had many injured me, and had lost (above all the rest) a precious husband, whom I entirely loved.[2]

Young couples sometimes had to start life living with relatives. This could happen in even rich families like the Thynnes of Longleat, Wiltshire. When, in 1576, the family was unable to secure possession of a house they owned, the newly married Joan and John Thynne had to live in his parents' household, not without some ill-feeling. In the 1650s Mrs Hannah Allen, who had lived with an uncle and aunt before her marriage, continued to do so afterwards because her husband, a merchant, was often away on business. After her uncle's death her husband went on a long voyage and she moved to the country with her aunt and later lived with her mother.

The stresses of marrying someone unsuitable were summed up by Mrs Delany. She wrote of her wedding in 1718 to a man forty years her senior, 'Never was woe dressed out in gayer colours, and when I was led to the altar, I wished from my soul I had been led, as Iphigenia was, to be sacrificed.'[3] Later she was to write, 'Why must women be driven to the necessity of marrying? A state that should always be a matter of choice!'

The experience of an unhappy marriage, in a period when death or desertion were the only escape, was terrible. Women found a variety of ways of dealing with this. Religion might be a comfort. Mary Burrill reported in the 1650s, 'I have been infinitely troubled

---

[1] And more often men's poetry than women's. Women's more often celebrates constancy, regrets absence and mourns loss.

[2] Henry Walker, *Spirituall Experiences of Sundry Beleevers*, London, 1651, pp. 60–1.

[3] Ruth Hayden, *Mrs Delany, Her Life and Her Flowers*, Colonnade, British Museum Publications, 1980, p. 24.

by my marriage to my second husband, and have been afflicted in conscience about it much, till the Lord gave me comfort that my sins were forgiven.'[1] One of the most harrowing accounts of an unhappy marriage is that by Lady Margaret Cuninghame. She married in 1598 and remained with her father for the next three years because her husband would not support her, though she was not so far estranged from him not to be able to produce a son in 1601. Her husband continued to refuse to support her and she had to stay in inns. After a promise of reform he boarded himself, her and their children (by now there were at least two) with a servant of his and 'turned to all his wonted iniquities, . . . he kept no duty to me, but became altogether unkind, cruel, and malicious', to the point where he turned her and her gentlewoman attendant naked into the night and they had to seek refuge with the minister. In 1608 she gave birth to a son and her husband did not come anywhere near her until five weeks after the birth:

and then he came to me and would have accompanied with me for his filthy pleasure, which I refused for divers respects, especially for his wicked life, at the present being excommunicate for slaughter; and also Jennet Campbell being with bairn to him, with many other heinous sins that he daily committed without any appearance of amendment.[2]

Lady Margaret finally said that she had had enough, especially as his sexual demands were greatest of her when she was pregnant, and that she would have no more to do with him. Unfortunately, we do not know what became of this unhappy woman.

Other women had to put up with less outright abuse but with men who could be very difficult. Lady Anne Clifford, a strong-willed woman, had to spend much time coaxing her first husband, the Earl of Dorset, to behave with ordinary decency towards her. In 1617 she recorded how

My lord went up to my closet and said how little money I had left contrary to all they had told him. Sometimes I had fair words from him and sometimes foul, but I took all patiently, and did strive to give him as much content and assurance of my love as I could possibly.[3]

Her diary is full of references to him giving her 'a cold welcome' and threatening to remove their daughter from her.

[1] John Rogers, *Ohel or Beth-shemesh*, London, 1653, p. 413.
[2] *A Pairt of the Life of Lady Margaret Cuninghame*, privately printed, Edinburgh, 1827, pp. 10–11.
[3] *The Diaries of Lady Anne Clifford*, ed. D. J. H. Clifford, Alan Sutton, 1990, p. 53.

How did Marriage Change in Early Modern England?

The work of Lawrence Stone and Alan Macfarlane has dominated the history of marriage in the early modern period. Lawrence Stone has argued that some time between 1500 and 1800 the patriarchal family gave way to the affective family, thus giving children a much greater say over their own marriage partners. Alan Macfarlane has argued that marriages for love took over from marriages for convenience because of the growth of individualism. Both of these historians have been criticized, but their work has shaped much of the current debate on the nature of early modern marriage, and whether the choice of marriage partners became freer, and, if so, when. Both of them have looked at marriage in the changing social and economic circumstances of early modern England, and at a change in sensibilities.

In the early sixteenth century, the upper classes married younger and had more children; by the late eighteenth century, it was those at the lower end of the social scale who married younger and produced larger families. More women became dependent upon waged labour for the family income, and fewer participated in family businesses. Material conditions may have contributed to lowering the age of marriage. By the late eighteenth century, skilled male workers earned more and needed a shorter period in which to save up to marry. They were also less likely to be committed to lengthy apprenticeships. Unskilled men earned less, and female rural employment became more precarious and worse paid, so there were now people who, however long they saved, were not going to make an appreciable difference to their material circumstances. The restricted work available for women meant that getting married early became a more important priority, instead of waiting until both partners were economically independent of their families. Previously women had been able to save money; now they could only survive by marrying, and in poorer families many had to take on paid work all their lives, rather than just during the period before they married. Incentives to defer marriage disappeared for both the poor and the better-off.

Marriage changed not just because of altered material conditions, but also because the institutions controlling it changed. The church courts became increasingly impotent and authority, where it mattered, was transferred to the secular courts. Matrimonial offences became thereby a much less public matter. No longer did church wardens have power over matrimonial matters. Instead, marriage became a matter of public order and material maintenance, rather than of morality. The move away from supervision by the ecclesiastical authorities to supervision by the secular authorities also led to the regularization of marriage. No longer were oral contracts or spousals valid; clandestine marriages, which had largely superseded them, were outlawed too in 1753.

Did all this lead to, or reflect, changes in the quality of marriage? Was there really a general move towards freer choice of partners? Most of the evidence we have about choice of partners is for those social strata most likely to exercise controls, for economic and dynastic reasons, over their children's marriages. Yet, even then, it is clear that partners were rarely obliged to marry against their strong wishes. Personal preference played an increasingly large part in the choice of partner in the higher classes. For the middling sort, the ability of the wife to participate in the family business, or to transmit gild rights to her husband, diminished in importance. Poorer people seem always to have had reasonable freedom, though in the later part of the period choice of partner became a more private matter, especially with clandestine marriages and the anonymity of city life. In all classes we see the diminution in the influence of the kin group or community, and the elevation of the individual's judgement – the Macfarlane thesis.

But what difference did this make to women? It excluded the influence of the larger community group from the making of a marriage; and it exposed women to the consequences of a difficult marriage without the support of that community. A freer choice of partner would seem to lead to a higher expectation of marriage, and to elevating the relationship of husband and wife above that of the family as a whole. To return to Stone's thesis, the external evidence of marriage manuals suggests that Protestant values did permeate English society, and enhanced the moral value of the wife in her husband's eyes. These ideas were of greatest appeal to the middling sort, a group which increased in size and influence between the sixteenth and eighteenth centuries. Such values seem also to have had some impact upon the upper classes; but it is very difficult to know if there was any change in the affection and regard in which plebeian couples held one another. We simply cannot say whether more such marriages were happier or unhappier, or whether partners had a greater or a lesser likelihood of experiencing satisfaction in their marriages.

CHAPTER FIVE

Women and Sex

Despite the work of investigators like Masters and Johnson, and Kinsey, there are many things which are never known about people's sex lives. We usually acquire information about such things only when they are publicized as a result of someone behaving in a fashion which is considered scandalous, or has caused outrage. It is particularly difficult to discover what women themselves thought about their own sexuality. Debates about the extent to which sexuality is socially constructed, and to which fertility is culturally determined, have affected our view of sexuality and fertility in the past, and have alerted us to the idea that these things may have been very differently regarded in other times.

Fertility

Christian marriage requires that the participants be sexually mature; but in early modern England the mean age of marriage, in the mid-twenties, was manifestly years after this, though we know little about the precise age at which people reached sexual maturity in past times. Youthful aristocratic marriages are not indicative of a low age of sexual maturity, since sexual relations were not expected to commence until the partners had reached maturity. In 1663, on the wedding day of his son, James Duke of Monmouth, who was fourteen when he married the twelve-year-old heiress of the house of Buccleuch, Charles II wrote, 'we intend to dance and see them both abed together, but the ceremony shall stop there, for they are both too young to lie all night together'.

Attempts have been made to establish the age of menarche (the onset of menstruation) in early modern England by looking at illegitimacy rates; but for much of the sixteenth, seventeenth and eighteenth centuries the illegitimacy rates were so low, less than 6 per cent of births, and the ages of the mothers so rarely recorded, that this does not provide much information. Peter Laslett has concluded that the mean age of menarche in medieval and early modern England was about fourteen years, but that it must have risen some time in the eighteenth century. Absence of menstruation in young women was associated with the complaint known as green-sickness, described as a condition of adolescent girls comprising a collection of physical and psychological symptoms. There is little evidence that class, race or climate affect age of menarche; there is good evidence to show that the attainment of a certain body weight is critical to its onset, which would result in observable differences between the ill-fed and the well-fed.

It is sometimes alleged that early modern women virtually did not menstruate because they were so often pregnant or recently delivered, or were suffering from amenorrhoea caused by illness or malnutrition. This is obviously nonsense. Even if the usual age of menarche was seventeen, this still left nearly ten years before marriage; and it is clear that lower-class women's pregnancies might be quite widely spaced, at intervals of two or three years. Menstruation and the processes of reproduction were considered to be the reason for women's inferiority, supported by the biblical view of menstruation as pollution. Sexual intercourse during menstruation was discouraged on the grounds that a child conceived then was likely to be puny and red-haired, most undesirable attributes. Absence of menstruation in a woman of appropriate age was a matter of great concern, because it was associated with infertility.

It is difficult to discover anything about the age of menopause. It is claimed that women generally did not live long enough for menstruation to cease, but we have seen that this is not so. The intervals at which children were born increased progressively as women passed through their thirties, but the evidence for Colyton in Devon has shown that women who married over the age of thirty had children at shorter intervals and continued to bear them later than women who had married younger and had their first child earlier. This suggests that the natural decline in fertility was, in the longer-married women, accentuated either by reduced sexual activity or by some deliberate means of contraception.

Lawrence Stone contends that birth control became thinkable in the eighteenth century only because of the liberation of sexuality from the constraints of theology. He cites as evidence that the upper classes' birth rate fell below that of the lower classes, whereas in the sixteenth century it had exceeded it. Others have argued that it was only with the Enlightenment that it became possible to separate procreation and pleasure. But the real subject of concern is not attempts to inhibit conception, but how people controlled fertility to maximize as well as minimize pregnancies.

Control of fertility means controlling who has children (in early modern England, married women); when they have them (from their mid-twenties on, and more at some seasons of the year than others); at what intervals (we have seen that the intervals increased when there were already other children); and up to what age (we have seen how late-marrying women continued to bear children until a more advanced age than those who had married early). All of these matters show evidence of human intervention in some degree. It was important for a woman's standing in society that she bear children, and that she enhance their chances of survival. It is, however, difficult to say how far women actually acquired status with children, rather than lost status by failing to have them.

The statistical evidence for the active control of fertility is uncertain, because of the difficulty of deciding what a 'natural' birth rate is, and whether any discernible rise or decline can be accounted for by other means. What little we know about attitudes to fertility is from medical textbooks, written by men, chiefly for use by men in families rich enough to pay a doctor and rich enough to be concerned about the passage of property and possibly a title. The evidence for Colyton, Devon, which has unusually complete records of births for the seventeenth century, shows that periods characterized by a high rate of marriage and a high birth rate were also periods of lower mortality. One historian has accounted for the marked reduction in the number of births by the practice of some kind of conscious control and another has attributed it to the effects of a period of plague in 1645–6.

It is likely that contraception was chiefly used by married women wishing to control the size of an existing family or to prolong the invervals between births, rather than by young women wishing to prevent pregnancy altogether. Information seems to have been distributed by means of a subculture of women rather than by any official medical means. Indeed, deliberate attempts to inhibit fertility were regarded as a sin. Advice was given in midwifery textbooks on how to promote conception and avoid miscarriages, some of which may have been a veiled form of advice upon how to inhibit conception or induce abortion.

The only techniques available until the early eighteenth century to prevent conception were *coitus interruptus*, abstinence and extended nursing. Abortion might terminate a pregnancy, and we shall look later at measures taken for disposing of unwanted children. It is unlikely that contraceptive measures were widely used because there are a number of women's writings which indicate that after a difficult pregnancy or birth the women dreaded the prospect of further pregnancies. Abstinence was prescribed for quite long periods, as for example when a mother was breast-feeding, and also during menstruation. Contraceptive devices began to appear fairly widely in the early eighteenth century. Sheaths were used for prophylaxis, chiefly against venereal disease. James Boswell wrote in 1763 of how he 'strolled into the Park and took the first whore I met, whom I without many words copulated with free from danger, being safely sheathed'.[1] By this period the use of tampons and sponges was becoming more common (though, unlike the French practice, without the douche which made the devices more effective).

The contraceptive effect of prolonged breast-feeding on demand was noticed in a medical text published in England in 1716. Women who worked as wet-nurses, and lower-class women who kept their children with them and fed them on demand for a relatively longer period, were likely to be less fertile than women who employed wet-nurses. Women who did not feed their own babies had a greater number of pregnancies, more closely spaced than those who did breast feed. Breast-feeding women whose children died had shorter intervals between births than those whose children survived. Lady Townshend of Stiffkey, Norfolk, had nine full-term pregnancies in ten years, while the women she employed as wet-nurses had pregnancies at intervals of two or three years. The decline of breast-feeding has been suggested as a contributory factor in the raised birth rate and the higher infant mortality of the second half of the eighteenth century. But nothing is known about the extent to which prolonged lactation was consciously used to inhibit maternal fertility. Modern studies show that it is only during lactational amenorrhoea (cessation of menstruation caused by lactating) that the contraceptive effect is pronounced. It may well last for at least six months; but when the menstrual cycle resumes, which it may do during breast-feeding, the contraceptive effect is much diminished.

Abortion was undoubtedly practised in early modern England, but we have little idea of how widely. It was the only method of fertility control which was entirely under the woman's control. The

---

[1] *Boswell's London Journal 1762–3*, ed. F. Pottle, Heinemann, 1950, pp. 230–1.

best-publicized instances were of single and widowed women; married women might have been able to terminate a pregnancy without attracting notice. In 1503, 'Being pregnant', Joan Wynspere, a spinster of Basford, Nottinghamshire, 'drank divers poisoned and dangerous draughts to destroy the child in her womb, of which she immediately died'. She was found guilty of the felony of killing both herself and the child in her womb. There is some statistical evidence in one Lancashire village that abortion may have been used systematically to control fertility. During the seventeenth century, the miscarriage rate there was between 26 and 96 per 1,000 live births (compared with rate of about 50 per 1,000 in London in the first half of the seventeenth century and a modern rate of about 10–20 per 1,000).

Abortifacients were sold under thinly veiled guises, and doctors, perhaps disingenuously, warned against tight-lacing and over-exercise for pregnant women. There were also various charms and amulets which were supposed to prevent conception, or to induce miscarriage. The physician James Rueff wrote in 1637 of how women 'by lacing in themselves straight and hard . . . may extinguish the feature, conceived in their womb'. It seems that people did not regard the foetus as having life until it had 'quickened', in the fourth month. To induce an abortion did not become a criminal offence until 1803.

Pleasure

Medical writers considered that the effects of sexual intercourse were generally beneficial for women, and they attributed to its lack many ailments of virgins and older widows. This view appears both in the specialist medical literature and in the popular medical advice given in almanacs. Gabriel Frend's late sixteenth-century almanac taught moderation for both men and women in work, food, drink, sleep and sex. This doctrine was widely accepted, as is witnessed by one woman's guilt at her behaviour during a period of religious despair: 'I followed and hunted after my lovers, having men's persons in admiration.'

Classical medical authors believed that conception was most likely to take place if both partners were not just willing, but actually took pleasure in sex. This was because conception was believed to take place only if the woman emitted a seed, which she would do only if the experience of sex was pleasurable. Barrenness was attributed to lack of love. The influential sixteenth-century

French physician Ambroise Paré, whose works were translated into English in the early seventeenth century, wrote that

> The sense and feeling of venereous actions seemeth to be given by nature to women, not only for the propagation of issue and for the conservation of mankind, but also to mitigate and assuage the miseries of man's life, as it were by the enticements of that pleasure.[1]

The midwife Jane Sharp (*fl.* 1671–1725), writing in 1671, followed popular precept in believing that barrenness often occurred when couples were married against their wills at their parents' behest. The Scottish medical writer McMath asked what woman 'would else impair her health . . . in breeding, bearing and bringing up of children, if not bewitched to this incredible pleasure excited in coition?' Even after the late seventeenth century, when physicians began to understand something of the workings of the ova, medical writers continued to believe that the woman's pleasure affected conception.

It was widely believed that women had larger sexual appetites than men. Popular chapbooks and almanacs, largely written by men, portrayed women as sexually insatiable. The seventeenth-century chapbook *Nine Times a Night* claimed that

> Nine times a night is too much for a man,
> I can't do it myself, but my sister Nan can.

There were also chapbooks written for women, often very bawdy, which suggest that women in seventeenth-century England were confident in their own sexuality and might openly take pleasure in sex. A new bride in *Art of Courtship* said,

> These happy days I ne'er had seen
> Till I had kept my vow:
> But now I find such solid bliss,
> That I'd not be a virgin now.

And a widow in *Cupid's Soliciter of Love* said, 'I had more pleasure in one night's lodging with my husband, than I have ever had since he died, which is the space of one whole month.'[2] A case about alimony reported in 1654 concerned a woman who 'immodestly said . . . that her first husband had done the part of a man, twelve times a night, but that this husband had done but eight'.

---

[1] Ambroise Paré, *The Workes*, London, 1634, Concerning the Generation of Man, book 24, p. 889.
[2] Quoted in Margaret Spufford, *Small Books and Pleasant Histories*, Cambridge University Press, 1981, pp. 159–60.

Medical and quasi-medical writers also subscribed to this notion of female insatiability. Nicholas de Venette claimed that women 'are much more amorous than men, and as sparrows, do not live long, because they are too hot and too susceptible of love', and he added, 'Excess is only blamed in the caresses of a woman, and held a capital crime when passing the bounds of reason.'[1] Men had a part to play in encouraging the woman's pleasure, especially if they wanted her to conceive. Ambroise Paré advised that 'When the husband cometh into his wife's chamber he must entertain her with all kinds of dalliance, wanton behaviour, and allurement to venery' in order to encourage the womb to 'strive and wax fervent with a desire of casting forth its seed'.[2] By the eighteenth century the idea of pleasure dissociated from procreation had acquired greater currency: 'By . . . hastily rushing into a woman's arms, a man may enjoy a great many times, without her, properly speaking, having enjoyed him once.'[3]

However, most of what we know about this is from men's writings. We know virtually nothing about the extent to which women conceived of their sexuality as being separate from reproduction, or the extent to which sexual initiatives by women were acceptable. The medical texts and handbooks place increasing emphasis on male activity and female passivity both in sexual encounters and in the process of conception.

While sexual intercourse might have been advocated as the remedy for many feminine ills, the same cannot be said for masturbation. During the sixteenth and seventeenth centuries, it was primarily objected to on religious grounds on the basis that all sexual activity not intended for procreation was a sin. However, during the eighteenth century, it became a matter of increasing concern to the medical profession. The anonymously published *The Ladies Dispensatory* (1739) gave an account of a woman who, having between the ages of fourteen and nineteen often masturbated, fell into fits where she would scream out, throw off her clothes, 'endeavouring to lay hold of any man she saw, that he might lie with her', and finally died in a 'sudden raving fit' aged twenty-three. The author concluded that 'We see then what, and how many, are the diseases and inconveniencies which the fair sex are

[1] Nicholas de Venette, *The Mysteries of Conjugal Love Reveal'd*, 3rd edn, London, 1712, pp. 66, 141.
[2] Ambroise Paré, *The Workes*, London, 1634, Concerning the Generation of Man, book 24, p. 889.
[3] *Ladies Physical Directory*, London, 8th edn, 1742, p. 70. Quoted in P. G. Boucé, 'Some sexual myths and beliefs in eighteenth century Britain', in P. G. Boucé (ed.), *Sexuality in Eighteenth Century Britain*, Manchester University Press, 1982, p. 43.

capable of bringing on themselves by an unnatural abuse of their own bodies.'

The beliefs that masturbation led to insanity, and that it was something from which sexually innocent children should be protected, became widespread in the eighteenth century. The subject was addressed specifically in an anonymous tract called *Onania: or, the Heinous Sin of Self-Pollution*, which ran to nineteen editions in the early years of the eighteenth-century. Girls' boarding schools were blamed for encouraging masturbation, and the author claimed that he had been reliably informed that it had become as common among girls as it was among boys. If allowed to continue, it led to a distaste for godliness and virtue, a weak bladder, hysteric fits and, worst of all, barrenness. Where women succeeded in having children, they were puny and unfit and unlikely to reach adulthood. Though intended to advertise a tincture against these adverse effects, it is clear that there was some recognition of masturbation as a female activity with particular consequences for women. That the symptoms from which women were said to suffer as a consequence were no different from those of the multitude of feminine ailments discussed in the medical texts suggests that the idea of women's bodies as mysterious and irrational organisms was very widespread.

Same-sex Relations

Heterosexual relations are hard enough to fathom, but even more speculative must be any comment upon same-sex relations. The history of same-sex relations is much influenced by contemporary attitudes to gay rights; and attempts have been made to identify historical characters with same-sex preferences. However, the idea of an exclusive sexual preference does not seem to have existed, and homosexual activity was probably only part of an individual's sex life. Certainly there was no concept of homosexual identity, in the sense that a person might define himself or herself as being exclusively interested in same-sex relations.

There is explicit evidence of sexual activity between individual men; in the case of women the evidence is much more tendentious. Since in England sexual acts between women were not criminal, unlike those between men, there are not even records of prosecutions. (In a number of European countries, such as France and Spain, lesbian acts were regarded in the same terms as acts of sodomy between men and were capital offences.) There are, however, occasional references such as the following, from that well-known gossip Horace Walpole, who wrote in 1750 of a Miss Shelley, who was known as Filial Piety 'for imitating her father in bearing affection to her own sex'. The author of the 1752 pamphlet on masturbation referred to its prevalance in boarding schools, both boys' and girls', which suggests that it may have been mutual as well as solitary. In 1737 John Smith and Elizabeth Huthall married at the Fleet in London; the registrar reported that his clerk had 'judged they were both women, he's a little short fair thin man not above 5 feet'.

Several seventeenth-century women have, on slender evidence, been claimed as lesbians. Aphra Behn (1649?–89) has been claimed on the evidence of her poem 'To the fair Clarinda, who made love to me'; so has Katherine Philips (1632–64), the poet who celebrated women's friendship in her writing. The evidence for sexual activity as opposed to romantic love and friendship between women is very scarce. Friendship between women was a popular subject in women's poetry of the late seventeenth century, but became less so in the eighteenth century.

Licence and Free Love

Despite the literary emphasis on virginity, brides were not necessarily expected to be virgins, and their marriage chances were not inhibited by the knowledge that they were not. However, sexual reputation was a matter of great concern to both men and women. In the ecclesiastical courts at York, three-quarters of all the cases of defamation, and 90 per cent of all those with a female plaintiff, were brought against people who had impugned the plaintiff's sexual reputation. Exchanges such as the following, which took place in Oxford in 1584, were not uncommon: 'Goodwife Hopkins called this respondent bastard and said she would prove her a bastard, and thereupon this respondent said unto her, whosoever saith I am a bastard I say she is a whore of her tongue.'[1] In the sixteenth and seventeenth centuries the preservation of women's sexual reputation was an extremely important part of their standing, but it diminished in importance in the eighteenth century, or at least there were fewer opportunities to go to law about it. Accusations of libertinism were taken as a terrible slur.

---

[1] E. R. C. Brinkworth (ed.), *The Archdeacon's Court: Liber Actorum, 1584*, Oxfordshire Record Society, 23–4, 1941–2, p. 171.

There were in early modern Europe people who preached sexual liberation; but it is not always easy to distinguish those who really did believe in it from those who were claimed to do so by their enemies. Then, as now, charges of sexual misconduct were directed against individuals or groups who challenged accepted values. There were calls for the reform of traditional relations between men and women, and these were associated with religious radicalism. Radical Anabaptist women in Saxony in the 1520s referred to priests as 'bath attendants' because of their role in baptising people; claimed that marriage and whoredom were one and the same thing; and were accused of denying their husbands sex. The women regarded themselves as the brides of Christ, and were chaste because they could not serve two masters.

The Family of Love, a sect which came to England from the continent in the mid-sixteenth century, gained a reputation for sexual licence. They believed in divorce and in holding property in common between members, which is always liable to give rise to speculation about free love. But they also held that true marriages could only take place between believers. There was an episode in a Surrey congregation of Familists which suggests that they countenanced adultery, but there is little other evidence that they preached or practised sexual licence. Their descendants survived into the seventeenth century, but were probably absorbed into other sects during the 1640s and 1650s. A pamphlet of 1641, concerned to show how they had tried to corrupt a girl, reported that

They have certain days which are dedicated unto saints as they call them, as to Ovid, who wrote the Art of Loving, to Priapus, the first bawdy butcher that ever did stick pricks in flesh, and make it swell, and to many others which they used to spend in poetizing in the woods.[1]

Sectarian women in the 1640s and 1650s were popularly associated with advanced views on marriage and divorce, though the principal sources for this are male commentators who disapproved of sects, and who saw women's prominence in them as confirmation of their opinions. An account of women preaching in 1641 claimed that Joan Bauford of Feversham taught 'that husbands being such as crossed their wives' wills might lawfully be forsaken', and there were reports of other women calling for freedom from tiresome husbands. We know very little about what women themselves believed, since even in the more radical sects they had little real power.

[1] *A Description of the Sect called the Familie of Love . . . Susanna Snow*, London, 1641.

Sexual freedom, and release from the constraints of marriage, were popular subjects in the 1640s and 1650s, and they were much aired in books and pamphlets by male sectaries and their enemies. The Ranters preached that sin lay not so much in outward acts as in inner thoughts, as Jacob Bauthumley wrote in 1650: 'He that looks on a woman with a secret and inward lust, hath committed the sin in spirit and heart; as if he had done the outward act, and is in God's account an adulterer.'[1] Laurence Clarkson chose to put this into practice, believing that 'to the pure all things, yea all acts are pure', and that 'till you can lie with all women as one woman, and not judge it a sin, you can do nothing but sin'. His wife, however, had loyally declared that she ought to lie with no other than her husband. Those who wished to vilify the Ranters made much of their supposed libertinism; one critic in 1650 wrote that 'These creatures are married to all, every woman is their wife, not one woman apart from another, but all in one and one in all.'

Others who had a reputation for sexual licence were Adamites, who supposedly preached nudity as a symbol of regained innocence, though it is impossible to say whether anyone actually was an Adamite in the 1640s or 1650. The doctrine common to both the Adamites and the Family of Love was that of Antinomianism, the doctrine that, by sinning more, the believer might achieve more grace. In the 1640s a group of divines debated the role of conscience with a man in Newgate prison due to be executed for having two wives.

In the later seventeenth century, there was a marked difference between the sexual libertinism of the royal court and the bawdiness of the lower orders, where sexual transgression was punished by illegitimate children, disease and the church courts. But did the Enlightenment bring a change of attitude? Male writers certainly elevated the naturalness of desire and there appeared a literature concerned with the practice of sex. The early-eighteenth-century *Pleasures of Conjugal Love Explain'd* spoke out against experiment, 'The action of love furnishing pleasure enough of itself without obliging us to seek for it by new figures', though it also claimed that the womb was 'better situated' for conception when the woman was on all fours rather than on her back.

---

[1] Jacob Bauthumley, *The Light and Dark Sides of God*, London, 1650, reprinted in N. Smith (ed.), *A Collection of Ranter Writings from the Seventeenth Century*, Junction Books, 1983, p. 246.

Prostitution

Organized prostitution was an urban phenomenon. There were well-established red-light districts or their early modern equivalents. Southwark, just south of the City of London across the river, was notorious in the sixteenth century for its playhouses, rings for animal baiting and 'stews' (brothels), as well as for its prisons. In 1546 an order was issued to close down the brothels, but they were reopened under Edward VI and remained open throughout Elizabeth's reign. In Chelmsford in 1567, two men and a woman, Mother Bowden, were presented for keeping brothel houses and a third man was presented for keeping a 'disordered house'. One of the chief objections to brothels was that they were liable to lead to disorderly behaviour, as in this case involving Mother Bowden:

Henry Cooe lived in great disorder with his wife, for that she reproveth him for his incontinent life and use of suspect houses, and on a time she went to the brothel house of Mother Bowden to see if her husband were there (which before was often denied). He slipped out of the house through the backside and his wife beat both the old woman and the harlot her daughter, and pulled her about the house by the hair of the head, which daughter came running into the street and made announcement that Cooe his wife would kill her mother.[1]

Even in the 1650s when the Puritan campaign to reform manners was at its height, prostitutes were said to be swarming over Covent Garden. In the 1760s James Boswell wrote of 'the splendid Madam at fifty guineas a night, down to the civil nymph with white-thread stockings who tramps along the Strand and will resign her engaging person to your honour for a pint of wine and a shilling'.[2] Literary evidence for eighteenth-century England, quoted by Olwen Hufton, suggests that, where commerce in sex was controlled, it was often in the hands of women.

Many women in rural England used sex as an informal way of securing the protection of a man, but formal prostitution in the countryside was unusual: it certainly rarely appears among the indictments in the church courts. It seems mainly to have been poor women, often vagrants, who wandered round the country with several children by different men. Generally, prostitution was carried out part-time and temporarily. Alehouses were often the location from which prostitutes worked, and the alehouses of suburban London were notorious in the early seventeenth century

---

[1] F. G. Emmison, *Elizabethan Life: Disorder*, Essex Record Office, 1970, p. 26.
[2] *Boswell's London Journal 1762–3*, ed. F. Pottle, Heinemann, 1950, pp. 83–4.

as places where prostitutes plied their trade. There were many attempts to clean up alehouses as the location of both vicious and seditious behaviour. A quarter of the twelve unlicensed victuallers presented in Chelmsford in 1567 were charged with keeping brothels. Alehouses in London were the centre for rather better-organized prostitution. But for much of the period prostitution was the last resort of the very poor. The Norwich census of the poor of 1570 listed a dozen prostitutes.

The commonest form of punishment for prostitution involved some kind of public disgrace, like the stocks or being displayed in a cage. Severer punishments involved being paraded through the streets on a cart, branding or being sent to the house of correction.

Venereal Disease

Much more has been written about men and venereal disease than about its incidence among and effects upon women. Syphilis arrived in Europe from America in the late fifteenth and early sixteenth centuries, and by the mid-sixteenth century it was well established in England. It is doubtful how clearly syphilis and gonorrhoea were actually distinguished before the nineteenth century. Mercury was widely used in the treatment and could cause as much suffering and be as fatal as any of the diseases themselves. The extremely unpleasant symptoms and effects of venereal disease, especially syphilis in its advanced stages, roused little sympathy, though rich, upper-class male sufferers were relatively well insulated from the execration with which poor sufferers were treated. Attitudes to the disease were much concerned with sin and punishment. It was considered to be a divinely ordained bridle upon sexual licence, and those who suffered from it were regarded as justly punished fornicators. Lady Anne Clifford recorded in her diary that in 1619 Sir Arthur Lake's wife died 'having been grievously tormented a long time with pains and sores which broke out in blotches so that it was reported that she died of the French disease'. Quack remedies abounded. In the *Female Tatler* of 1710 there was an advertisement for the Tomb of Venus 'or a plain and certain method by which all people that ever were infected with the venereal distemper may infallibly know whether they are cured or not; with effectual remedies to eradicate all noxious remains'.

It was widely believed that women spread venereal disease, perhaps as an extension of the sin of Eve. People who became infected were often said to have been 'burned'. Prostitutes figured largely in the search for scapegoats, and the closure of brothels was often recommended as a remedy against the spread of veneral disease. James Boswell was extremely indignant to find that he had caught some kind of venereal infection from a woman he regarded as a lady. 'Am I, who have had safe and elegant intrigues with fine women, become the dupe of a strumpet?', he raged in 1763. 'There is scarcely a possibility that she could be innocent of the crime of horrid imposition.' Nevertheless, the church courts, which had an interest because of their concern with promiscuous behaviour, did acknowledge that women might be the victims. In 1564 a Walthamstow woman was taken in adultery with a man 'who did burn her'.

Between the sixteenth and the eighteenth centuries there were changes in attitudes to sex. Many subjects which had been moral matters, dealt with by the church courts, became matters either of public order or of medical concern. The idea that pleasure might be punished remained, but they were man-made rather than divine punishments. Whether one can say that we see the death of sin is debatable, but we certainly see the substitution of the doctor for the minister.

CHAPTER SIX

Motherhood, Family and Friends

Motherhood, like sexuality, is socially constructed: the idea that women are 'naturally' disposed to care for their children – or, indeed, for other people's children – now has little currency. The anguish which accompanied the relations of step-mothers and the children in their care is clear evidence of that. Many women in early modern England spent most of their adult lives engaged in bearing and rearing children, and the ideal of a good woman was inextricably linked with motherhood. But motherhood took place in the context of a family, and was part of a web of complex relationships with both relatives and friends.

Pregnancy

The detection of pregnancy was a considerable problem, and the competent authority on this was considered to be married women rather than the medical profession. When a woman was found guilty of a capital crime, a jury of matrons was empanelled to adjudicate on whether she was pregnant, and if so, a stay of execution was granted. All kinds of techniques were used to diagnose pregnancy, none very successfully. Many women claimed to know that they were pregnant, even with a first child. Mrs Alice Thornton, writing in the 1650s of her first pregnancy, claimed that she knew that she had conceived seven weeks after her marriage. Having established that a woman was pregnant, the length of the pregnancy was estimated as about forty weeks from conception.

Lack of children was a cause for great concern and disappointment, and was a public matter. The newly married Earl of Huntingdon consulted his uncle in 1672 on how to penetrate his bride's particularly resistant hymen. Childlessness was usually attributed to the woman's supposed barrenness. About a quarter of all marriages were childless. Infertility accounts for about 12 per cent of all marriages not producing children: the other families had children who did not survive.

Married women regarded their first pregnancy with gratitude, though, as we have seen, many lower-class women were several months pregnant when they married. Pregnancy was regarded as a blessing, but not necessarily an unalloyed one. Mary Rich, Countess of Warwick (1624–78), noted that after having two children very close together she was 'troubled when I found myself to be with child so soon', but Hester Thrale, writing in the mid-eighteenth century, crowed 'five little girls too, and breeding again and fool enough to be proud of it'.

Pregnancy was often regarded as a period of ill-health, and anxious grandmothers-to-be frequently advised their daughters not to travel in carriages or undertake strenuous activity during their pregnancies. Women themselves said little about their pregnancies, and if they did it was usually after quickening (the fourth month) when the likelihood of miscarriage was less.

Many women's pregnancies were blighted by anxiety about the outcome, both for themselves and for the baby; especially if they had a history of difficult deliveries. In the 1650s Mary Cary (fl. 1636–53) wrote in the apprehension that she would die giving birth to her fourth child. An anonymous woman wrote in the late seventeenth century of how, when she was pregnant, she was

very distressed as to my bodily health; and as my time drew near I had reason to conjecture that I was with twins, which occasioned much fear in me, thinking, that upon the bearing of one child, if it should be told me that I had another to bear immediately, it would be much more terrible to me than death.[1]

She had good reason for anxiety, because her child was born dead. The next time she was pregnant 'I fell under such terror and consternation as was like to sink me to death.' Fortunately this time she had an easy and safe delivery. Frances Boscawen wrote in 1747, 'The fear of my labour terrifies me.'

The risks of death in childbed increase with the number of pregnancies, especially after about the fifth. However, mothers in their later pregnancies are also older, and risks to the mother increase with age, so that a mother of forty, irrespective of how many or few pregnancies she has had, will be at greater risk than

[1] National Library of Scotland, MS 1035, f. 7.

one of twenty-five. French evidence also suggests that a third of maternal deaths were from high-risk deliveries like still-births and multiple births. Mrs Hodgson of York, who died aged thirty-eight in her twenty-fourth labour, is an extreme example. This explains why women in early modern England might greet the discovery of their pregnancies with sentiments of hope, thankfulness, duty and trepidation, rather than with unalloyed delight.

Delivery

A statute of 1624 forbade the concealment of a birth; so most births were attended by someone, even if it was only neighbours. Even very poor women might expect to have some kind of birth attendant. In 1688 the churchwardens of Quainton, Buckinghamshire, authorized a payment of 7s. for a midwife and a nurse for a travelling woman and, as it sadly turned out, a grave for the child. Plainly eighteenth-century English midwives had some reputation, for Mrs Stanley, a midwife established in Savannah, Georgia, who had delivered 128 babies, decided to be delivered herself in England in 1737, not caring to trust herself to the other midwives of Georgia. It was the usual practice for husbands to be nearby at the births of their children, but there were usually only women actually at the bedside. In the late sixteenth century, Lady Margaret Cuninghame considered that her husband had behaved very badly to have left it five weeks from her delivery before he came to her. In the 1670s, Mr Veitch, an exiled Scottish minister, had to leave his wife eight days after the birth of one of their children, 'upon which', she wrote, 'I fell under a great exercise of mind, mischief and an ill heart got the mastery of me'.

Many women were intensely anxious about the prospect of labour. Elizabeth Countess of Bridgewater (1626–63), wrote a number of prayers and meditations on pregnancy, labour and the birth of her children.

> I beg of thee to have compassion on me in the great pain I am to feel in the bringing forth of this my child. . . . When that I come to the cruel groves of labour, in this my travail give me patience, and sure confidence in thee. . . . Give me no untimely birth,[1]

she prayed when pregnant with her third child. The helplessness of midwives and doctors is indicated by her prayer for 'When I continued with child after I thought I should have fallen in labour'.

[1] British Library, Egerton MS 607, pp. 44–5.

Elizabeth, Viscountess Mordaunt (d. 1678), wrote a whole series of prayers of thanksgiving for the safe delivery of her children born in the 1660s and 1670s. What could make the delivery particularly distressing was that a mother commonly knew she was dying. When Frances Drax was told in the 1670s by the minister that she was dying, she replied that she was willing to die and hoped that God would receive her.

More women's labours were difficult than nowadays, and there were few pain killers. Mrs Alice Thornton, who had been very ill after several of her pregnancies, wrote of the birth of her fifth child in the 1650s, 'I was upon the rack in bearing my child with such exquisite torment as if each limb were divided from other.' This labour lasted only two hours, but the child was born feet first and dead. Of her nine full-term pregnancies only three children survived for more than a few weeks.

At its worst extreme, an obstructed delivery could lead to the deaths of both mother and child, since Caesarean sections were not successfully performed until the nineteenth century. Medical textbooks wrote of how to dismember a dead child *in utero* to save the mother's life. We simply do not know how often this kind of expedient had to be resorted to. The desire for children and the need for heirs could suppress women's fears. Lady Willoughby wrote to her husband in the 1580s, after the death of their only surviving son, to say that, though she had lived apart from her husband for some years and was over forty, she was prepared to be reconciled with him and would hazard her life for another child to continue the house of Willoughby.

In a chillingly titled article, 'Did the mothers really die?', Roger Schofield argues that the risks to mothers of death in childbed from the process of child-bearing were not as great as was previously believed. He claims that the greatest risk is at the first birth, especially if the mother is still in her teens. Since the age of marriage was high, there were few teenage pregnancies and most women had six or seven full-term pregnancies, only a sixth of pregnancies were at high risk. Schofield argues that an increase in infectious diseases was the cause of the rise in maternal mortality between the late sixteenth and the late seventeenth centuries, and that the decline during the eighteenth century was the result of improvements in obstetric practice (especially the use of forceps) and the diminution of infectious disease. Women in their final months of pregnancy, or newly delivered, are more susceptible to common diseases like smallpox, TB and influenza than is the population at large, because the mother's immune systems are directed to retaining the foetus, and her resistance to disease is consequently reduced. However, evidence from France suggests that infection was not a major source of death in childbed in the period 1660–1714. Schofield's article has not been challenged, but the anecdotal evidence of deaths in childbed, whether actually giving birth or immediately afterwards, is of a higher mortality than he suggests.

One group of women whose deaths in childbed are more visible than most is the hapless young women who gave birth to illegitimate children. They appear in the coroners' reports, often because their children were found dead. In 1753 at West Kington, Wiltshire, the coroner recorded the death of a male infant, supposedly the son of Mary Banning. Mary was 'apprehended in a stable in a very weak condition and, being immediately sent to bed, she languished for an hour and died'. In 1755 at Easton Grey, Wiltshire, Elizabeth Vizzard was found dead with a dead girl child beside her. The coroner concluded that 'for want of proper assistance in her delivery she languished and died'. A particularly tragic case was that of Ann Hale, whose illegitimate daughter died because Ann was disabled by a paralytic stroke and, no one being present at the birth, the child fell to the ground and was killed by hitting her skull.

These tragic outcomes were a real source of fear for both parents, but children were welcomed at their arrival with thanks for their safety, for the mother's safe delivery and for God's mercy in sparing them both. Mothers were more inclined than fathers to express obvious pleasure, and this becomes increasingly evident during the eighteenth century. In the later years of the century, Frances Calvert wrote of her child's birth, 'Oh joyful moment! Never, never to be forgotten', and Melesina Trench delighted in her baby, 'when I looked in my boy's face, when I heard him breathe, when I felt the pressure of his little finger'. Did this change in expression, in the possibility of parents taking delight in their children, come about because of a reduced sense of God overseeing the whole process and stepping in to prevent pride? Or was it because of a real feeling that mothers and children were more likely to survive? The figures suggest that mothers became more likely to survive and children less likely, though we know little about whether infant mortality among the diary-keeping classes rose at the same rate as among the population as a whole.

Lying-in

It was usually agreed that women in childbed should be governed according to their respective constitutions, and that labouring women required different treatment from persons of quality. Women's delicacy was believed to be related to their status. Many women suffered ill-health after childbirth. Mrs Alice Thornton suffered fits, fevers, sweats, and faintings, she lost her hair and fingernails, and her teeth became loose and turned black after her first pregnancy in the 1650s. She was afflicted by prolonged illness after her later pregnancies with much loss of blood and fainting.

Women might suffer psychological disorders in the immediate aftermath of giving birth. Some modern writers have sought to associate these with the increasing proportion of hospital births, but since the 1850s, when records of this kind of condition first started to be kept, the incidence has remained fairly constant. Nowadays 50–80 per cent of women suffer from some kind of maternity 'blues', 7–30 per cent from post-natal depression, and 0.1–0.2 per cent from puerperal psychosis. In the mid-seventeenth century, the physician Charles Lepois noted that some women developed mental disorders during childbirth or delirium immediately after childbirth (though this could have been a consequence of puerperal fever), and he attributed these disorders to dark humours. References to mild post-partum depression started to appear in the medical literature in the early nineteenth century. It is difficult not to see something of these conditions in these two descriptions from the 1650s:

About some nine years ago at the birth of a child I had very great temptations of destroying myself and have had oftentimes a knife put into my hand to do it, so that I durst not be left by myself alone.

I had a temptation by Satan to drown myself in a pond near Leeds in Yorkshire, whither the devil led me . . . and I was by him drawn out thither, and came to the pond side, but by the providence of God, having a great love to a young infant I had then, I took that child in my arms; and when I came to the place, I looked upon the child, and considered with myself, what shall I destroy myself and my poor child?[1]

Melancholy was the commonest post-partum condition, but Mrs Elizabeth Walker's daughter was seized by a state which 'took her head, which deprived her of her understanding'. Sometimes these states were exacerbated by grief. Mrs Walker (1623–90) wrote in the

---

[1] H. Walker, *Spirituall Experiences of Sundry Beleevers*, London, 1651, pp. 26–7, 37.

1690s after the stillbirth of her eighth child, 'In this lying-in I fell into melancholy, which much disturbed me with vapours, and was very ill.'

Twenty-eight days after the birth, women were expected to undergo the ceremony of churching, one of the few church ceremonies in which women were the centre of attention. Churching had a twofold function as both a thanksgiving and a marking of the return of the new mother into the community. She was attended by women, commonly those who had attended the birth, the midwife having an important position. The father of the child played a distinctly inferior role. The drinking and feasting which followed was often the occasion for considerable rowdiness, and marked the end of the isolation of the new mother.

In the pre-Reformation church, the ceremony signified purification. Between 1558 and 1642 its ritual significance varied with the temper of the local clergyman; but the majority of women attended a churching service (even if the child had not survived), despite strong Puritan objections to it. Puritans objected in particular to the woman wearing a veil and kneeling before the altar. In the 1630s Mrs Hazzard, wife of a Church of England clergyman and one of the founders of the Broadmead congregation of Baptists, would offer succour to women who 'would come out of other parishes, and be brought to bed there at their time of lying-in, to be in Mr Hazzard's parish, to avoid the ceremonies of their churching'.

Churching ceased during the Civil War and Interregnum; it was officially restored in 1660, but because of nonconformist objections it proved impossible to reinstate it to its pre-Civil War position. Until then it was more than an empty ceremony. Clergymen might threaten the mother of an illegitimate child with refusing to church her unless she divulged the name of the father, and such women were expected to undergo penance in front of the congregation before being churched.

Infants and Children

The most important aspect of care of the newborn was feeding, and it was agreed that it was preferable for women to feed their own children rather than to put them out to wet-nurses. Nevertheless, large numbers of children were put out to nurse and the numbers increased in the eighteenth century. Some were the children of noblewomen and gentlewomen, some were the children of poor women who had to work for a living, and some were children who had been abandoned. The majority of children were sent to live with the wet-nurse, especially if they lived in London or another city, when they went out to the surrounding countryside. Only the richest parents kept a wet-nurse at home. Usually the nurse would come to the parents' house when the child was born and stay there for a few days, and then return to her own home, having full care of the baby there.

Advice about weaning was exchanged between women, and it took place when the child was between nine months and two years of age. The age at which weaning customarily took place seems to have declined from nearly two years in the sixteenth century to between nine and twelve months in the mid-eighteenth century, and it was at this age that the child would be returned to its parental home.

Motherhood was approved of and sought after for married women, but it was not considered desirable for unmarried women. There was the moral position, from which arose the question: who was to be punished? There was the economic question: who would support the mother and child? And there was the social question: who would be responsible for the child? Merely being the parent of an illegitimate child was not a civil crime, but magistrates might order punishment for breach of the peace. The penalties of the law weighed more heavily on women than on men, and more heavily on poor women than on women able to support themselves and their illegitimate children. If the child's maintenance fell upon the parish, the mother might be whipped, have her hair cut off, or be sent to prison or a house of correction. Attempts might also be made to prosecute the putative father, to exact from him money for the support of the woman and child.

The church courts might impose penalties for immorality. A woman was expected to do her penance before being churched, though often on the same occasion. Under canon law a child became legitimate if its parents later married, no matter how long after its birth. The common law courts did not take this line and illegitimate children, even if their parents subsequently married, had no automatic rights of inheritance. The likelihood of the mother of an illegitimate child marrying varied greatly according to local circumstances – the sex ratio, local employment and courtship practices.

Illegitimacy was uncommon in the sixteenth and seventeenth centuries, reaching its lowest incidence in the 1650s, and gradually rising during the eighteenth century. Bastardy was most apparent in times of economic hardship. There was, for example, a short-term rise in some places in the 1590s, a period of acute economic difficulty. As economic conditions improved in the seventeenth century, bastardy rates declined. During the eighteenth century, the opportunities for women's employment diminished, the age of marriage declined and the illegitimacy rate rose. The connection between generalized economic hardship and a rising number of illegitimate births seems to be that economic hardship leads to postponed marriage because hard times make it difficult to secure sufficient financial independence to make marriage possible. Normally sexual relations took place because marriage was intended. Illegitimate births may well have had more to do with courtship practices than with sexual promiscuity.

There were also marked regional patterns: there were places where the rate of illegitimate births was persistently high over several generations, and sometimes even over centuries. For example, of the thirty-three illegitimate children born in Earls Colne, Essex, between 1600 and 1627, thirteen were born to only three women. No satisfactory explanation for this has yet emerged, but it lends support to the thesis that there were bastardy-prone societies, and also bastardy-prone families where illegitimate children were born to successive generations.

But what of those children for whom there was no care? We have seen that abortion was publicly associated with young unmarried women, or with widows, or with women whose husbands were absent. Like abortion, infanticide was most readily detected when committed by a young unmarried women whose whole livelihood was threatened by having a child. In sixteenth-century Middlesex infanticides made up 7 per cent of all criminal homicides. Men and married women were rarely charged with it, and it was difficult to detect when it took place in a family with several children, or in the vagrant population. Female children were not singled out as the victims of infanticide.

Most infanticides were murders of newborn babies by their mothers, usually unmarried women, who commonly were servants. Poverty was an important factor. In 1792 Mary Goodenough was sentenced to death for infanticide, having had sexual relations with a neighbour in return for food for her two children. Older children were sometimes murdered by their mothers. One of the seven cases of murder tried at the Essex assizes between 1559 and 1561 was by a spinster who pushed her six-year-old son into 'a fiery furnace' so that he died a fortnight later. She was found guilty but was remanded because she was pregnant.

Another solution to the problem of an unwanted child was to

abandon it. Abandoned children became a charge upon the parish, which had to find a wet-nurse, then someone to care for the child after it had been weaned (though children seem often to have stayed with the wet-nurse as a kind of foster-mother), and then someone who would take the child as a parish apprentice. In London children might be sent to one of the paupers' hospitals like Christ's Hospital, which had become a school by the seventeenth century. The numbers of children abandoned by their parents rose to unusually high levels in the period 1690–1720, when a thousand children a year were abandoned, and the majority of these children were almost certainly not bastards. The opening of Thomas Coram's London Foundling Hospital in 1741 aroused considerable controversy on the grounds that it encouraged irresponsible behaviour by parents. Foundling hospitals were established in an attempt to combat infanticide and as part of a general scheme to reorganize poor relief and care for the mentally and physically disabled.

Many foundlings had physical defects or disabilities, boys outnumbered girls, and most were abandoned in the winter. Children were often abandoned in or near churches, a very ancient practice. Mothers who were detected abandoning their children might be whipped at Bridewell. The children themselves were initially sent out to wet-nurses in outlying parishes and then educated for some trade in the foundling hospital before being sent out to an employer.

Abandonment was the response of some parents to children with disabilities. Many such children simply did not survive, though we cannot tell to what extent there was any deliberate lack of care for them. Parents regarded disabled children as a punishment for earlier sins. Elizabeth Countess of Bridgewater wrote a prayer in the 1640s for when she was in labour: 'bring me out of this my extremity, and fill my mouth with honour and praise to thee that I may see my dear child without any deformity'. In 1670 Elizabeth Turner wrote that 'My child was not only free from deformity, but a goodly, lovely babe.' In 1701, when Thomas Boston's daughter was born with a double hare lip which prevented her suckling, he wrote 'my afflicted wife carried the trial very Christianly and wisely'. There was a considerable amount of both popular and scientific interest in what were known as monstrous births, often because they were believed to foretell some kind of disaster.

There were occasional stories of children being abducted. Parliament was informed in 1645 that 'divers lewd persons do go up and down the city of London and elsewhere, and in the most barbarous and wicked manner steal away many little children'. Law officers were to apprehend anyone found stealing, buying or receiving stolen children, and powers were given them to search ships.

Mothers seem to have had the chief responsibility for children up to the age of about seven. Children began to leave home for service or apprenticeships from the age of about twelve or thirteen. Parents might be separated from their children for long periods, but social status determined at which stage of their childhood children left home. Much has been made of the comments of foreign visitors, like this Venetian of about 1500:

> The want of affection in the English is shown clearly in the case of their children. After they have kept them at home till the age of seven or nine at the most, they put them out, both boys and girls, to hard service in the households of others, contracting them there for another seven or nine years. These are called apprentices.[1]

Families might comprise children by previous marriages as well as those of the husband and wife themselves. In one case, in Chichester in 1636, John Brookes and his wife Ellen were forced to live apart because their children by previous marriages 'cannot well agree, making debate between them; therefore for a more quiet and contented living, keep two several houses, and come and go one to another when they think well'.[2]

Children's lives were fragile: they might die from disease or in accidents. Katharine Ross reproached herself when her child died from being overlain by his nurse, 'which was no small aggravation . . . I had warning of it before . . . having never any nursed but by myself before'. Little boys, allowed to stray away from the home, often drowned. In north Wiltshire in 1753 the coroner recorded the death by drowning of two two-year-old boys, one in a ditch, the other in a tub of wort; the following year there were two more such deaths, one in a well and one in a brook. Boys were also killed by carts. The number of girls drowned was smaller, and they most commonly died by falling into buckets and wells rather than into ditches and rivers, suggesting that they stayed closer to home. The attitude of mind which devout parents needed to cultivate was summed up by the woman who wrote, 'Amongst the various cross dispensations by which I have been chastised, the deaths of my children were not the smallest. But that which was most at heart with me was the salvation of their souls.'[3] Apprehension of a child's

---

1 Quoted in Frank Davies, *Teaching Reading in Early England*, Pitman, 1973, p. 52.
2 Quoted in Lawrence Stone, *The Road to Divorce*, Oxford University Press, 1990, p. 5.
3 National Library of Scotland, MS 1037, f. 21.

death was nearly as terrible as the event itself: the same woman wrote of her daughter, 'when she was dying I was in extreme grief and fear of her being lost'. Parents were able to face more straightforwardly than nowadays the possibility that their child would die. There were no wonder drugs or operations, only miracles; hence the significance of prayer even among those who were not otherwise particularly devout. Praying was the only action open to them.

Adult Sons and Daughters

Generally, adult sons and daughters did not live with their parents, or widowed parents with their children. Occasionally, young married couples lived briefly with one or other set of parents, but this was normally only a temporary expedient. Among the poor, daughters lived with their parents if they were pregnant or had been deserted by their husbands.

The incidence of geographical mobility was such that it must have been common for adult offspring to be separated from their parents by considerable distances. For Lady Twysden this was a real source of anguish during her father's last illness and death in 1649 at his house, Nonsuch Park, in Surrey:

> There was six by him at the time of his death, he wanted no help . . . my sister and brother Warham who lived with him was then on business gone in to Dorsetshire, and I to my grief was in Kent so could not know of his illness, to be with him, he was 87.[1]

Lady Anne Clifford recorded in her diary in 1616 that 'Kendall came and brought me the heavy news of my mother's death which I held as the greatest and most lamentable cross that could have befallen me.' Alice Thornton wrote in 1659, 'I took the saddest leave of my dear and honoured mother as ever a child did.'

Evidence of parents' concern for their adult or near-adult children can be very touching. Lady Katherine Paston, writing in 1626 to her son William, a student at Corpus Christi College, Cambridge, worried about the effects of playing too much tennis: 'If thou lovest my life let me entreat thee to be very careful of thyself for overheating thy blood.' In the winter she wrote,

I pray thee have a great care to keep thyself very warm and put

---

[1] *The Diary of Isabella, wife of Sir Roger Twysden*, ed. F. W. Bennett, Archaeologia Cantiana, 51, 1939, pp. 128–9.

somewhat about thy neck for thou art very much subject to pain in thy throat, and if need be wear a cape. There can be no harm in keeping warm.[1]

Lady Bridgeman, writing in 1690 to her son Orlando ('Orle'), a student at Oriel College, Oxford, advised him likewise:

I have writ to Judith to hasten your Indian gown which I pray accept from me, and also the cap to keep you warm. Pray have care of catching cold. . . . You shall never want anything from us that may be for your own good.

She concluded her letter, 'Dear Orle, Your most entirely affectionate mother'.[2] Clothing could be a source of embarrassment too. Dudley Ryder wrote in the early eighteenth century that 'My mother is very much to blame for wearing clothes that make her friends blush for her and ashamed of being seen in her company.'

Affection might be overlaid by disappointment. Mrs Veitch, wife of a covenanting minister, who to avoid persecution left Scotland for England in the 1670s, was disappointed when her sons preferred being soldiers to ministers. Long periods passed without her seeing them because they were away serving in the Netherlands and America; but when the eldest died, she remorsefully wrote, 'I fear I have been too preremptory with God in desiring to have all my sons ministers.' And Mrs Johnson wrote to her son in 1684 to oppose his joining the army.

Deaths of daughters in childbed were devastating to parents. Mrs Elizabeth Walker, only two of whose eleven children had reached adulthood, survived them both. She fell into a deep melancholy after the death of her daughter Mrs Margaret Cox. Her other daughter died in 1675 shortly after giving birth to a son: 'The disease took her head, which deprived her of her understanding.'

But relations between adult sons and daughters and their parents could be very bitter. Thomas Wilbraham and his wife, Elizabeth Mytton, a considerable heiress in her own right, had a serious dispute with his parents about their non-fulfilment of their side of the marriage contract. In a letter of the 1650s he wrote to his mother, 'I am far from offering to threaten my parents, what I desire tends much to your reputation and quietness of mind and soul.' Plainly part of the problem lay with the relations between Elizabeth and her parents-in-law, for the letter continues,

[1] *Correspondence of Lady Katherine Paston 1603–1627*, ed. R. Hughey, Norfolk Record Society, 14, 1941, p. 97.
[2] Bradford Papers, Staffordshire County Record Office, P/IV 96–1098, 28 Oct. 1690.

My wife says she can hope of no favour from you in what's in your disposal. We may not enjoy what was promised her, the retaining of which may be a high motive to prevent her settling her estate. My wife presents her humble duty with mine to my father and your ladyship and could have confirmed the news of her great belly had she thought it more authentic from herself than from me.[1]

Unsuitable marriages were perhaps the most bitter subjects for dispute among those who wrote letters. Mary Boyle's father refused to see her when she announced her intention, in 1638, to marry Mr Rich. In the 1640s Anne Halkett's mother refused to speak to her for fourteen months, except to reproach her over her desire to marry Thomas Howard.

Other Relations and Friends

While families might not all live together, there is considerable evidence of the importance of blood relationships outside the household. Female testators frequently left bequests to their grandchildren with considerable expressions of affection, and where women had outlived their own descendants or had none, nephews and nieces appear as beneficiaries. We should remember, however, that this is not necessarily evidence of personal intimacy, for relations often lived at considerable distances. What it does show is the strength of feeling that one should do the best thing possible for one's family, and that one's assets were part of a family's property. This is as much a part of a system of patronage as evidence of bonds of affection between blood-relations. There is, however, evidence of affection in correspondence such as that between Sarah Duchess of Marlborough, and her granddaughter Diana Spencer, wife of Lord John Russell, but such sources are unusual.

Close friendships between women from the higher ranks of society are much easier to chart than those between other women, because they were able to write letters and could afford to celebrate or, on occasion, to commemorate their relationship. In 1627 the Countess of Totnes erected a monument to Mrs Amy Smyth, her waiting gentlewoman for forty years, in the church at Stratford-on-Avon, Mrs Smyth having expressed the desire to be buried there, knowing that that was where the countess was to be buried. Certainly there were often close relationships between

[1] Bradford Papers, Staffordshire County Record Office, 18/4/4/4.

noblewoman and gentlewomen and their female retainers. Such friendships were often recognized in bequests. Elizabeth Hampton, spinster of Oxford, in 1661 left two of her 'fairest pewter platters' to her former servant, Elizabeth Major. There are also cases of servants leaving their possessions to their employers.

The poetry of Katherine Philips (1632–64) celebrates friendships between women; she created a circle of women friends in which she was known as Orinda, and her friends by other pseudonyms. Anne Owen, the woman in the circle to whom she was closest, was, as Lucasia, celebrated in many poems:

> The compasses that stand above
> Express this great immortal love;
> For friends, like them, can prove this true,
> They are, and yet they are not, two.

Katherine Philips was trying to create a philosophy of friendship, and she commemorated in her verse not only friendship, but also betrayal. There were many women's poems on friendship in the Restoration period, a subject which tended to disappear from women's writing in the eighteenth century.

It is difficult to know how far it was acceptable for women and men to be friends. There are many cases of noblewomen taking under their wing writers and clergymen, and there are also instances of devout women of lower social rank being on close terms with members of the clergy. Ralph Josselin's very obvious grief at the death in 1650 of Mrs Mary Church is a case in point. The Essex minister had seen her shortly after her death, and then preached her funeral sermon two days later, after which he wrote 'God hath taken from me a choice special friend. . . . When Mrs Mary died my heart trembled and was perplexed in the dealings of the Lord so sadly with us.' Anne Newdigate had male friends after her marriage, one of whom, Sir William Knollys, took it upon himself to advise her on how to bring up her children.

The Affective Family, or Did parents love their children?

Much recent literature has taken it for granted that the primary relationships in all women's lives in early modern England were within the family, and that therefore the family was a sufficient basis upon which to study women. But many women were members of more than one family, and evidence of their loyalty to one family rather than to another provides insights into family relationships, though inevitably this tends to relate to women of higher status. Women who were unhappily married often continued to identify themselves with their father's family, especially if they were heiresses. Lady Anne Clifford (1590–1676) commemorated her own ancestry in her buildings, in the monuments she erected to her mother, and above all in her own monument which gives the Clifford family tree and scarcely refers to her two husbands, the Earls of Dorset and Pembroke. That she left only daughters may have been a consideration, but Lady Carey (1546–1630), who inherited a large estate in Northamptonshire and left several sons, set up a monument at Stow-Nine-Churches, Northamptonshire, to commemorate her ancestors, herself and her children, but not her two husbands, Sir John Danvers and Sir Edmund Carey. On the other hand, the Countess of Rutland (died 1671) was concerned with celebrating her husband's family in her reconstruction of Belvoir Castle in Leicestershire; and nearby, at Stapleford, Lady Sherard erected a splendid monument to her husband commemorating his ancestors rather than her own. There is, then, no single family type in which to look at women.

Lawrence Stone has put forward a thesis about the changes in the structure of the early modern family and in relationships within it. He has argued that relationships within the family, influenced by the omnipresence of early death, were less loving before the mid-eighteenth century than afterwards; and that there was a discernible change in the emotional quality of family relationships, most especially in the relationships between parents and children. He has also urged, 'Thou shalt not assume the ubiquity in the past of modern emotional patterns – neither premarital love, nor conjugal affection, nor maternal devotion to children.' What we are concerned with here is the position of women in the family: women's family relationships and whether these changed.

Among the evidence which Stone and other historians use is the brutal discipline imposed upon children, the use of stern and corporal punishments, and the way in which many children were separated from their parents at a young age. But this is still a matter for debate, because other historians have found evidence that child-rearing practices were not as brutal and unfeeling as has been argued. This debate depends partly upon the kind of sources consulted. Conduct books, necessarily counsels of perfection, tend to emphasize discipline and, as many of them have a religious bent, the natural sinfulness of children. Evidence of parents' own feelings, from diaries, letters and personal papers, suggests that the emotional content of family relationships changes little.

Sending children away from home had a long and honourable history. Children left their parental home under the medieval custom of oblation (giving children to be brought up in a monastery), or fostering (sending children to be brought up in another family). There is some evidence that wet-nurses and foster-parents and their charges had a special relationship. In the early seventeenth century, Anne Newdigate was advised by a friend not to breast-feed her own child, on the grounds that it would make her grief the greater if he should die. Recent work on apprenticeship in sixteenth and seventeenth century England is questioning the extent to which children who had a family of their own were actually sent away at the age of twelve: those who were may chiefly have been orphans. When children were sent away in their early years it was into another parent-like relationship. The early age at which children left home was evidence not of lack of affection, but of a belief that the family was a network of obligations, of which children were as much a part as adults. Sending children away was a way of extending the family's range of contacts, since many parents both dispatched their own children and received other people's: they were not negating parental feelings.

Parents' reactions at the deaths of their children also offer an insight into the quality of the parent-child relationship. It is easy to believe that parents were more callous about their children when they had the expectation that some would die in childhood. It is much more likely that they found different ways of dealing with their grief. The evidence of women who lost their children suggests that, far from caring for them less, the loss of a child was just as devastating a blow as it is today. What parents did have, however, was a highly developed set of responses which promoted resignation after the first overwhelming grief. Most of the evidence we have of women's responses is from literate women, or from the wives of literate men, but occasionally there are reports of the feelings of women of lower rank. This description is by a woman speaking in 1650:

> Two years ago I buried a child, which was a very great trouble to me to part with, and then I was more fully convinced of sin, which caused my burden to be the greater, so that I could seldom have any other thought but of desperation.[1]

One might argue that her faith increased the burden of her grief, but that would be an anachronistic explanation. Her sense of sin

---

[1] Henry Walker, *Spirituall Experiences of Sundry Beleevers*, London, 1651, p. 26.

did at least give her an explanation for such an otherwise senseless event. There are many cases of people being concerned that they loved their children too much. Another woman said that

> The Lord stroke the elder of my two children then living, which was a boy, my other, which is a girl, I did not so much value, but now I do, and know God's mercy in sparing her, but my child that then died, was the chiefest comfort that my heart was fixed upon in this world, which hath been so great a grief to me, that I have slept few nights quiet since.[1]

The Countess of Bridgewater wrote a prayer when expecting her third child: 'If it be thy good will, lay not thy heavy hand of justice and affliction on me, in taking away my children in their youths, as thou pleased to take my last babe Frances.'

Parents recognized, more readily than they do in a society with low infant mortality, that children might die. High infant mortality does not diminish parents' feelings, but it encourages the development of resignation and the acceptance of death, qualities which may be confused with lack of affection. Indeed, what is very striking is that parents' expression of their love for their children embraced their apprehension of the fragility of their children's lives.

[1] Henry Walker, *Spirituall Experiences of Sundry Beleevers*, London, 1651, pp. 69–70.

PART THREE

Women's Material Worlds

CHAPTER SEVEN

Health and Strength

Disease and diet affect everyone's physical condition, but they are even more important in women when pregnant or lactating, or, indeed, when seeking to become pregnant. Poverty, too, as we see in modern debates about nutrition, influences child-bearing, child-rearing and health in general. Poverty may have been less significant in relation to the power to purchase medical attention and medicines, since they were rarely efficacious in this period and some medical practices may actually have caused harm. We shall look here at what expectations women had of good health at different stages of their lives, bearing in mind the diseases to which they were subject, the food which they ate, and the kind of care that the sick and infirm might receive.

Disease

The commonest microbial epidemic diseases in early modern England were bubonic plague and typhus. Bubonic plague is predominantly an urban disease, and it is associated with warm weather since very cold weather kills the eggs of the flea which spreads the disease. Plague was feared much more than the other epidemic diseases, and it was responsible for more social disruption: 60 per cent of cases were fatal. It was estimated at the time that over 70,000 Londoners died in the plague of 1665–6, and this may well be an underestimate. This was the last great epidemic of the disease in England, though there were isolated outbreaks for about the next ten years. Until then London had been stricken every twenty-five or thirty years. Smaller cities experienced outbreaks at longer intervals. Market towns occasionally suffered epidemics, but when they did mortality could be devastating, as in Penrith,

Cumberland, in 1598, when 33 per cent of the town's population died. There is disagreement about whether plague caused higher mortality among men or women; in general, in England it seems to have affected them equally, but it was particularly devastating for those aged between fifteen and twenty-five.

Epidemic typhus is carried by human body lice. Epidemics usually began in winter, when clothes and bodies were washed least, and tailed off in the warmer weather. It rarely kills children if they are healthy, but it is very commonly associated with famine, and the combination of typhus and starvation kills disproportionately large numbers of children. Other common epidemic microbial diseases were influenza and smallpox. Influenza did not usually result in a very high mortality and epidemics rarely lasted long, usually no more than about seven weeks, though the effects might be protracted by secondary infections such as pneumonia. Smallpox did not become an epidemic disease until after the seventeenth century, and it was chiefly confined to urban areas. Until then it was rarely fatal, though its effects could include severe disfigurement. In 1718 Lady Mary Wortley Montagu introduced the first smallpox vaccination, but it was not widely used initially. Whooping cough, unlike other infectious diseases of childhood, is much more severe in girls than boys.

The incidence and severity of epidemic disease varied because local populations might develop immunity to common local diseases. Travellers might import new diseases to which the local population was more susceptible; this is one of the reasons why life in the cities was so much unhealthier than life in the country. The shifting population constantly imported new strains of diseases to which most of the population, having not previously been exposed to them, lacked immunity.

Epidemics might have a different impact upon men and women. Both epidemic disease and starvation inhibit human fertility: that is to say, births, measured by baptisms, fall in number. (Demographers say that conceptions fall, but there was normally no record of pregnancies which failed to reach full term.) It is generally assumed that it is the woman's fertility which is most affected, because illness and starvation frequently lead to amenorrhoea (cessation of menstruation). Given the marked seasonality of conception and births among the rural population, one can see that diseases associated with certain seasons might have devastating effects upon pregnant or lactating women. Distinguishing between the effects of disease and the effects of dearth is problematic; generally, births seem always to have declined as a consequence of starvation, but only sometimes as a result of an epidemic.

Another perennial problem was infestation. Fleas, bed-bugs and lice were commonplaces of life, even among the most affluent. Samuel Pepys's wife, cutting his hair, found about twenty lice on one occasion. Lice cause itching and carry a number of diseases such as typhus; one species of flea carries bubonic plague. There were also worms and fungal infections which were difficult to cure. The commonest condition (over a quarter of all patients) seen by the seventeenth-century Somerset physician John Westover was the 'itch' or scabies. In fact skin conditions in general made up a high proportion of all his cases, probably because of their unsightliness. After the itch, worms was the commonest condition he saw in children.

Malaria and tuberculosis were endemic and could lead to death or severe disability. Malaria was endemic in England until the nineteenth century, when the draining of marshes and the increased enclosure of drains reduced the habitat of the malaria mosquito. Its distribution and incidence varied considerably, and there were some parts of the country where it was endemic but where the local population had developed partial immunity. In the early modern period, malaria was generally identified as 'ague', with different types defined in terms of the frequency of the fevers, quartan and tertian. Malaria is characterized by chills, fevers and sweats which can come on at any time and may go away altogether spontaneously. It makes pregnant women more vulnerable to other infection and may cause abortion or stillbirth. The birth weight of first children born to malarial mothers is reduced, but the weight of subsequent children is not affected.

Tuberculosis (TB) has a variety of forms of which the most familiar is TB of the lungs, a disease which can be exacerbated by a polluted atmosphere. There is evidence that deaths from TB declined, but that deaths from other lung diseases increased, in the late eighteenth and early nineteenth centuries. Another commonly occurring form was TB-affected lymph glands (scrofula or king's evil), the disease which it was believed was alleviated by being touched by the king. TB may advance slowly or fast, but its progress in a recently delivered mother is particularly rapid. It also becomes a dangerous disease if associated with the hormonal changes which accompany puberty and pregnancy; and adolescent girls were especially susceptible to TB, smallpox and other serious infections.

The decrease in the population in the late seventeenth century was characterized by a marked increase in child mortality, but not in adult mortality. This suggests that disease must have played an important part, since adults and children are equally vulnerable to environmental factors, while children are more vulnerable to infectious disease. Since the disease was not plague it may well have been measles, though seventeenth-century physicians did not always distinguish between the various diseases which produced rashes and fevers. Measles was common and often fatal, but it was also confused with other similar diseases such as rubella.

Mental Health

Humoral pathology, the prevailing medical philosophy of the sixteenth, seventeenth and much of the eighteenth centuries, assumed an intimate and fundamental connection between the mind and the body. In the earlier part of the period, women with psychological maladies were as likely to consult a minister or astrologer as a physician. Psychological well-being was considered to be a spiritual state as much as a physical one. A young mid-seventeenth-century woman who had attempted to kill herself was attended by a doctor and two ministers. Given the inability of physicians to effect real cures, their presence at the bedside of anyone with an intangible psychological disorder, even if it was an advanced mania, can have offered no more than reassurance.

In the early seventeenth century, the physician and astrologer Richard Napier saw nearly twice as many cases of mental disorder in women than in men. Later in the century John Westover saw three times as many cases of melancholy among women as men, and more than twice as many cases of female 'distraction' as male. He also noted familial tendencies to melancholy. In 1680 he built a small hospital to which some of his patients with mental disorders were admitted. Anne Lewis was there for four weeks suffering from melancholy, and Anne Young and Alice Stevens were there for twenty weeks and thirty-one weeks respectively, with madness.

Religious or quasi-religious explanations for insanity gave way increasingly to psychological and physiological explanations. By the eighteenth century, neurological and psychiatric conditions were beginning to be recognized separately and in their own right. Ideas of possession by evil spirits, and of the disadvantageous conjunction of astrological phenomena, gave way to explanations based upon age, or stage of life, or some direct physiological condition or act like the menopause or masturbation. Allied with this was the development during the eighteenth century of institutions for the insane, where doctors might observe numbers of people afflicted with similar disorders. Five new hospitals were built in London and thirty-one in the provinces, some of which admitted mentally disturbed patients.

It is particularly important not to be constantly trying to look over one's shoulder from the present to the past or to attach modern labels to historical conditions. Apart from the difficulty of identifying symptoms from descriptions, people often had the symptoms of more than one condition. They also gave different conditions different values from those which would nowadays be attached to them. In the absence of any kind of chemical analysis, all diagnosis had to be made from external symptoms. Furthermore, many acute states, or states of extreme emotion, were perceived in religious rather than psychological terms. Ecstasy, for example, had a religious value and might be highly prized among enthusiastic sects. Hearing voices was not considered to be abnormal unless the advice the voices gave was patently anti-social. Self-doubt was associated with the passage to finding true religious faith. Despair and suicidal feelings were associated with the temptations which the true believer might have to undergo to find God. Suicide was the ultimate sin, and suicidal feelings prompted deep religious difficulties.

Suicide was surprisingly common, though male suicides outnumbered female. Of the forty-seven women's deaths recorded by the Sussex coroners between 1500 and 1558, twenty were suicides (43 per cent); and of the sixty-eight women's deaths recorded by the Nottinghamshire coroners in the same period, twenty-one were suicides (31 per cent). Fewer than 2 per cent of those found to have committed suicide in the period 1485–1660 were found to be *non compos mentis*; the majority were found to have committed a felony. Yet by the mid-eighteenth century the figures were more or less reversed. Suicide was strongly associated with poverty, economic distress and pre-marital pregnancy (though the confiscation of the property of someone who had died by suicide may have prejudiced coroners against verdicts of suicide for the very wealthy).

Women's mental health was, in the eyes of the physicians who wrote about it, very much connected with their stage of life. Most physicians divided women's lives into three periods during which they were believed to be particularly susceptible to certain conditions, with, to us, a puzzling and changeable collection of both physical and psychological symptoms. Virgins and young girls were believed to suffer from chlorosis or green-sickness; married woman from suffocation of the mother, suffocation of the womb, or mother-fits; and widows from a variation of this. Suffocation of the mother is now identified as hysteria, but no two physicians could agree on its precise symptoms. Originally it was believed to be the result of diabolic possession. In the early seventeenth century, Edward Jordan tried to demonstrate that it was not the result of possession, preferring a more physiological explanation. Later in the century, the physicians Thomas Willis and Thomas Sydenham described it particularly as a complaint of virgins and widows and those who led a sedentary life, 'Such as work and fare hard are quite free from every species of this disorder', and they held its causes to lie more in the mind than the body.

Though I have come across no accounts by women themselves of them suffering from mother-fits, physicians' notebooks record a number of cases, and so do male observers. The seventeen-year-old sister of the seventeenth-century minister Philip Henry swooned with mother-fits, which continued for the best part of a year. Recipe books for remedies, both doctors' and housewives', contain prescriptions for remedies for hysteric disorders. The remedies clearly distinguish between hysteric and menstrual disorders; other disorders of the womb; and lunacy and melancholy.

Eating Disorders and Nutrition

Concern about eating disorders, and women's relationship with food, is often identified as a particularly twentieth-century phenomenon. But early modern women were not unaware of fatness and thinness. Queen Mary wrote to Lady Mary Forester in the 1690s, 'I am not changed in my humour, though I am in my shape, but that not by so good a reason [pregnancy] as you had when I saw you last, but mere fat.'[1] Pica (eating inedible substances) and anorexia nervosa were not unusual complaints in early modern England, and they generated a considerable medical literature.

Pica was a commonly described medical condition, associated particularly with diseases of virgins and pregnant women. James Guillimeau wrote in 1612 that such women were often troubled

---

[1] Historical Manuscripts Commission, 9th Report, Appendix, part III, Stopford Sackville MSS, p. 7.

with 'this depraved or immoderate appetite' for 'raw or burnt flesh, yea, even to long after man's flesh, ashes, coals, old shoes, chalk, wax, nutshells, mortar, and lime'. The influential French physician, Ambroise Paré, whose works were published in English in 1634, described how pregnant women were often afflicted with

loathing and waywardness . . . whereby it happeneth that they loathe meats of good juice, and long for and desire illaudable pleasures, and those that are contrary to nature, as coals, dirt, ashes, stinking salt fish, sour, austere and tart fruits, pepper, vinegar.[1]

Nicholas Fontanus, writing in the 1650s, put the matter more robustly:

Women are sometimes so extravagant and preposterous in their appetite, that they refuse wholesome meat, and long after coals, chalk, a piece of an old wall, starch, earth, and the like trash, which they devour as ravenously as a hungry ploughman will wind down a good bag pudding.[2]

In the 1650s a young woman herself described how 'the devil did tempt me to rend the pillow, and pick out some of the feathers to swallow them down, which I did, which had like to cost me my life'.

A condition which we would call anorexia nervosa was quite commonly recognized by early modern medical writers. Nicholas Fontanus, describing in the mid-seventeenth century the condition of melancholy proceeding from the womb, wrote of women who 'have no stomach to their meat, and being taken with a strange loathing of aliment, their bodies waste and consume'. It was not until the nineteenth century that not eating for psychological reasons, rather than physiological ones, was recognized by the medical profession; however, fasting for supernatural reasons was well known in the early modern period, and had been associated with the cessation of menstruation. Usually the reason given was some kind of spiritual crisis, like this girl in the 1650s, speaking of her progress towards the discovery of God's goodness: 'I was much distempered in my mind . . . I feared to eat any thing lest they should poison me.' Mortification of the flesh was not one of the aspects of Roman Catholicism which commended itself to Protestants, so it is interesting to see extreme privation surviving as an aspect of the religious life of more radical Protestants. Fasting girls were as likely to be attended by a minister as a physician.

---

1 Ambroise Paré, *The Workes*, London, 1634, Concerning the Generation of Man, book 24, p. 890.
2 Nicholas Fontanus, *The Womans Doctour*, London, 1652, pp. 156–7.

During the sixteenth and seventeenth centuries there were a number of celebrated cases in Europe of self-starvation, usually by adolescent girls, but occasionally by women in their twenties, or boys. These were widely reported, both as aids to faith and as medical curiosities. Martha Taylor, who in 1668–9 took nothing but the syrup from stewed prunes or raisins, was the first well-known English case, and there were several more in the eighteenth century. John Reynolds presented a paper to the Royal Society in 1669 entitled *A Discourse upon Prodigious Abstinence: occasioned by the Twelve Months Fasting of Martha Taylor, the Famed Derbyshire Damozell: Proving that without any Miracle, the Texture of Human Bodies may be so altered, that Life may be long Continued without the Supplies of Meat and Drink.*

Food was the object of these women's predicaments and was recognized as a source of difficulty by both patients and physicians alike. Food had a considerable presence in medical literature, because of the importance that was attached to diet in humoral pathology. Also, in the absence of effective medicines, changes in the diet or special foods might at least diminish people's feelings of impotence when faced with intractable medical problems. Sufferers from different conditions were to be given different things to eat and drink. Newly delivered women, for example, were to be given soothing drinks. How far these medical recommendations actually found a place in popular practice is difficult to establish, and there is often little distinction between the preparation of remedies and the preparation of food, both of which, in all but the largest households, were done by women.

Starvation and Nutritional Deficiency

The effects of a general shortage of food were not a matter of much interest to early modern medical writers, though they were of great concern to law enforcers, who rightly saw food shortages as a threat to public order when otherwise peaceable citizens, including women, would take to the streets. More recently, food shortages have interested historical demographers. They have been engaged in a fierce debate as to whether mortality crises (periods when the death rate rose sharply in a short space of time) were caused primarily by epidemic disease or by food shortages (indicated by grain prices). Shortage of food might lower resistance to disease, especially if there were repeated epidemics. Severe weather combined with a poor diet could also have serious effects upon people's chances of survival. February 1762 was exceptionally cold and the accidental deaths (four of them of women) recorded by the coroner for Wiltshire were all attributed to the severity of the weather.

By the early seventeenth century, England had ceased to experience nationwide famines, but there were regional mortality crises in which food shortages played a part. In the north of England in 1623, burials in many places increased to two or three times their normal level (from 30–40 per 1,000 per year, to 60–120 per 1,000 per year) chiefly because of food shortages. In 1740 a combination of scarce food, bitterly cold weather and disease (dysentery, typhoid or typhus) led to greatly increased numbers of deaths. But what did poor people eat? England was becoming a wheat-eating society, and it was only the poorest people and people living in distant upland areas who ate rye and oats. Peas and beans were used to stretch supplies of scarce grain. In times of hardship these cheaper foodstuffs were more popular, but increased demand might send prices to three or four times their normal level.

Starvation can cause death by itself or can exacerbate the effects of disease. However, in the London bills of mortality (the weekly lists of the numbers of people who had died and their cause of death, kept in the first half of the seventeenth century), only infants are identified as dying of starvation. Eating rotten or unsuitable food (tree bark, for example) was a common contributory cause of death in times of dearth. In early modern England, episodes of crisis mortality rarely lasted for more than a few months, but their effects on the population could be more enduring. Extreme shortage of food inhibits ovulation, reduces the number of conceptions and increases foetal mortality. The effects on the birth rate may be seen for eighteen months after a crisis has ended. Severely malnourished mothers are more likely to give birth prematurely, to have difficult labours, or to give birth to underweight, full-term babies. It is not clear whether malnourishment affects the quality or quantity of mothers' milk. Malnourishment takes a particular toll of children aged one to four.

In starvation, people simply do not eat enough; in malnutrition, they may have enough volume but their diet is deficient in some elements essential for good health. The effects of an unsuitable diet must have affected many people chronically.

Nothing was known about iron-deficiency anaemia, to which menstruating, pregnant and lactating women (especially those with an inadequate diet) are particularly prone. Vitamin D deficiency was also a particular problem for women. Vitamin D is found in oily fish such as herrings, and in egg yolk and milk; it is also synthesized when skin is exposed to ultra violet radiation. Known now as rickets when it occurs in children and affects growing bones, and as osteomalacia in adults, it leads to mal-formation of the long bones, ribs and pelvis. In particular, it leads to narrowing of the pelvic opening and thus to terrible obstructive complications in childbirth. If a pregnant woman is in poor health, her child may be more susceptible to rickets; and repeated pregnancies, and suckling a child during pregnancy, also increase the likelihood of children suffering from the disease. The symptoms of rickets were first described in a recognizably modern form in 1650, but it was believed to be a contagious disease because in children, apart from bone malformation, it leads to feverishness, irritability and sleeplessness. With the increase in smoke pollution in cities it came to be a characteristic conditon of the urban poor because of inadequate exposure to sunlight, as well as insufficient diet. Doubtless some of these deficiency conditions diminished as the standard of living rose during the eighteenth century, but their incidence among poor people cannot have been significantly reduced.

Care of the Sick and Infirm

Women were responsible for much of the treatment of illness in the household, and they had at their command considerable numbers of home-made remedies for the commoner complaints. There has been much discussion among historians about the extent to which the male medical profession (apothecaries, barber-surgeons and physicians) was, during the period 1500–1760, trying to extend the scope of its activities at the expense of work traditionally done by women. Women's position was eroded in the sense that by the end of the period there was less scope for women to occupy career positions than there had been. There was a serious attack by men on female midwives; and male midwives achieved a prominent position during the eighteenth century. But throughout the period the burden of actually carrying out daily care for children, the sick and the elderly fell on women, either as relations or as servants.

As an extension of their household responsibilities, some women became known in their communities for their skill in medical matters. In the 1730s James Fretwell described his Yorkshire mother's skill in 'surgery', and she often gave assistance to those who could not afford to pay for medical treatment. He also referred to Mrs Skipton

who was a woman that was very serviceable in her neighbourhood, let the physicians laugh at old women and their medicines as long as they please, yet she did a great deal of good, sometimes beyond their expectations, and often (I'm afraid) contrary to their wishes.[1]

This kind of help added to women's authority in the community. Parishes might pay poor women to do nursing and laundry for the sick and infirm.

For those able to afford the attention of a physician there were various kinds of doctor available. Most practised in towns, but there were also some rural practitioners. Richard Napier (1559–1634) treated more women than men for both physical and psychological disorders. John Westover (1643–1706) ran a practice from the village of Wedmore in Somerset. Contrary to modern figures, more of his patients were men than women, but this may reflect the fact that doctors had to be paid. It is evident from a comparison of the writings by male physicians with women's own accounts of their diseases that there was a very considerable gap between popular diagnosis and treatment and professional medical practice, especially as much of the popular diagnosis and treatment was in the hands of women.

It is easy to assume that because of the short average life expectancy in early modern England there were few of the elderly, and that those who did reach an advanced age must have been very infirm. But attitudes to old age were rather different then. The elderly were not singled out as a distinct group, nor was old age considered to be synonymous with infirmity. There was no retiring age and those who needed to work for their livelihoods continued to do so until too sick or feeble to continue though the type of work they did might change with their altering physical circumstances and health.

Much of the provision for the elderly infirm was in the form of out-relief (money, food, fuel and clothing), though many parishes had some form of residential assistance. Workhouses were introduced in the eighteenth century. Some almshouses provided for equal numbers of men and women, but many, like Sir William Cordell's foundation of 1570 at Long Melford in Suffolk, accommodated more men than women. At Cordell's Trinity Hospital there were places for twelve men and two women, and at the Jesus

---

[1] 'A Family History Begun by James Fretwell,' *Yorkshire Diaries and Autobiographies in the Seventeenth and Eighteenth Centuries*, Surtees Society, 65, 1877, p. 221.

Hospital, Canterbury, founded in 1595, there were places for seven men and four women. Archbishop Abbot's almshouses at Guildford, established in 1619, required that the twelve men and eight women be over sixty years old, celibate and natives or long-term residents of the town. After the middle of the seventeenth century, benefactions were usually for equal numbers of men and women, or were simply for a certain number of poor people whose sex was not specified.

There was an increasing tendency during the seventeenth century for almshouse provision to become specialized. For example, William Goddard's Jesus Hospital at Bray in Berkshire, completed in 1627, was for forty poor persons of whom six were to be freemen or women of the Fishmongers' Company, and the rest parishioners of Bray over fifty years of age. In the late seventeenth century, Trinity House in Hull provided thirty seamen's widows with 16d. a week and fuel. Apart from accommodation, there was a chapel, and above the chapel was a room for storing sails which the widows made. Clergymen's widows were accommodated by Bishop Seth Ward in 1682 in the College of Matrons in Salisbury, and by Sarah dowager Duchess of Somerset in 1686 at Froxfield, Wiltshire. During the eighteenth century, the endowing of almshouses became a progressively less popular form of charity.

Charitable benefactions allowed the donor to govern from the grave. In the sixteenth and early seventeenth centuries, bene-factors who left money for almshouses would specify how many people of each sex were to be accommodated and the minimum age for admission. It was also quite common for clothing to be provided (often some kind of uniform) and for there to be a requirement to fulfil certain religious duties. Women were usually required to be widows or spinsters; men, if they were married, might be required to live apart from their wives. In 1632 an almsman in Dulwich was expelled for trying to seduce an almswoman. Rich women left money for charitable purposes, sometimes specifying what it should be spent on, sometimes leaving it to executors or trustees to decide. In her will of 1711, Mary Bridgeman of Castle Bromwich Hall, Warwickshire, desirious of leaving part of her fortune for charitable purposes, left £500 to be administered by the Bishop of Bristol, the Speaker of the House of Commons, and her son John to buy an estate whose income was for charitable uses in Castle Bromwich.

The peak of almshouse endowment was the 1580s. Benefactors were increasingly people who had made their money as merchants and traders. The advantage of almshouses was that they could fit almost any pocket. Lady Lumley endowed almshouses for twelve people at Thornton-le-Dale, Yorkshire, in 1657, a grammar school there, and more almshouses in Shoreditch in 1672. At the other end of the scale, in 1725 Deborah Hampden endowed an almshouse for one 'poor maiden who shall have lived in good reputation to the age of forty years'. Those too poor to endow the most modest almshouses might give money for some form of outdoor relief, and this became a more popular form of benefaction by the later eighteenth century.

The term 'hospital' came to stand for something rather different in 1760 from that which it had stood for in 1500. In the early sixteenth century, the majority of hospitals were almshouses and leper houses which did not provide medical care. During the seventeenth century, hospitals providing care for the sick increased in number. During the eighteenth century, specialist hospitals, especially lying-in hospitals, became more common. The form of hospital which requires the greatest leap of the imagination is the institutions in which those regarded as mad were detained. Since madness was not necessarily seen as a medical problem, these institutions were refuges rather than hospitals in the modern sense.

It is sometimes argued that people in past times never enjoyed positive good health, but merely varieties of ill-health. This was certainly the case for women on whom child-bearing and poverty had taken their toll. Nevertheless, as we have seen, many women, if they survived these vicissitudes, lived to what was even by modern standards a great age. We should not let the absence of modern comforts and medical techniques distract us from the fact that people are very resilient and can survive and recover from a surprising amount of illness and discomfort.

CHAPTER EIGHT

Women's Livelihoods

This chapter is concerned with debates and speculations of historians about the work women did. It is also concerned with the place of women's work in the economy; the changing role of domestic production; and debates about proto-industrialization as they relate to women's work. Chapter 9 is concerned with some of the occupations by which women earned their livings independently of men.

The subject of women and work has exercised people in a number of academic disciplines in recent decades. The issue attracting most attention has been the extent to which the industrial revolution altered women's working lives. For some writers pre-industrial England was a society where women might participate in a wide range of crafts and trades, and where they were able to exercise choice, and be independent. For other writers it was a society in which women were shackled to the home, identified only through the male members of their immediate family, a situation from which women were liberated by the free labour market of the industrial revolution. To a large extent the study of women and work in pre-industrial economies has been conditioned by this debate.

The nature of women's work in the early modern period was described in 1580 in a book of advice to housewives: 'Some respite to husbands the weather may send, but huswives' affairs have never an end.' More recently, Mary Prior has written,

> The division of labour between the sexes was efficient and inequit-able. . . . The realm of work was . . . divided into two parts. What men did was definite, well-defined, limited. . . . What the women did was everything else. . . . So the realm of work was divided without residue.[1]

---

[1] Mary Prior, 'Women and the urban economy: Oxford 1500–1800', in Mary Prior (ed.), *Women in English Society 1500–1800*, Methuen, 1985, p. 95.

Women's work then (and to a large extent now) was the jobs which get done all the time and are not therefore worthy of comment, like housework, or the things which need to be done in an emergency or seasonally. Though there were some changes between 1500 and 1760 in the kinds of occupation open to women, this residuary function remained the characteristic feature of women's work, or, rather, of their lives. Even the exponents of early modern England as a society of economic opportunity for women cannot deny that women were poorly paid and that their work was regarded as inferior long before the industrial revolution.

Women's work in early modern England was arranged informally and rarely involved contact with official bodies. Women rarely exercised authority over anyone outside the home, or appeared in public places; and their work lacked formal standing. Women were identified not by their trade, as men were, but by their marital status. These characteristics were the result of much women's work taking place in the household: their own, or someone else's.

The Daily Round

The word 'work' has for us connotations of waged labour, but most women's work was unwaged. Work was what women did in the household towards the general maintenance of the family. Household manuals laid down how the good housewife ought to spend her day. Thomas Tusser's *Five Hundred Points of Good Husbandry* of 1580 gives as morning activities: cleaning the floors; spinning and carding wool; preparing ingredients for cooking and brewing: preparing breakfast; feeding the cattle; brewing; baking; dairy work; laundry; malting; and preparing dinner at noon. In the afternoon the housewife (the mistress of servants) should chivvy her servants back to work; use up the left-overs from dinner; sew; save feathers for pillows; and make candles. In the evening she should feed the hens and pigs and milk the cows; lock up the hens; bring in the washing; and lock up the house. Then she should serve supper; amuse her husband; tell the servants what to do the following day; and go to bed having washed the dishes, laid 'leavens' (prepared yeast) and saved the fire. In summer she was advised to go to bed at 10 o'clock and rise at 4, in winter to bed at 9 o'clock and rise at 5. Many of the jobs were occasional, weekly or seasonal; and in urban households, and some rural households, goods like candles, bread and beer were bought ready-made.

A study of accidental deaths recorded in the coroners' inquests for the later Middle Ages gives a fascinating insight into the way in which real women spent their days. Morning accidents were commonly concerned with fetching water and preparing meals, working with livestock and brewing. The number of accidents rose as noon approached and women became tired and hungry. Afternoon accidents were predominantly concerned with laundry or seasonal agricultural work. Drowning and burning, and accidents connected with fetching water, and with laundry and cooking, were much the commonest causes of accidental death for women. They took place both in their own homes and in the homes of neighbours.

The evidence of inquests held in the sixteenth century suggests several changes in women's daily routines. The greater use of chimneys had improved domestic safety. Relatively few women died in fires, and of those who fell into the fire, several were described as ill at the time of their deaths. Accidents fetching water were common; indeed, drowning was the commonest cause of death recorded by coroners. Young girls, often servants, fetching water early in the morning when it was still dark, fell into ponds and down wells. So early were some of these accidents that it is clear that Tusser's times of waking were not necessarily just a counsel of perfection. Agnes Ellyot, a Sussex woman, drowned in 1554 when, going to fetch water at a water pit at 4 a.m., the stake on to which she was holding gave way.

But it was not accidents in the home which were most likely to kill women; it was accidents outdoors. Falling off a branch while picking pears, being struck by falling pieces of timber, being caught by pieces of machinery like the cog of a malt mill or the arm of a horsemill, all caused deaths in the sixteenth century. Travelling, too, was attended by all sorts of risks, especially in the vicinity of a large river. The river Trent was particularly treacherous: nine women were drowned in a boat in 1510, and a further accident in 1543 killed one woman, three men and three mares. There were many accidents involving carts and horses which resulted in fatalities. The number of travelling accidents appears to have diminished in the eighteenth century, but this may be a consequence of the way in which accidental deaths were recorded rather than a consequence of women travelling less or of roads and transport becoming safer.

For most of the period 1500–1760 poor women spent their time at home, looking after their children, fetching water, cooking, sewing and doing laundry, spinning and, at certain seasons, agricultural work. They might keep poultry, do petty trading, brewing or gardening, and take part in their husbands' trades. There were variations in this daily round. Extreme poverty cut down both cooking and cleaning, since there was nothing in which to cook or prepare food, and no possessions to need cleaning. Living in the town, especially for the poor, probably meant buying prepared food from cookshops. Sufficient wealth to employ a servant added directing the servant's activities to a woman's work. Even in the eighteenth century, when country houses were often divorced from the agriculture which supported them financially, women took a serious interest in the management of the household, though slightly shamefacedly. Mrs Lybbe Powys recorded in 1756 that Lady Leicester of Holkham Hall was often to be found in the kitchen and was once spotted there at 6 o'clock in the morning, 'thinking all her guests safe in bed, I suppose'.

We have seen that the household was likely to consist of parents and children, rarely other relatives except for short periods, as well as servants and employees. There were also lodgers. Many people in towns lived in lodgings, and running lodgings was an extension of women's ordinary domestic work. But there were lodgers in the countryside too. The 1589 poor relief statute, which laid down that no cottage might be erected without four acres of its own land, also specified that its only inhabitants might be the family. There were many indictments in the later sixteenth century for having 'inmates', or lodgers living in cottages in the country where they were not permitted. These prosecutions probably arose from a fear that such people were likely to become a charge upon the parish (because they were usually very poor), or because of suspicion of immorality. The large number of such cases in the late sixteenth century suggests that there was a serious housing shortage.

Waged work was, for most women, associated with a particular period of their lives, between childhood and marriage. It was the opportunities for such work which contributed to the independence of young women and their relatively late age at marriage during the sixteenth and seventeenth centuries.

Starting Work

Women's days were filled from beginning to end with tasks concerned with the welfare of their families, but not classed as employment from which they might legitimately take a holiday. Men's work, being clearly demarcated, began and ended at certain times, and allowed them leisure. Thomas Baskerville, travelling round England in the 1660s, drew a different conclusion. He observed that Suffolk women

go spinning up and down the way . . . with a rock and a distaff in their hands, so that if a comparison were to be made between the ploughman and the good wives of these parts, their lives were the more pleasant, for they can go with their work to good company, and the poor ploughman must do his work alone.

And in Gloucestershire at 4 o'clock in the morning he saw

many women of the older sort smoking their pipes of tobacco and yet lost no time. for their fingers were all the while busy at knitting and women carrying their puddings and bread to the bakehouse lose no time but knit by the way.[1]

We know very little about the age at which women began paid work. The notion of unsuitable employment for children was a nineteenth-century one, and until reformers began to inveigh against child sweeps, miners and midshipmen, it was expected that children would contribute to the livelihood of the household. It was quite usual for children to start to do so from the age of about ten. Accidents involving girls described as servants are recorded for girls of eleven and twelve in the sixteenth century. In the 1650s a girl of twelve from a gentle family was expected by her father to take her dead mother's place as house-keeper, mother to ten children, and mistress of six servants.

For many children, girls as well as boys, work began with apprenticeship. This could be of two types, either a regular craft apprenticeship or a parish apprenticeship. Both were seen as a means of training children to a craft or trade in someone else's establishment, because, until the eighteenth century, it was unusual for children to be apprenticed to a parent, or to close relatives. The premium paid to the master by the parents or guardians was quite large, so considerable efforts were made to ensure that apprentices were appropriately placed. The normal age for beginning an apprenticeship was the early teens, though girls were often apprenticed younger than boys, and parish apprentices younger than craft apprentices. Farm service was a form of training, but it did not involve the legal arrangements of apprenticeship. Young people were taken on for a year at a time, and lived with the farmer, working at a variety of tasks on the farm. Girls

---

[1] Historical Manuscripts Commission, Portland MSS, vol. II, pp. 266, 303.

might do farm work, work in the dairy or tending poultry, or domestic work looking after the male farm servants.

There is a good deal of uncertainty about the extent to which girls were apprenticed, because of the confusion between parish apprenticeships and craft apprenticeships. In sixteenth-century London the number of girls apprenticed was small: fewer than 2 per cent among thousands of boys. In eighteenth-century Warwickshire more girls were taken on, numbering about 6 per cent of the total number of apprentices. Some of these Warwickshire girls were obviously being taken on as apprentices to women, chiefly in trades connected with sewing. Others were probably being taken on as domestic servants, like Mary Alpot, apprenticed in 1742 for five years to John Smallwood, yeoman; or for dairy work, like Sarah Barnes, apprenticed in 1741 for four years to Joseph Blunt, a dairyman. Mary Addyes, taken on in 1753 until she should reach the age of eighteen, by William Richards of Birmingham, pistol-maker, was probably doing domestic work. The premium which was paid for her was very much larger than was usual, £16 instead of under £10. The girls who were apprenticed to weavers and tailors may have been working in that craft or they may have been doing domestic work. Quite a few Warwickshire women took on apprentices, some in female trades, such as mantua maker, some taking on apprentices in their husbands' businesses, such as brushmaker. The periwig maker's apprentice could have been male or female.

Parish apprenticeships were for pauper children and were a combination of outdoor relief and occupational training. Children were placed younger and in less skilled trades than craft apprentices. Of the seven girls apprenticed in Kingston upon Thames between 1610 and 1658, five were poor children. They might not be particularly welcome. Elizabeth Clark, a widow of Trent in Somerset, informed the assizes in 1642 that she had no work for the nine-year-old Edith Durnford who had been placed with her, and that she was 'of mean capacity to do service'. The case was referred to two local JPs, who found Edith another place the following year. How successful the scheme for parish apprenticeship was can be judged by the fact that less than half of those taken on completed their indentures.

Of those girls who were apprenticed, the majority were apprenticed in housewifery, some form of sewing, or retailing. In mid-sixteenth-century Bristol many of the girls who were apprenticed as housewives or shepsters (tailors) had no father. These girls came from the same kinds of backgrounds as the male apprentices:

about half from tradesmen's families, and about a third from landed and agricultural backgrounds. During the century formal apprenticeships for women declined, but informal ones, especially the parish apprenticeships, continued, so that by the seventeenth century the majority of girls apprenticed in Bristol were parish apprentices. Alongside this development is an increasingly clear distinction between male and female occupations. The history of women's apprenticeship in Bristol is replicated in other places. For example, in Rye in the late sixteenth century, most apprentices were orphans and of local origin. Here it is clear that apprenticeship was primarily a means of providing young fatherless girls and boys with a parental relationship, as it was in seventeenth-century Colyton in Devon.

Ending Work

Work today may end very abruptly with retirement, but in early modern England it did not come to an end at a specific age. There was no retirement age, and there were no regular pensions for the elderly. Simply being old was not itself a qualification for claiming parish relief.

Women, though they worked in the sense of having occupations, often tiring and time-consuming ones, relatively rarely had jobs outside the home. Those who needed to work for their livings continued to do so until too sick or feeble to continue, though the type of work they did might change with their altering physical circumstances and health. Many of the older women in the surveys of the poor in early seventeenth-century Salisbury earned something spinning. A reason for inability to work was assigned to even the oldest of the poor, like the 75-year-old Widow Bagges, 'lame in her hands'; the 85-year-old Maud Sawnders, who was 'feeble'; and the 80-year-old Widow Cowltee, who was almost blind. Women were also often responsible for young children until well on into their forties, and it was not uncommon for a woman to have her last child at the same time as her eldest children were producing their first offspring. But as it was unusual for more than two generations to live together, there was rarely much opportunity for women to have any responsibility for their grandchildren. Indeed, given the distances which people migrated, it was quite likely that they would see them only infrequently.

A change which one would expect to find in women's occupations is that they would cease to do fine sewing as they became more long-sighted with age. Spectacles were a considerable novelty, and they were expensive and difficult to obtain. Lady Bridgeman, living in Warwickshire, ordered some spectacles from London in 1698, but was not satisfactorily fitted until 1701 after a great deal of correspondence. The Norwich census of the poor in 1570 suggests that women over fifty were unlikely to do work like embroidery, lace-making and button-making. This is corroborated by work on women's occupations in late-seveneenth-century London. Young women did domestic work; women in their thirties and forties did sewing; older women did washing, nursing, hawking and domestic work by the day, which is evidence that older women who needed to work to maintain themselves tended to come from the lower social levels. A high proportion of women over sixty maintained themselves, often in very menial occupations; and they might continue to do so until an advanced aged, like the woman of eighty-six who sold fruit and vegetables from a cellar in Bloomsbury, London, in the late seventeenth century.

Poverty and old age were associated. About 7 per cent of the population of sixteenth-century England was aged over sixty, yet 15 per cent of the Norwich poor were over sixty, and over half of these were women. In places where there was a system of parish relief beyond the statutory minimum, it might be possible to stop working. High social status was defined partly by employing power; and employers, out of a sense of responsibility to their dependants, might keep older people, giving them different tasks with advancing age. They might support them in other ways, for it was common for employers to leave legacies of money to their servants.

In cities, gilds and companies offered some relief for their members and their members' families who had fallen on hard times. Grants were made to widows, wives of men in prison, women abandoned by their husbands, and orphaned children. In the sixteenth century, the London clothworkers' company granted 26s. 8d. a year to the widowed Mrs Pettinger. She married a member of another company, who then ran away, whereupon the clothworkers resumed their pension to her. In Oxford in the early seventeenth century, the cordwainers' company paid widows a sum of between £2 and £5 at their husbands' death, the amount depending upon the husband's rank in the company.

Domestic Production

Women's work, both paid and unpaid, was usually based in the home, either their own or someone else's. There was little distinction between what they did as mothers, wives and daughters, and what they did as wage earners. Many of the paid occupations open to women were simply an extension of the kinds of thing which women were expected to do anyway. Agriculture and manufacture largely relied upon a workforce which was resident at the place of work. Farms were based upon households where many of the farm servants lived, and manufacture was based upon workshops where many of the employees lived.

Women might be involved in the household's economic activities in one of two capacities: as paid employees (chiefly as domestic or farm servants) or as unpaid members of the family helping out in the business. It is clear that the town gilds which regulated the conditions of work in various trades recognized that women were active in various unpaid capacities even in trades where woman were not normally employed, like coopering or gunsmithing. In this unpaid capacity women had no status unless they were widows who were carrying on the business after the death of the husband and master craftsman. Even as widows their status was lower than that of a man, and on remarriage they forfeited such status as they had.

Historians have long debated whether women were better or worse off under a system of domestic production, or of factory production. There is a general consensus that in the later Middle Ages women had considerable freedom to run businesses on their own accounts, but that this freedom started to be eroded during the hard times of the sixteenth century and was further reduced at the Civil War. Alice Clark, writing in 1919, argued that domestic manufacture gave women a valued place in production. The development of capitalist production and specialization led to the wives of the richest merchants becoming idle. The work of the wives of small craftsmen went unrecognized, leading to a reduction in their status, and in their economic independence; and the work of the poorest women became progressively less skilled and more undervalued. As early as 1678 an anonymous writer expressed concern that the wives and daughters of the more prosperous tradesmen lacked the skills to assist in the man's business, and he urged them to learn double-entry book-keeping. Ivy Pinchbeck, writing in 1930, however, argued that domestic production oppressed women by denying them any status or choice in what they did, and by concealing the contribution they made. She argued that specialization and factory production, or at least the separation of production from the home, liberated women.

The household declined greatly as the principal locus of economic life during the seventeenth and eighteenth centuries. It is also clear that the part that women played in domestic production became more specialized; that the enforcement of exclusively 'male' trades affected women's opportunities, and pushed them into certain clearly defined occupations. It is not clear that factory production improved their position, since there was a marked sexual division of labour in factory production. But much more important than this is the fact that domestic service remained much the most important source of employment for women and virtually the only one where a woman could certainly keep herself. Paid work in manufacturing was only a very small source of women's employment.

An important feature of the early modern economy is that the distinction between agriculture and industry is not coextensive with the distinction between country and town. The production of food took place in and around towns, especially market gardening, and livestock were to be found in towns. Much industrial activity, especially manufacturing, took place in the countryside; and many of the households where manufacturing took place, especially the production of cloth, were in the countryside.

The Sexual Division of Labour: Agriculture

From earliest times, men and women did different kinds of agricultural work, though some work was done by both sexes. This was usually less skilled and more seasonal than the work which was reserved for men or for women alone. In the seventeenth century, the tasks which both sexes did were: reaping, binding, carrying corn, shearing sheep, thatching, spreading manure and breaking stones for road repair. There is even some evidence for women ploughing and following the harrow, though these were normally reserved for men.

The availability of temporary work has always been of particular importance to women because it fits in with their family and household commitments. The seasonal rhythm of work in agriculture produced marked seasonal peaks in marriages and births. Marriages peaked in the early summer and autumn, and births (including second and subsequent births) in the early spring (with conceptions in the late spring and early summer). Grain-growing areas produced the greatest seasonal fluctuations in employment, with the highest level of demand being in the summer at harvest time and the lowest in the winter. For women the main work was weeding, harvesting and gleaning. The Lincolnshire justices of the peace set women's wages in 1621 for 'shearing' wheat, rye or other grain at 2d. a day with food and drink, or 6d. without (the rates for men were 3d. and 8d. respectively); and for women cockers of barley and peas they were ld. a day with food and drink, or 4d. without (men's rates were 2d. and 6d. respectively).

Hiring fairs in grain-growing areas were often in September. In areas where livestock farming predominated, the time of greatest unemployment was in the late spring and early summer, just after calving and the busiest time in the dairy; and here hiring fairs were often in May. Dairy pasturage provided women with dairy work, butter- and cheese-making. Sheep farming provided work with wool. For men the national level of employment in agriculture was as its highest in June to September and at its lowest in November to February. The pattern for women was similar until about 1750, when their peak period of employment was in the spring as well as at harvest time, though with not such high levels of harvest employment as formerly. This suggests that women were being used less for harvesting, but more for other kinds of work, indicating a growing sexual division of labour.

Women were usually paid less than men for the same work. Eighteen people were employed in the gardens of the Duke of Chandos in 1721: the sixteen men were all paid 1s. 2d. a day and the two women, who did weeding, 8d. In Lincolnshire in 1621, women's wages for shearing grain were two-thirds of men's; for cocking barley and peas, only half. Women's real wages for work in arable farming areas fell after 1760, unlike men's, which rose. This may have been because in areas like East Anglia there was an increasing tendency to specialize in grain growing. Grain growing increasingly relied upon the use of new tools by skilled male labour. In pastoral areas, women's wages kept pace with men's, possibly because of greater specialization in animal husbandry and dairying, and the enhancing of the position of female farm servants, who traditionally found more employment in pastoral than in arable agriculture. However, the large-scale commercial dairies which opened in the eighteenth century began to employ male managers; otherwise the only work men did in dairies was unskilled. During the eighteenth century, women's work in agriculture was increasingly restricted to animal husbandry, and women were excluded from harvest work. As a result, the seasonal pattern of women's employment diverged from that of men, and their overall wages from agriculture fell.

One change which excluded women from skilled and remunerative work in arable regions was the use of the long-handled scythe for mowing in place of the short-handled sickle for reaping. Scything was regarded as a skilled job which warranted higher pay and required a strong man. The scythe was originally used for grass, barley and oats, though there were regional differences in its use, but by the eighteenth century it was being used for wheat and rye. Women were not employed as mowers, though they continued to be employed as reapers. The scythe could mow faster, but left the crops in greater disarray than the sickle. This did not matter with grass, but it mattered with grain crops because more people had to be employed to sort the stalks, bind them and stack them – work that was often done by women. But even so, fewer people were required than when a sickle was used and, apart from the mower, their work required less skill.

Changes in working practices reduced women's opportunities both for skilled and well-paid agricultural work, and for seasonal work. The decline of farm service meant that there was less opportunity for young women to make a good living before they married, or for married women to take on extra work to supplement the family income. Farm service during the sixteenth and seventeenth centuries occupied an important time in young women's lives, when they prepared themselves for marriage, learned skills and saved their wages, but were in someone else's charge, living with the farmer as they would have lived with a master to whom they were apprenticed in a town. Women farm servants ran the dairy; milked the cows, cared for small animals and poultry, and did weeding and other seasonal tasks, as well as domestic work like making ale, cooking and looking after the male farm servants. Increasingly, farm service, undertaken on an annual contract under which servants were paid regardless of whether there was work for them, and under which they lived in the farm house, was replaced by day labour.

In many rural areas, women did specialized work which supplemented the family income, and which was separate from any household industry like textile manufacture. Straw plaiting and lace-making were found in Bedfordshire and Devon respectively. Towns with weavers might keep many women busy spinning in the surrounding countryside, as, for example, round Norwich and the West Country clothing towns. Such activities were increasingly found in arable regions where men were employed as day labourers.

In the seventeenth century, rural families often had diverse sources of income, and also greater access to common land than they had later following enclosure. Increasingly, women were restricted to weeding and stone picking in the spring, and occasional work at haytime. Root crops and beans sometimes provided work, but not for more than a few days. Under this regime there was rarely work for women for more than four months of the year. The impact of the decline in work for women was exacerbated by the increase in the number of families dependent for their livelihoods upon wages alone.

The use of the scythe increased the proportion of corn lost or damaged, but it is not clear whether or not it affected the amount of corn left for gleaners. Gleaning was a customary right and was always done by woman and children – indeed, in many places able-bodied men were expressly excluded from gleaning. Especially for the poor it was an extremely important right, and even in better-off households it might contribute up to an eighth of the household's annual income. Until the later eighteenth century, gleaning was a far from marginal economic activity, though it was of greatest benefit to those who were marginal in the rural economy.

Though there were divisions in the work done by women and men in the fields, the barns and the dairy, women might manage farms. The late-eighteenth-century diary of Mary Hardy records her involvement in many decisions regarding the running of her farm: for example, settling matters to do with a brick kiln; offering advice on the management of meadows; and ordering the sowing of barley.

Agriculture, employing the majority of the population, was radically restructured between the sixteenth and the eighteenth centuries in such a way as materially to affect women's lives. Their opportunities for skilled, well-paid work were reduced, more families became dependent upon the wages of landless labouring men, and there were fewer opportunities to supplement the family income with seasonal work. The progressive impoverishment of women, the feminization of poverty, may well have contributed to lowering the age of marriage in the eighteenth century, as there was little incentive for them to work before marrying if they did not earn enough to save anything.

The Sexual Division of Labour: Manufacture and Proto-industrialization

There is much uncertainty about the relative sizes of the industrial and agricultural sectors of the economy, the number of people working in them, and how far there were changes within and between these sectors during the early modern period. This is in part because agriculture and industry are almost impossible to separate. Such statistics as have been collected relate to the occupations of adult men, not of women and children. Furthermore, men, like women and children, often had more than one occupation, and in the countryside many people worked in both agriculture and manufacturing.

The view traditionally held by economic historians is that underemployment in the countryside made the development of alternative sources of income imperative. However, Joan Thirsk has pointed out that there was nothing accidental or temporary about the combination of agriculture with manufacturing. Pastoral farming and industrial employment were complementary activities in an integrated economic system. The development of the woollen industry depended not just upon people keeping sheep, but upon the industries which processed the wool and turned it into cloth. This kind of activity was particularly suited to the household. The independent operators of the north and west were in a very different position from the agricultural labourers of the south and east, dependent upon a hierarchy of employers bent upon paring labour costs to a minimum.

The importance of industry to the rural economy varied from place to place. It was more important in areas of pastoral farming than in areas of arable farming, as is illustrated by the case of the West Yorkshire clothiers. The greatest concentration of worsted manufacture was to be found in the area west of Halifax, where the soil was too poor for anything but grazing, and local inheritance customs had given rise to small landholdings. Worsted was traditionally made by the putting-out system, by which central merchants supplied wool and sometimes owned the looms. From the first half of the eighteenth century, putting-out workshops might consist of several journeymen employed in a single premises by a large clothier. The workers rarely had any land or agricultural work to supplement their wages, and normally they participated in only a single stage of a manufacturing process requiring a number of stages; so they needed no training or apprenticeship. Central merchants received the manufactured cloth, and in effect paid the workers wages. Woollen manufacture by small independent producers who owned their own materials and equipment was concentrated to the east of Halifax, where the soil was more fertile, and where there was mixed farming and greater seasonal fluctuation in the requirement for agricultural labour. These small independent workshops produced blankets and coating material, a finished product, and usually combined the work with some kind of agriculture. It was possible for these workers to accumulate their own capital.

There were also other kinds of industry which were related to highly local specializations. An example is woad, which was grown and processed as a dyestuff in Lincolnshire and in one or two other places. A treatise of 1586 on its preparation claimed that forty acres of woad would keep in work 160 people, chiefly women and children. Several industries relied upon recycling materials, such as metals or rags, but few statistics survive because the second-hand market was virtually unregulated. Apart from manufacturing there were other forms of rural work which were neither agricultural nor domestic. Very little is known about how far women worked in mineral extraction, which was, in many parts of the country, an important source of employment. Some workers in the extractive industries worked in agriculture as well; but the more specialized the mining or processing, the less likely this was to be the case. Joan Isted, a widow ironmaster in the Weald of Kent, employed five French workers in 1544. In 1631 several women, wives of men employed in the mines, were paid for winding and washing at the royal lead mines at Thieveley, Lancashire. There was also work in mills of various kinds, and at furnaces and forges; and in areas where there was suitable clay, women made bricks and pottery, usually as casual workers.

Economic and social historians have been much taxed during the last hundred years to locate the origins of the industrial revolution. Some historians have identified what they call proto-industrialization: industrialization before the industrial revolution. The discussion of the origins of industrialization is of significance to the history of women's work because it concerns the development of rural industries and their relationship with agriculture. It also raises the question of why it became so unsatisfactory to have people working at home at their own pace, and with their own machinery; why it was better for producers to build factories, mechanize production, institute time-keeping and pay a workforce wages.

The debate about the extent to which the process of industrialization worked to women's detriment takes as its starting point the assumption that few women were engaged in wage labour before the later eighteenth century. Women were involved in the putting-out system, and it has been argued that this system effectively reproduced the processes of factory production and the payment of wages, except that people worked in their own homes. Putting-out was most prevalent in the manufacture of textiles, especially the more modern types; of clothing like hosiery; of leather goods; and of small metal goods. Most of the production techniques were quite simple, and did not require a high degree of skill, or much equipment.

Putting-out may have faciliated the division of labour. Work could be put out over a wide geographical area, and the merchants at the centre of the transaction came to retain large numbers of out-workers. The income provided by putting-out also came, during the eighteenth century, to occupy a higher proportion of the livelihoods of the workers. Machinery such as spinning wheels and looms was usually owned by the worker, though the new knitting frames of the seventeenth century were often rented, usually from the central merchant. Crafts which were least likely to go over to the putting-out system were those which had low capital require-ments, and where one producer could conveniently carry out all the processes alone. Independent producers continued to make coarse woollen cloth in Yorkshire; small metal goods in and around Birmingham; and cutlery in and around Sheffield.

Most historians are agreed that modern industrialization may be said to have begun with the introduction of factory production, and with the employment of large numbers of people in unspecialized jobs in specialized workplaces, mass-producing manufactured goods for wages. For Adam Smith, writing in 1776, the division of labour was certain to lead to 'that universal opulence which extends itself to the lowest ranks of the people'.

The model of proto-industrialization suggests that there was a considerable degree of industrialization before the introduction of the factory system, to the point that many rural producers might be said to have been working for wages, and that the people who directed these operations were able to accumulate capital as a result of their investment. It also presupposes that capitalist (as opposed to subsistence) agriculture had developed to a substantial degree, and that there were significant numbers of landless people living in the country dependent upon wages of some kind for their livelihood. This model has been criticized on a number of grounds. It is said to neglect the very high degree of regional variation and different practices within industries; the fact that some of the working practices described as part of proto-industrialization had been present since the thirteenth century; and that, in some of the areas where proto-industrialization was best developed, no industrial revolution followed (indeed, the term 'de-industrialization' has been coined to describe what took place).

Women were not prime agents in the movements towards mechanized production and capitalist agriculture. They did take part in protests against mechanization, but such protests were effective only when they fitted in with the economic climate. In 1455 a five-year ban on the import of manufactured silk goods was brought in after complaints against foreign competition by the silk women and spinsters of silk in London. In 1675 demonstrations swept London when weavers rioted against the use of the new engine looms. It was reported that thousands took to the streets in such traditional textile-producing districts as Moorfields and Spitalfields. Of the 201 who finally appeared in court, eleven were weavers' wives: an indication of the continuing involvement of women in domestic textile production. In 1689 women silk workers in London rioted against the government's attempts to encourage the use of woollen cloth. Women might seem to have been trying to stand in the path of progress, but it is by no means clear that this progress brought them many advantages.

CHAPTER NINE

Varieties of Waged Work

Urban and Rural Trades

The gilds and companies which regulated trade in towns were not in the later Middle Ages formally closed to women. The charter of the London company of innholders of 1514 admitted sisters as well as brothers to livery: that is, they might be full members. However, it is not clear how far this was simply a provision to allow the widows of liverymen to continue to run businesses after the deaths of their husbands, which ensured that apprentices were able to complete their indentures and that any loan made by the company to a business would be repaid. Married women were normally unable to engage independently in a craft or trade, though the custom of some towns made some exceptions. Single women had no access to companies or gilds except occasionally by patrimony, and even then they might forfeit their rights on marriage. However, single women might buy and sell property and incur debts which married women might not.

In London, custom allowed the wife of a merchant to be regarded as a *feme sole merchant*, provided that she practised a different trade from her husband. In Bristol, women might become free of both the gild and the city, but a married woman taking on an apprentice required the signature of her husband on the indenture. In Oxford, in the sixteenth and seventeenth centuries, widows of cordwainers were allowed to continue their husbands' businesses, but had to pay a fee to join the company of cordwainers. The membership of the Oxford tailors' gild was described as being the master, wardens, commonalty and widows. Women were generally excluded from positions of power within the gild and from the wider civic rights which membership of a gild might confer. Some companies restricted the activities of women members, requiring all apprentices to be presented by men and then transferring some to women masters. Even when widows' rights were recognized, the number of women fully operating as masters of a trade or craft was small. In sixteenth-century London, widows engaged fewer than 2 per cent of the 32,000 apprentices enrolled in seven companies; and of the apprentices taken on, only seventy-three were female. Remarriage might affect a widow's entitlements, especially if her second husband was a member of a different trade from her first. The ordinances of 1608 for Kingston upon Thames specified that a woman might continue in her late husband's trade so long as she 'continue a widow and use and exercise the same trade that her husband did'. It was also possible in some circumstances for the new husband to join his wife's company. The pattern of allowing women to be gild members was similar in provincial towns to that in London, but women's membership was restricted earlier. The gild merchant in Preston, Lancashire, had sixteen women members in 1397, six in 1415, one in 1542 and none after that, despite a reaffirmation in 1592 of women's right to membership.

The extent to which women might participate in 'men's trades' was connected with the prevailing economic climate. In the early sixteenth century there were few restrictions, but with the price rises of the 1540s, companies and gilds became much more protective of their male members' interests. The London weavers' company effectively excluded even widows in the 1550s; bakers were prohibited from employing women in 1547. Other companies restricted women's activities in various ways, often to do with their visibility, preventing them from working outside the house or in open places. For example, in 1547 the carpenters' company complained about women purchasing building materials on their husbands' behalf. Nevertheless, in the seventeenth century widows continued to run workshops. In Kingston upon Thames, still a provincial town separate from the metropolis, the widowed Mary Dodson took on several apprentices into her cooper's business between 1618 and 1623. Ellen Dodson, also the widow of a cooper, kept the business going for her son. She took on her first apprentice in 1626, then in 1633 she took on her son James.

In the 1640s, during the Civil War, the regulations governing trade, apprenticeships and employment were relaxed, especially in London where the majority of the parliamentary forces were recruited. The bills for food and clothing for the armies indicate that there were large-scale suppliers of food (especially bread and cheese) and ready-made clothing for the troops. The people who made these things cannot all have been men because military conscription was introduced in 1643 by both sides. Women were already working in the dairying and victualling trades and in the less skilled forms of tailoring, but there is no evidence of them going into shoe-making or the manufacture of arms, armour or ammunition. The army of the Eastern Association bought 11s. worth of bread from Widow Day; Elizabeth Addison and Anne Addison each supplied a cow for meat; and Elizabeth Ashburne received £14 for four cattle. Widow Phillips ran a carrier's business and received £1.4s. for bringing a consignment of armour for 260 men and twenty barrels of bullets from King's Lynn to Cambridge.

After 1660 it proved impossible for gilds and livery companies to regain their hold over trade regulation. During the later seventeenth century there was a progressive decline in their power. The example of the goldsmiths shows how deregulation affected that craft. From the middle of the seventeenth century it came to include a multiplicity of trades: silversmithing, making buckles, spoons, hilts, cases, watches, toys, spurs and other large and small items, and, after 1770, Sheffield plating; all of these were done by women as well as men. With increasing specialization and diversification in manufacture, there developed a separation between making and trading, so that by the late eighteenth century there were goldsmiths, women among them, who bought and sold silver and gold goods without running their own workshops. In 1726 there were forty active women goldsmiths in London running their late husbands' businesses and several female apprentices to London goldsmiths. But the chief work for women was provided by the splitting up of the trade and the creation of lower-status occupations paid on piece rates, such as polishing and finishing.

Other London companies continued to admit women. In 1665 James Windus and his wife Anne took on Elizabeth Billingsley as an apprentice scrivener, and the following year they took on Lucy Sanderson. In 1677 James, with a new wife, Christian, took on Margaret Alsop as an apprentice. Sarah Dutton, daughter of Thomas Dutton, was admitted a member by patrimony in 1675. The scriveners' company was founded in the early seventeenth century and another late established company, the company of wheelwrights, founded in 1670, admitted women from the beginning and had as members widows, daughters by patrimony, and female apprentices.

Although gild regulations in the late seventeenth and eighteenth centuries continued to allow women to run their late husbands' businesses, a declining number did so; and when they did it was rarely for long, unless it was a trade traditionally practised by women. In early-eighteenth-century London about 5–10 per cent of businesses were run by women. Insurance company records show that, of the businesses which had taken out insurance run by widows, over a third were in the food, drink and entertainment trades, and almost another third in textiles and clothing (all trades in which women commonly served apprenticeships). The variety of widows' trades is considerable: butcher, tallow chandler, linen draper, wholesale stocking dealer, and engraver in stone. But, except in those trades where they were recognized as having expertise and status, the actual numbers of widows was small. Widows of London master craftsmen were much more likely to remarry than widows in the provinces.

Church court records have recently been used by Peter Earle to identify female occupations in London in the late seventeenth and early eighteenth centuries. A very high proportion of London women were dependent on their own earnings for their livelihood, though this might as easily be taking in lodgers as waged work. This was a period of war when more married women were obliged to work in the absence of husbands who were soldiers or sailors, or in trades associated with the transport and equipping of the army and navy. None of the wives of gentlemen, men in the professions and masters, and few wives of skilled artisans, had any kind of paid employment. It was the wives of the worst-paid men, especially women in their twenties and thirties, who were most likely to take waged work. It was unusual for women at this social level to work at the same trade as their husbands; those who did were usually in some form of victualling. This runs counter to Alice Clark's thesis that the *majority* of women worked in their husband's businesses. However, it is likely that women's work in family businesses was under-recorded.

Women in provincial towns practised a similar variety of trades. Several ran successful goldsmiths' for decades, like Katherine Mangie who took over her late husband's workshop in Hull in the 1680s and ran it for about fifteen years on her own, and then in partnership with her son and daughter. After Mrs Mangie's death in 1725 at the age of eighty-eight, her children ran the business, her daughter continuing on her own after the death of the son. As in London, too, there was a wide variety of work done by women, but the numbers outside the food, drink and clothing trades were negligible. In eighteenth-century Oxford, women appear in many specialized occupations in these trades – sausage maker, bacon-monger and hop dealer, for example – and in some occupations connected with transport, such as running livery stables, and as bargemasters and wharfingers.

The returns of papists, a census of Catholics made in 1767, give a further insight into the variety of work done by women in provincial towns in the mid-eighteenth century. There is no reason to suppose that Catholic women's occupations were unrepresentative of the population as a whole, except that midwives required episcopal registration to practise, which barred Catholic women. In the city of Durham we find a schoolmistress, a cheesemonger, an innkeeper, an 'idle fortune teller', a petticoat quilter and a huckster (a pedlar or seller of small goods) as well as servants. In more fashionable York there were laundresses, washerwomen and charwomen, milliners, lace-makers, seamstresses, mantua-makers with journeywomen and apprentices, and a glove sewer. Even as late as 1767 there were some widows running their husbands' businesses, such as the female cutler in Sheffield, a 42-year-old widow.

Young women migrated to towns in search of work and to improve their opportunities of finding a husband. A high proportion of the women working within towns were in domestic service before they married. Apart from the variety of work available in towns, different towns had different kinds of work to offer women. The development in the eighteenth century of spas and urban resorts, like Bath and Ludlow, catering for people with money and leisure, offered particular opportunities for women. In such towns more households were headed by women, there was more domestic service for women, and there were more occupations for women in services like laundry and in trades like millinery. The rural hinterlands of such towns also provided work for women in dairying and in market gardening to supply the town with food.

The great difference between country and town for women was the variety of work, or rather jobs. In the country the majority of women in employment were household or farm servants. There might be variety within their work over the seasons. Judith Carpenter, a servant in Norfolk in the 1720s, used at harvest time

to go every day with the tithe cart into the fields, and to rake after the cart, and at other times to do all the commercial business of the house, as looking after the dairy, dressing the fowls for market, and if the business of the house was over she used to spin.[1]

Farm servants had yearly contracts and were employed in a variety

---

[1] Bridget Hill, *Eighteenth Century Women: an Anthology*, George Allen and Unwin, 1984, p. 185.

of jobs on the farm and in the house. Other occupations listed for the women of rural Lancashire in 1767 were spinner and house-keeper, which seems very limited in comparison with the work available in towns.

Whether a woman worked in the town or in the country, most women's waged work was associated with tasks which women traditionally performed in the home. There were all the jobs to do with cleaning houses and clothes, there were many jobs which involved sewing (but not tailoring or anything with specialized designing skills) and jobs to do with the preparation and sale of food and drink.

Retailing

Women were very active in retailing and this was recognized in law in the provision for *feme sole merchant*. They operated as small traders in market towns and villages. Country women took consignments of dairy produce and other small goods into town, either to sell directly at weekly markets or to supply retailers. In villages there were resident sellers of bread, meat, candles, fish and cheese, as well as ale. All of these trades had the advantage for women that they could be done occasionally. It was not necessary in a small community to be a professional, full-time trader.

With increasing specialization in agriculture and manufacturing in the eighteenth century, opportunities were reduced for the kind of small-scale retailing that women had traditionally done. In theory, with the relaxation of trading restrictions in many towns in the eighteenth century, opportunities for women should have improved. In fact, they worsened in all but a very few trades. While gild regulation of trading declined, new forms of licensing suitable for larger-scale trading were introduced. Many more transactions were conducted in private rather than in the open market, and there was an increasing tendency towards engrossment, the development of a wholesale market in commodities under the control of large-scale traders. Both developments worked to the detriment of women retailers because they required a larger scale of operation. It is unusual to find women as merchants dealing with wholesaling or factoring. The number of women with stalls in the covered market in Oxford declined during the eighteenth century as informal occasional market selling declined. The move to London trading and away from fairs and provincial towns probably also operated to the disadvantage of women: for example, the luxury trade of skinners moved from York to London. Increasing regulation of the drink trade and the development of commercial brewing restricted opportunities for running alehouses on a small scale, as many women had done, and the number of victuallers' licences issued to women declined.

Women's presence in retailing was not, however, simply a tale of continuous decline. Women continued to take advantage of the possibilities for occasional work afforded by retailing. A considerable number of women turned retailers when times became hard, and when times improved they ceased. Licences issued to women small traders in eighteenth-century Oxford increased in years of dearth, as in 1766. Small-scale retailing could be run successfully as a part-time or occasional business, to fit in with the family and household. But the increasing restriction of small-scale retailing reduced the level of women's participation.

Credit and Capital

Women were particularly important in the maintenance of small-scale rural credit. Inventories from the period 1635–1735 suggest that on average about 16 per cent of the property of those men and women rich enough to leave wills was in the form of credit owed to them at the time of their deaths. This proportion rose to 20 per cent in the period 1685–1709 and fell to 5 per cent after 1735. Some of this might have been deferred payments, but some of it was certainly loans.

Borrowing and lending were essential to the economic life of the countryside, and in most rural communities certain people were known to be ready to make loans. The interest charged was in the order of 4½–6 per cent per annum, though rates of 10–30 per cent for small short-term loans have been recorded. In an age without accessible banking, cash had to be kept somewhere and people did not invest in government stock until the late eighteenth century. Spinsters, widows and bachelors without business or family commitments invested their surplus cash in loans to their neighbours. A half or even two-thirds of the property of widows might be tied up in loans at interest in sums between £45 and £90, lent to a number of people. To lend money at interest was technically illegal and during the sixteenth century several statutes were passed to control the practice; however, the right of widows to lend capital and preserve their inheritances was defended by many writers and the law was not actively enforced.

In eighteenth-century London, women provided credit; they were more than twice as likely to be creditors as debtors in bankruptcy proceedings. They were also active in pawnbroking and in second-hand sales, both of which were businesses which were connected with credit. As their role in running other kinds of business declined, women seem to have become more active in the small-scale credit market. Widows also owned a large amount of the housing stock and derived income from rents.

Women were involved in small-scale financial transactions in the local community, but they played very little part in the wider commercial world. Merchants' widows rarely ran their husbands' businesses, and if they did, it was almost always in association with a man. Women sometimes appear among the lists of ship owners, such as Lady Margaret Crumpe, one of five owners listed for the slave ship *Dorothy*, bound for Jamaica in 1707, or Anne Carnaby who, with John Carnaby, ran coal ships from Whitby in the eighteenth century, or another Whitby woman, Alice Reynolds, who invested in shipping. These women were probably investing capital rather than engaging in the shipping business; Catherine Stroud, on the other hand, was rather more active as a slave ship owner with Walker Stroud in Bristol in the second half of the eighteenth century.

Service

Domestic service was an important source of employment for women, and became more so as time advanced. In the early sixteenth century, the members of a household, as well as having functions to perform, contributed to the head of the household's status. The number and status of male retainers kept in the Middle Ages was an intrinsic part of the social standing of anyone who had claims to gentility. So in a nobleman's household there was a hierarchy of dependants ranging from relatives to bottlewashers. It was usual to find young men and women, the sons and daughters of other aristocrats, who had been sent to live in the household for their education. The nobler the household, the more people of noble or gentle birth were to be found there under the protection of the head of the household. The number of women employed in noble households in the sixteenth century was small, and they generally did such menial tasks that they were not part of the household's display. Noblewomen often had a couple of gentlewomen in attendance, but again this did not contribute substantially to the respect in which the household was held.

The presence of people of many different ranks meant that the distinction between master or mistress and servant was far from clear-cut. Lady Willoughby, chatelaine of Wollaton Hall, Nottinghamshire in the 1570s, had a couple of women who were the equivalent of ladies-in-waiting in her household. She and her husband were on the border between the upper gentry and the minor aristocracy. The house had about forty-five or fifty servants of whom only eight were women, consisting of the two gentlewomen, two children's nurses, three other women, and someone who was referred to as Mary 'the fool', and various messengers and wet-nurses as required. Women servants were chiefly responsible for laundry, dairy work and the nursery. In a more modest household, Sir Thomas Tresham's at Horton in Northamptonshire, there were in the 1580s eleven men and five women servants: Maudlin 'the French woman' (presumably some kind of governess, for she received £10 a year), a chambermaid for the children, a cook and two other women.

Many of the jobs performed by women in great households run on old-fashioned lines were seasonal or casual. The household accounts for the 1620s and 1630s for Hatfield, the house of the Earl of Salisbury, show that the earl had a male housekeeper at Hatfield, and another at his London house. The full-time staff at Hatfield consisted of about eleven women and thirty-five men. Women were employed for occasional help in the kitchen; for cleaning the house and the brass and pewter when the family was not there; for preparing the house for their arrival; and for laundry. The sums they were paid in no case amounted to more than a few shillings. Very similar kinds of payment were made to women working at the same period at the house of the Earl and Countess of Sussex at Gorhambury, Hertfordshire. Women were paid 5d. a day for weeding, and also worked in the scullery; at cleaning plate; at laundry; at airing the chambers and the bedding; and at gathering watercress. Many of these odd jobs were done by the same person, Goodwife Mason, whose husband and daughter were also employed in the house and garden.

By the early seventeenth century, the practice of great households migrating from one house to another was becoming increasingly unusual, though people who were active in politics or the court might keep a London house and a country house. Lady Anne Clifford was one of the last people to keep up the way of life of a medieval magnate, having as a girl attended Queen Elizabeth's court. She inherited the Clifford estates in the north of England and lived on them from 1649 moving from castle to castle. In 1649–53 she lived at Skipton and Appleby castles, spending between nine months and a year at each; then she started to use Brougham castle as well, and during the 1660s brought into use a further three castles. In the last eight years of her life she confined her movements to three castles quite close to one another with occasional visits to a fourth which was not far distant. She travelled in splendid style, in a horse litter and with an entourage which included members of the local gentry, tenants and neighbours. In 1675, the year before her death, her household, which she habitually referred to as her 'family', consisted of two gentle-women, four laundry maids, a washerwoman, two gentlemen, eleven men, her male housekeeper and a man referred to as a clerk. Such an entourage, indeed such a way of life, must have seemed old-fashioned in the extreme in the 1660s and 1670s.

In the sixteenth century, there were rarely separate servants' quarters in even the largest houses. Male servants slept all over the house on pallet beds in closets and cupboards, and female servants slept in dormitories in the attics. But as a greater segregation developed between those who waited and those who were waited upon, so this was expressed in the arrangements within houses. Servants were provided with accommodation in quarters quite separate from those of their employers, and back stairs and access passages were built so that servants might do their work without being seen.

Between 1500 and 1760 the proportion of women servants in households increased. In the early sixteenth century, noble house-holds were served predominantly by men. By the eighteenth century, instead of amounting to a quarter of the domestic staff, women often amounted to a half, and in more modest households might outnumber men. In 1683 the Earl of Nottingham employed twenty-one men and fifteen women at Kensington, and in 1742 Lord Petre had nineteen men and fourteen women at Thorndon Hall, Essex. By 1797 Lord Salisbury had equal numbers of men and women in his staff of thirty-six at Hatfield. However, despite the decline in the numbers of men employed in domestic service, they and not women servants continued to be the measure of a household's status.

An important feature of life in the seventeenth century was the extension to lower social classes of the custom of having living-in servants. It was uncommon for yeomen, for example, to have living-in servants until the mid-seventeenth century. As nobler people separated their houses from farm buildings, those lower down the scale did so in a more modest fashion, removing animal houses from domestic accommodation, and making more space in their houses for servants. There may, however, have been considerable regional differences in the employment of servants, for although about a third of households in the seventeenth and eighteenth centuries employed living-in servants, local economic circumstances might raise or lower the proportion. Evidence of the large number of new households set up by the *nouveaux riches* of the eighteenth century is the great increase in the number of household manuals which were published from the 1760s advising employers upon how to manage their servants.

Domestic service changed during the seventeenth and eighteenth centuries as it employed more women. By 1655 there was an employment agency in London which dealt with men- and maid-servants and children's nurses. The casual end of the market seems to have increased in cities, but there was also more work for women of higher status who had fallen on hard times: widows and penurious daughters of the gentry were able to find work as housekeepers and governesses. More specialized skills were required as people wanted cooks, and the need for specialization made the career prospects better for the older woman. Domestic service seems to have become less an occupation for a restricted period of women's lives and more a career, possibly compensating for the reduced opportunities in domestic manufacture, though it remained predominantly a young women's occupation. In mid-eighteenth-century London, nearly 60 per cent of servants were aged between fifteen and twenty-nine and about 20 per cent were over forty. Servants' wages seem to have remained pretty static, but we do not know what they received apart from money, or whether there was any change in the perquisites which were expected.

Employers were not the only people who might have social aspirations. The anonymous author of the early-sixteenth-century *Discourse of the Commonweale of thys Realme of Englande* wrote regretfully of the days when a serving man was content to wear a simple frieze coat in winter and a Kendall coat in summer, while now he would be content only with 'a coat of the finest cloth that may be gotten for money . . . a prince or great lord can wear no better if he were clothed'. In the eighteenth century this complaint had been transformed into one against the expensive habits of servants who had learnt to ape their masters and mistresses in drinking tea. By the 1750s it was common for women servants to insist on tea or tea-money in their agreements with their employers, leading to complaints about their 'expensive appetites and tastes'.

There was a definite hierarchy of skills in domestic service, especially in rural households where more of the household's needs had to be met by making goods which might be purchased in towns. The wage rates set in Lincolnshire in 1621 were 24s. a year for a women servant who would take charge of malting, 22s. for one who could bake, brew and dress meat, 18s. for the second maid servant, and 14s. for the youngest. One of the few jobs in domestic service which changed little over the period was that of lady's maid, though only rich women were able to have a personal attendant. In the same list of pay rates in Lincolnshire, rates for female farm servants were given: common servants who could mow and sow were paid 33s. 4d., while those who could not mow and sow who were over sixteen years of age received 20s. (Compare this with the eighteenth-century rate of £3–5 a year paid to general servants in London, where wages were generally higher than in the provinces.) Living-out servants in towns were not considered to be respectable, and such work was mainly done by the very poor or by married women needing to supplement the family's income. The authorities did not like charmaids (as they were called) because they were so difficult to regulate. It is important to remember that relatively poor people might employ a servant to do heavy work. The London artisan Nehemiah Wallington had three servants in the 1620s, two men and a woman.

Historians of servants are accustomed to dwell upon the attractions of the life of a servant, especially for a woman, because of the security that it gave. Certainly if the board, lodging and clothes which normally accompanied the post of a living-in servant were of a reasonable standard, this might be true. The value of these combined with wages was probably greater than poorer artisans were able to earn in wages alone. However, the wages were not high, though they might vary considerably according to age, length of service, skills and location. The most important feature of domestic or farm service is that it was virtually the only occupation in which a young unmarried woman could keep herself and even save a little money. Most other women's occupations did not pay a living wage.

Very little is known about life from the servant's point of view. A rare instance is a 46-year-old woman who was a member of a London sectarian congregation in 1650. She was literate and had spent her early adolescence 'sat often in corners studying what way

I might come to God'. She left home to live with another family when she was sixteen and was troubled by the fact that they hindered her in the practice of her religion. She went on to live with a number of other families where she had similar problems, but being in London, she was able to go out and listen to sermons by godly ministers. Her career as a servant ended when she got married.

Domestic or farm service was primarily the work of young women, the means by which they left home, were trained for work, and managed to save up some money upon which to get married. They then married and left service. But what became of them afterwards? Some of them presumably became the wives of men with trades or farms in whose running they became involved. Others took up retailing or running an alehouse, or some other trade connected with victualling. Some let lodgings, an important source of income for many women in towns. They were not servants in the sense of having an employer, but the work that was involved was closer to that of a domestic servant than anything else. Another occupation which was open to former servants was to become a wet-nurse. Only a relatively small proportion of women seem to have been career servants, continuing in domestic service until middle age, though this became less unusual in the eighteenth century.

Nursing

There was no training in nursing, but caring for the very young, the old and the sick fell to women. Nursing was considered not just a woman's work, but her duty. The 1595 statutes of Sir Henry Bayntun's almshouses at Bromham, Wiltshire, provided for six poor people over fifty years, four men and two women. 'When any of the poor men shall be sick and diseased . . . then the women shall do their best endeavours to keep and attend them, which if they shall refuse to do then to be removed.' These were the only circumstances in which residents of the opposite sex might enter one another's rooms. If the women fell ill, other women were brought in to attend them. Caring for the sick or the old, since it generally took place at home, was seen as part of women's normal activities, though the women concerned might be the mistress of the house or the domestic servants. Most nursing of the sick, if not done by immediate relatives, was done by domestic servants. There was a particular need for nurses during the 1640s and 1650s in the Civil War, but what happened illustrates the casual nature of most nursing. Medical care for soldiers on the field was of the most rudimentary kind: surgeons and apothecaries travelled with the armies, but there was little they could do for injured soldiers, who were left behind in the care of local people, usually women, when the army moved on. Mary Burd submitted a petition in 1644 to be paid for looking after one sick soldier; she did not mention a sum but asked for 'what you shall think good', and received 10s. Mrs Judith Massey from Epworth, Lincolnshire, evidently made a business of looking after sick soldiers, for she was paid £10 for caring for 150 soldiers after the battle of Marston Moor.

In the later part of the period, care began to be institutionalized with the foundation of different kinds of hospital for lying-in, for foundlings and, latterly, for the sick. Institutions for women, such as lying-in hospitals and the London Asylum for Orphaned Girls founded in 1759, employed mainly women as did the new infirmaries. These recruited women staff to do general supervisory tasks, cleaning, distributing food and medicines, and watching over patients, but the qualifications were the same as those for domestic service. The women who supervised these staff were often widows from a higher social stratum.

Women were involved in the manufacture and sale of remedies, working with apothecaries and barber-surgeons, though it was difficult for them to obtain licences to practise in their own right. Women also worked in the less respectable end of the market. Several London newspapers of 1655 announced the arrival at Mr Web's house in Long Lane of 'the gentlewoman so famous for the cure of all cancers in the breast', who had 'lately performed that great and excellent cure of Mrs Farrow in Gunpowder Alley, who had the cancer in her breast for twelve years standing, whom the College of Physicians had concluded incurable'.

After members of the household, the most important part in the care of the sick was by local women who had a reputation for knowledge in medical matters. These self-employed women might be paid by the parish for caring for the local poor. In 1630, during a plague epidemic, the Norwich corporation paid Mrs Sandcroft to make provision for the infected poor in the pest house and to take them water, for which she was paid 7d. Sometimes they were women who would otherwise have been receiving parish relief themselves. How far such women were separate from midwives and the women who came to lay out corpses is not always clear. It is the part-time and intermittent nature of this work which makes it so intangible to the historian. Certainly there were some women with a considerable standing in the local community who worked as midwives. They accompanied the mother to the ceremony of churching after the birth of a child.

Even in the early seventeeth century, before the debate about male midwives had begun, the male medical profession was seeking to preserve its monopoly of professional expertise. In 1612 James Guillimeau wrote, 'I must admonish women in childbed not to regard the words of their nurses or keepers which continually preach to them.' The attack on women's attendance at births started in earnest in the eighteenth century, but by the later seventeenth century there was already an increasing preference for 'science' embodied in the medical profession over 'superstition' embodied in traditional medicine and its practitioners. George Counsell, writing in 1758, averred that

> It is a truth too well known, that mothers and their children are daily, if not hourly, destroyed (such is the practice of midwifery in our days) by ignorant wretches, in almost every state of life, a pack of young boys, and old superannuated washerwomen, who are so impudent and so inhuman as to take upon them to practise, even in the most difficult cases.[1]

He believed that the moment there was any sign of difficulty it was imperative to send for a male midwife for assistance. In 1760 Mrs Elizabeth Nineth launched her attack upon male midwives, mentioning the ingratitude of the male midwives of Paris to the women who had taught them their art. The appropriation of midwifery by men deprived women of both social and economic standing.

Midwives cared for mothers, but not usually for children. As an employment agency advertisement of 1655 indicates, children's nurses were a separate category. But there were also several kinds of children's nurse and it is also not always obvious what the distinction between a wet-nurse and a nanny or child-minder was, since wet-nurses provided both kinds of child care. Wet-nurses might be poor servant girls or mothers of illegitimate children, who were supported on the parish poor-rate and who became wet-nurses for orphans and foundlings. The London Foundling Hospital, opened in 1741, instituted a network of inspectors, both male and female, who supervised the wet-nurses all over the country to whom foundlings were sent. Nurses were paid 2s. 6d. a week, with a bonus of £10 after a year if the child had survived. Most of the nurses were married with their own families. They were women in their thirties, the wives of agricultural labourers and artisans, with families of about three or four children who took

---

[1] George Counsell, *The London New Art of Midwifery*, London, 1758, Preface, p. x.

on foundlings in the middle or towards the end of their own child-bearing. The youngest child of the nurse was usually about a year old when the foundling was taken on, and the foundling usually stayed between three and five years. Women rarely took on more than three or four foundlings. With their own families and older foundlings, they were running households of six or seven children. They were, in effect, foster-mothers as well as wet-nurses.

Round London, in the seventeenth and eighteenth centuries, there were large numbers of wet-nurses, sometimes less well regulated than those employed by the Foundling Hospital. These came from many different social statuses and might attend the birth of the child in London (the most important source of children) and then take him or her back with them to the country a month or so later. Some were plainly respectable women who took on children one at a time; others were little more than baby farmers for poorer Londoners. The women who became wet-nurses to the nobility and gentry usually lived in the country and were very respectable. Parents and doctors alike were agreed that the moral standing of wet-nurses was crucial because the nurse's qualities were transferred to the child. These women kept the child until it was weaned, at a year or eighteen months.

A study of wet-nurses employed by the Townshends, a Norfolk family of the upper gentry, shows that women who had formerly been servants in the Townshend household and who had been on terms of some intimacy with Lady Townshend might be employed. Between 1627 and 1637 Mary, wife of Sir Roger Townshend, gave birth to eight live children, all of whom were put out to wet-nurses. Four of the women employed can be identified, one of them having twice nursed Townshend children. Three of these women had been servants in the household and had left to get married. Two of them lived in comfortable enough circumstances to employ their own servants, two were the wives of yeoman farmers and one the wife of the village carrier. Their own children ranged in age from a few weeks to about six months, and they were paid about £10 per annum as nurses, rather more than they would have received as servants. Lady Twysden in 1647 paid her nurse £10 for her wages and expenses for a year. In Aldenham, Hertfordshire, in the seventeenth century, nursing supplemented families' income rather than providing the whole of it. It was usual to provide wet-nurses with fuel, food or clothing.

The development of institutions during the eighteenth century provided a new level of career for the gentlewoman who had no trade but needed to work to live. Work as supervisors in infirmaries and as the inspectors of wet-nurses offered paid employment of a kind which had not previously existed.

Performing Arts

From the second half of the seventeenth century, the performing arts were one area where women were able to practise a profession and to excel. But public performance was not considered a respectable *métier* for a woman and there were considerable social pressures against women making a profession out of the arts. Respectable women were discouraged from developing their performance beyond the level of a ladylike accomplishment. Many women who made a living out of performance had a male manager, sometimes their husband or father, so it is clear that performing was not necessarily a way of attaining an autonomous career.

Women's religious music more or less died out at the Reformation. Even in the early sixteenth century, few English convents were large enough to support choirs or much musical activity. The largest and richest convent in the country, Syon abbey in Middlesex, had choir sisters and brothers (the Brigettine order to which they belonged was a dual order with both monks and nuns). There were fifty-two choir sisters when the convent was dissolved in 1539. After the dissolution of the monastic orders, religious music was preserved in the all-male choirs of secularized collegiate churches. Women had sung in the civic pageants of the later Middle Ages, as in the Shearmen and Tailors' pageants in Coventry, but the female parts in the plays were taken by men.

The only female institutions which could form choirs were schools, and one of the best-known pieces of music composed in the seventeenth century, Henry Purcell's *Dido and Aeneas*, was revised in 1689 to be performed by the young ladies of Josias Priest's boarding school in Chelsea. The music was arranged for amateur singers, unlike the works which Vivaldi was writing slightly later for the orphan girls of the Pio Ospedale della Pietà, who were professional musicians. From the middle of the seventeenth century, theatres employed female musical choruses and much more was made of singing parts in plays. Shakespeare's plays were rewritten with more songs and the *Beggars' Opera*, first performed in 1728, provided many women singers with successful careers. Mrs Albegg (*fl.*1758–63) made her living for several years singing in the chorus of Garrick's rewriting of *The Winter's Tale*, in *Macbeth* and in *The Merchant of Venice*. She was paid 5s. a night in 1760 and £70 for the season in 1761. Italian women singers were much in fashion in Restoration London, and Charles II seems to have had 'Italian Musick' in which a number of women were employed. Women who earned their living from music were usually singers. Few women worked as instrumentalists except for keyboard players, and many women harpsichordists also worked as singers. Harriet Abrams (1760–1825) was unusual in being the composer of a number of songs with titles like 'A Smile and a Tear' and 'The Friend of my Heart', as well as singing, sometimes with her sisters.

For much of the sixteenth and early seventeenth centuries, women's parts in plays were taken by boys. Speaking on the stage was considered to be very unladylike in the early seventeenth century. Although royal and aristocratic women appeared in court masques in the early seventeenth century, there was no question of them uttering, however magnificently they might be dressed.

The Restoration saw the first possibility of a successful career on the stage for women. Plays like *The Beaux' Stratagem* and *The Recruiting Officer* had a number of good parts for women. Elizabeth Barry (c.1658–1713) made a particular name for himself as Lady Brute in *The Provok'd Wife*. The popularity of actresses meant that, though the ratio of men's parts to women's was about 2:1, some companies had nearly as many actresses as actors. Popular actresses would appear in male roles: for example, Mrs Baxter (*fl.*1706–11) played Lord Foppington in *The Relapse*. But the theatre provided livings for more than performers. Charlotte Cibber Charke (1713–60) managed the Little Theatre, Haymarket, and Lady Henrietta Maria Davenant (d.1691) ran a company of actors after the death of her husband William. During the period when she ran it, they performed at Dorset Garden and she appointed actors and controlled the repertoire. Some women in the later seventeenth and eighteenth centuries who made a living from the stage did so both as playwrights and actresses. Aphra Behn (1649?–89), Eliza Haywood (1693?–1756) and Susannah Centlivre (1667?–1723) all made careers as writers, having in their early years been actresses. The stage was unequivocally a career open to women, but the fact that so many women had to do more than one thing, whether singing and acting, or writing and acting, suggests that it was not easy for a woman to make a living on the stage, especially once she reached middle age.

Women made livings in other kinds of performance. There were equestrian performers like Miss Astley (*fl.*1773), who rode in her brother's circus. Mrs Mary Bateman (1763–1826) gave subscription breakfasts with the transvestite fencer Mme d'Eon at which they gave exhibitions of sword play. Charlotte Cibber Charke ran a puppet show in the 1730s and 1740s. Mrs Alchorne (1683–1787) was exhibited by her husband in the late 1750s as a strong woman and used to lift an anvil with her knee-length auburn hair.

The changes which took place in both rural and urban working conditions between 1500 and 1760 substantially replaced the household by the employer. The locus for employee–employer relations began to move from the family to a workplace, and the family, more particularly the father, no longer provided the model for the conduct of the employer. The variety of women's jobs in the countryside contracted as great houses ceased to operate as the focus for the economic life of agricultural estates, and as hired male labour replaced tenants' labour as a family unit. In towns women lost access to the high-status trades, but were still active in a tremendous variety of jobs, chiefly as employees. Opportunities for domestic work expanded in both town and country, and leisure and entertainment provided new types of work for women, as well as providing an arena for women to appear in public.

CHAPTER TEN

Women and Material Culture

Thanks to the heritage industry, the material worlds of women in the past are more familiar to us than many other aspects of their lives. Even poor women exercised choices about the clothing and household goods they bought with the small amounts of money they had. Richer women not only exercised choices, but dictated fashions in clothing and consumables and in buildings and gardens. Furthermore, some of these women were disposing of their own money: they were not simply spending their husbands'. Early modern England was a society in which consumption was becoming an increasingly important part of economic life and thus of the way in which people spent their time.

Possessions

Recent work by Lorna Weatherill on seventeenth- and eighteenth-century inventories for probate, of which women's constituted about 15 per cent, has provided an insight into the kinds of goods which women owned and how these differed from men's. There are no inventories for the very poor, but people of quite modest means left wills, and therefore inventories of their possessions were made. The only household article which men were more likely to have than women was a clock. Women had more pictures, prints, looking glasses, table linen, curtains and silver than men. There were regional variations: for example, earthenware was more common in areas where there was a local pottery industry, and pictures and prints tended to be found in the areas round London, closer to the printing industry. Widows were more likely to have gold and silver than spinsters, but their estates were often not worth very much, possibly because the husband's goods were partly distributed at his death. On the other hand, a widow might have considerable property to distribute on her late husband's behalf. Frances Matthew, widow of the Archbishop of York, Toby Matthew, gave his library of over 3,000 volumes to the Minster when he died in 1628.

There was a great increase in the use of domestic articles like curtains, chair-covers, tablecloths, carpets, cutlery and crockery, all of which were usually regarded as part of a woman's personal estate. This increase in consumption was attributed to the increasing idleness of tradesmen's wives, who had nothing to do but go shopping, but these goods penetrated much lower down the social scale and we see the beginnings of a recognizable consumer society.

Where did people buy these things? Many country people bought most of their manufactured goods not in the local town but from travelling traders, chapmen and chapwomen, whose numbers much increased from the 1670s. They usually lived in market towns and travelled on foot with their wares, sometimes as a family, or with a companion. They sold all sorts of things – printed ballads, almanacs and chapbooks, soft furnishings, clothing accessories. They travelled with patterns for simple garments to be made from the cloth they carried, while heavier garments were made by local tailors.

Many things which people owned were old. Not only was there a market in recycled materials, but there was a large market in second-hand goods, especially clothing. People sold their own clothes when they were really short of money, but they also sold clothes which had been given or bequeathed to them, and there was a considerable market in stolen clothes – 27 per cent of urban larceny cases in the eighteenth century involved clothing. Dishonest servants made off with their employers' wardrobes, and entire washing lines full of clothes disappeared as well as consignments of dirty laundry on their way to be washed. 'Clothes brokers' were often tailors, but there were a good many women second-hand clothes dealers. Anne Lenson, a London clothes dealer, was robbed in 1742 of stock of ornamental clothing valued at £2. She expected to mark up the clothes by 50 per cent for sale. Second-hand clothing and pawnbroking were related trades; clothes dealers were the more numerous in late-seventeenth- and early-eighteenth-century London, but even so, 10 per cent of the women who insured businesses were pawnbrokers.

At a more elevated level there were dealers in antiques and curiosities. The really great collectors, like the Earl and Countess of

Arundel, had agents who travelled abroad for them, but there were also agents in England, like Mrs Harrison who sold the Duke and Duchess of Somerset a black lacquer cabinet in 1695 for their house at Petworth, Sussex, and supplied much of the duchess's collection of oriental porcelain.

Fashion and Personal Adornment

England was one of the few European countries where there were effectively no sumptuary laws, dictating what people of various classes and conditions might or might not wear. The absence of such controls enabled fashions in dress to penetrate to lower social levels than elsewhere. However, extensive consumption of high fashion was restricted to those of wealth and metropolitan tastes. In the early Stuart court the amounts of money spent on clothing, personal adornment and feasting far exceeded those spent upon more durable works of art. Charles I bought Henrietta Maria a pair of earrings which cost more than the ceiling of the banqueting house at Whitehall which Rubens painted. A common butt of comedy in Restoration plays is the man or woman who has exaggerated or misconstrued the fashions of the moment. But fashion is also to do with much smaller and less ostentatious changes of dress – the type of apron worn, or the petticoat, or the placing or style of a piece of decorative embroidery. This kind of fashion was accessible to a very large number of women throughout the country.

Shopkeepers and chapmen were the disseminators of knowledge of new styles and fashions in the provinces. Until well into the eighteenth century there was a marked difference between town and country fashions in clothes. Fashion also merited lengthy descriptions in the provincial press. In the seventeenth century, prints of interior furnishings circulated, and by the eighteenth century fashions in clothing were depicted in this way and were an important ingredient of the women's magazines which started at this time. The first fashion plate to be published is said to be in *The Lady's Magazine* of 1759. The spread of fashion plates combined with the development of the Lancashire textile industry did much to make fashions in clothes much more uniform over the whole country.

Sewing was regarded as an important accomplishment for women, but in the household it was chiefly for mending clothes and household linen. Women did not usually make clothes themselves, except underclothes like the loose shift which both men and women wore underneath their jackets and breeches and bodices and skirts respectively. Adam Eyre, little more than a yeoman, recorded in 1647 that 'John Wainwright came to make my wife's apparel'. Those who could not afford this level of service could buy second-hand clothes or ready-made clothes from 'slop' shops. From the mid-eighteenth century the ready-made industry expanded greatly into garments like gowns, especially in the area round Manchester where it was associated with the Lancashire cotton industry.

The only specialist clothing trades in which women worked and in which they took female apprentices were millinery and making straw hats, mantuas and various kinds of trimming, notably lace. A mantua was a kind of loose cloak, but mantua-makers also made night-gowns, petticoats and other women's garments. Many of the garments worn in the sixteenth and seventeenth centuries required complicated and skilled processes of tailoring. They were lined and stiffened and seemed almost to hold their wearers up rather than flowing with their bodies, though most of the clothes which we have seen were people's best clothes, specially chosen for having their portraits painted in. We know relatively little about the clothes that people wore every day, or which poor people wore. There was a large ready-made clothing trade, as well as sales of second-hand and bespoke clothing. Women's clothes might be made very rapidly and many early-eighteenth-century dresses were made in a very slipshod fashion, though dressmaking techniques improved greatly during the century.

Hairdressing was usually done by maids and manservants, but Lady Anne Clifford recorded in 1619 that her friend Lady Manners came to dress her head. Her daughter's hair was trimmed by a manservant. Lady Anne also did her own hair, reporting in 1617 that 'I began to dress my hair with a roll without wire.' Make-up came into greater use. John Evelyn, writing in 1654 at the height of the English Republic, observed 'how the women began to paint themselves, formerly a most ignominious thing and used only by prostitutes'.

Attitudes to personal adornment are much tied up with ideas of status and beauty. In early modern England the archetype of beauty was predominantly a feminine one, but male beauty was not ignored. The followers of the Duke of Monmouth in the 1680s were as much entranced by his appearance as by his cause. The lovingly painted young men of the miniatures of the Tudor court and the proud, silk-clad young men of Van Dyck's portraits suggest a favourable attitude to male beauty. Puritan antipathy to personal adornment was concentrated upon hair. In 1644 *A Looking-Glass for Women* sought to demonstrate the unlawfulness of 'any outward adorning of any attire of hair, either in laying forth, or in crisping [curling] of the hair, or in broidered hair in all women', and a Puritan woman who preached against long-haired men was satirized in a pamphlet of 1641.

Needlework and Other Media

Many women concerned themselves with interior decoration, not least because it involved arts in which they themselves might be proficient. Professional male upholsterers and embroiderers were employed to make large pieces, but women did a great deal of the smaller work – indeed, the word 'work' was synonymous with needlework – and the creations of an accomplished needlewoman were objects of curiosity to visitors. In 1771 Mrs Lybbe Powys went to Fawley Court, Buckinghamshire, to see the sofa and chairs covered by Mrs Freeman and the bed in the best bedroom. She also went to Windsor to see the new bed built for the queen: 'a most curious piece'. Church furnishings were also made and donated by women. Mrs Horner, a munificent benefactor to various Dorset churches in the mid-eighteenth century, gave an embroidered altar-piece designed by Mrs Prowse to one church. Mrs Powys draws attention to the fact that, while women might not be expected to express their taste in architecture, painting or sculpture, arts where convention and learning played some part in the formation of taste, in clothes and soft furnishings they were expected to exercise taste and to respond to fashion.

From the early seventeenth century, pattern books were available with designs for embroidery, and some women used their interest in plants to provide themselves with patterns. There was a fashion during the eighteenth century for copying paintings in needlework. Horace Walpole praised the work of Miss Gray whose needlework pictures were to be seen at Earl Spencer's house at Wimbledon, for one of which, a copy of a Van Dyck painting of three figures, the earl had given £300. Walpole singled out for praise the work of Lady Caroline Conway and Mrs Morritt. Mrs Morritt took two years to copy a medium-sized Rubens; Lady Caroline could complete a substantial piece in four months.

Women who had leisure, and the numbers of these increased during the eighteenth century, sought ways of filling their time.

There developed a fashion for making objects out of all sorts of unlikely materials like straw and paper. Mrs Lybbe Powys made decorations from straw, paper, shells, coins and dried flowers. Many women decorated grottoes with shells and mineral specimens. In the 1740s Sarah Duchess of Richmond (d.1751) and her daughter lined a grotto with shells at Goodwood, Sussex. The Duchess of Portland (1715–85) shaped amber while her friend Mrs Delany decorated such objects as fireplaces and picture frames with shells. Mrs Montagu (1720–1800) did feather pictures and had a room lined with feathers which was visited by the king and queen and for whose opening she gave a party attended by 700 people. These activities might appear to be crafts rather than arts, but their practitioners reached a very high level of competence, as can be seen by the example of Mrs Delany's 'mosaicks', cut paper pictures of plants.

Food and its Preparation

The choice, purchase and preparation of food was largely in the hands of women. The development of a consumer market and the spread of fashion to the lowest levels of society influenced the consumption of food. Richer people during the early modern period changed their eating habits, eating increasingly in private, avoiding conspicuous consumption of food, the contrary of developments in France. It is likely that admiration for fat people declined in the upper classes as food became more plentiful, though they may still have been admired among the poorer sort.

The humblest houses did not have ovens and it was quite usual for those who wanted to bake something to use the baker's oven. Unless a household was very large or very remote, bread was bought from the baker, and by the eighteenth century quite small villages in the south of England supported their own bakers. There were fewer country bakers in the north of England where less wheat bread was eaten. Oat bread could be made on a girdle rather than in an oven, and this remained an important item of diet in northern upland regions. In towns there must have been many households where very little food was prepared; there was a large market in ready-cooked food, both take-away and pub food.

Most people's diets were very restricted, and for much of the period bread was the staple food. Richer people ate a great deal of meat, and the amount they ate increased from the late seventeenth century with the introduction of winter fodder crops which allowed animals to be fed during the winter. The introduction of new foodstuffs from other parts of the world had only a limited impact upon ordinary people's diets. It is likely that the diet of the rural poor became less varied as they had less access to land where they might grow a few things for themselves, or to common land where they might keep livestock. By the late eighteenth century, it was said that they lived chiefly on bread and cheese. From 1671 restrictions were imposed on taking game and it became un-fashionable to eat many species of birds, such as seabirds, which had formerly contributed to the variety of people's diets. The urban poor at least had the possibility of a more varied diet supplied by the multiplicity of cookshops.

Men prepared food for sale, as butchers, bakers, pastry-cooks and brewers, and worked in households large enough to need chefs and specialist under-chefs in the kitchen, but they were essentially tradesmen performing well-defined tasks. By the eighteenth century, large taverns were beginning to offer organized entertainment involving food, and they employed male chefs to prepare it. The idea that women lacked the aesthetic sensibility to be really great chefs began quite early.

Women bore general responsibility for the preparation and service of food in the smaller household, even in those where there were servants. By the eighteenth century, people of the middling sort were employing women cooks who might or might not have other duties, depending upon the size of the household. These cooks were specialists, often older women paid more than their younger and less specialized colleagues.

Women also provided much of the labour in food retailing. The widowed Isabel Langcaster did commercial catering for Hull corporation. At her death in 1637 she left her late husband's servant all the spits and racks which she kept at the mayor's house. Food was prepared for sale in a variety of places, and taverns and alehouses were popular eating places. During the sixteenth century, there was a considerable increase in the number of alehouses because of the shift from ale drinking to beer drinking. Ale was simply made and perishable, suitable for making and drinking at home. Beer, which contained hops, kept and travelled much better, was more complicated to manufacture, and was a more commercial product. During the sixteenth and seventeenth centuries, alehouse-keepers brewed beer, but brewing and retail-ing were increasingly separated with the development of a specialized brewing industry using male labour.

Running an alehouse was not necessarily a full-time occupation.

Alehouse-keepers were often recent arrivals in the vicinity, poor and female. The nature of the work made it particularly suitable for women, since it required little capital and might be done part time. From 1552 there was a national system for licensing alehouses. At Bideford in 1660 about a quarter of the licensed alehouse-keepers were women and this was a characteristic figure. In Chelmsford in 1567, ten men and two women were presented at the quarter sessions for selling beer without a licence. Unlicensed alehouse-keeping was one of the commonest legal charges brought against women. By the seventeenth century, it became less of an occupation for the very poor, as the licensing regulations required alehouse-keepers to find sureties. Greater restrictions upon the issuing of licences led to a decline in the number of women selling ale.

Women were involved in other aspects of commercial food production. Dairy work was almost exclusively female, and this could take place on a considerable commercial scale as the provisioning accounts for cheese for the army and the navy reveal. Timothy Avery received £650 in May 1651 for supplying the army with cheese, much of which must have been made by women, and with corn. With the growth in the size of cities, dairy retailing became more important, and housewives selling dairy produce, poultry and eggs at a weekly market gave way to specialized dairy shops. However, with the introduction of new machinery into cheese and butter making in the late eighteenth century, the expertise of men started to replace that of women.

The earliest cookery manuals described very straightforward techniques, but were intended for professional chefs. Manuals of housewifery were for women and assumed that their readers lived in the country and produced many of their own foodstuffs. They offered detailed instructions for domestic brewing and food preservation, but contained little about cooking. The emphasis of these books, on frugality, health and good management, contrasts with the medieval custom of alternate fasting and feasting. In the eighteenth century, women began to produce books on cookery and housewifery. These concentrated upon good, plain food and were rather dismissive of messed-about foreign dishes. French food was associated with extravagance and waste. These manuals were far from just cookery books, containing advice on making medicines and other remedies, on brewing, preserving, dairy work and planting, and on how to run a household and manage servants. Their authors, Elizabeth Moxon (*fl.*1749–58), Hannah Wolley (*fl.*1675–85), Hannah Glasse (*fl.*1742–70) and Ann Cook (*fl.*1760), came from a variety of backgrounds. Hannah Wolley had been a governess and schoolteacher and was married to a school-master. Ann Cook was a trained cook. Hannah Glasse trained her own servants to cook.

Building

Many of the people who worked in gardens and on building sites were employed as day labourers and were often illiterate, so there is only a record of them if they were paid by someone who kept accounts. Women often weeded gardens; in 1721 among the eighteen people employed in the Duke of Chandos's gardens were two weeding women paid 8d. a day. Women rarely worked as builders' labourers, though they were among the citizens of a number of towns building siege-works and fortifications during the Civil War. The newspaper *Special Passages* reported in August 1642 that at Northampton '500 men and 100 women have wrought all yesterday and this night carrying earth to strengthen our walls and places of fortification'. Women also worked in brickmaking and in quarrying, both of which were rural occupations which people did alongside agricultural work.

Some women dealt in bricks and tiles. In the early seventeenth century, Widow Crane provided 1,000 bricks and Mrs Holbache supplied 1,000 bricks and 3,000 tiles for building the Eyffeler almshouses in Warwick. Alice Jory, sometimes with her husband but usually alone, was paid about 1s. 6d. a week for 'bearing' the lime, lime ash and sand for building the new shambles at Plymouth in 1606. She carried building materials when the Guildhall was built in the same year, and in 1614 she and her husband carried some of the materials for building the hospital for orphans.

Women also ran businesses connected with building and decorating. In 1698 Lady Bridgeman commissioned from Louis la Guerre a picture to go over her closet fireplace, and the receipt for the seven guineas it cost was signed by Eleanor la Guerre. The widow of the York glass-painter and stainer, William Peckitt, made and erected a window to his memory in the church of St Martin-cum-Gregory in 1796. Mrs Eleanor Coade (1742–1821) ran the factory in London which, from the 1760s, manufactured artificial stone to a secret formula.

We know little about the houses of the very poor, but we may suppose that women took part in building wattle and daub cabins for their own occupation. A poor Wiltshire widow, Edith Curtis, described in 1628 as 'being destitute of a house to live in, by the help of her friends about five years sithence did build a cottage upon the waste ground and commons'. She 'took in a little plot of ground out of the said waste to make her garden'. During the eighteenth century, rural houses were increasingly built of stone and brick, and were less commonly simple timber constructions. There must then have been less opportunity for women to be involved in the construction of houses, but presumably the very poor continued to build the kind of temporary squatters' house that Edith Curtis and her friends built.

Women played a greater part in directing and commissioning building works and gardens, acting under their husbands' names, than the records indicate. The rebuilding of Belvoir Castle in the 1650s is often attributed to the 8th Earl of Rutland, but it was in fact his wife (d.1671) who commissioned John Webb to design a new mansion on the site of the castle, which had been destroyed in the Civil War. The Marchioness of Ormond (d.1685) conducted an extensive correspondence in the 1660s and 1670s about the restoration of Kilkenny Castle and the building of Dunmore, both in Ireland, and about her husband's house, Moor Park in Hertfordshire. In 1674 she was negotiating to buy the marble doorcases and chimney-pieces from the Earl of Strafford's former house at Naas, Co. Kildare. Lady Bridgeman (d.1713) corresponded with her cousin William Winde about the alterations which she and her husband, Sir John Bridgeman, were making to their house at Castle Bromwich in the late 1680s.

Few women engaged in grandiose construction projects, because they did not have the disposal of their own funds; and those who did were often in the straitened circumstances of widowhood. Only a very small number of women could afford to commission architectural projects or gardens on their own accounts. For many men architectural projects were a way of displaying their wealth and status, their taste and education by their references to foreign and classical examples. Women were not under the same pressures to display their taste and learning in this way.

Nevertheless, there were important women's commissions. Perhaps the best known is Hardwick Hall, 'more glass than wall', a fine example of the spread of Renaissance architecture to the provinces and so famous that its builder is now simply known as Bess of Hardwick. Elizabeth Countess of Shrewsbury (1518–1608) started building at Chatsworth in Derbyshire, which she bought at the time of her first marriage to Sir William Cavendish in 1549. Her third husband was George Talbot, 6th Earl of Shrewsbury, and she was almost certainly the moving spirit behind his new house, Worksop Manor. She started Hardwick after his death in 1590 and it was complete by 1597. The house had a number of idiosyncratic features, most obvious of which are the great initials E.S. on the tops of the towers, dominating the decorative scheme where other patrons might have chosen classical or heraldic motifs. The state rooms were in an unusual position, on the top floor, as they were at Chatsworth and Worksop, a position feasible in the house of someone who did not expect to have to entertain the queen.

Mary Sidney, Countess of Pembroke (1561–1621), was more concerned to demonstrate her taste. She was a woman of considerable intellectual gifts, coming from a learned and cultivated family; she wrote herself, and was patron to a number of writers. After the death of her husband in 1601, she spent her summers on holiday, smoking, dancing and target shooting. In 1615 James I granted her the manor of Houghton Conquest, Bedfordshire, and there, possibly employing Inigo Jones, she built a splendid H-shaped house of a modern plan whose ruins survive. She was an active member of the court circle presided over by James I's queen, Anne of Denmark, which included several other building women like Lucy Harington, Countess of Bedford, and the Countess of Suffolk.

Those women who did engage in building projects sometimes did so with their husband's money, like the Countess of Rutland; sometimes with their widow's jointure, like Mary Sidney; and sometimes with their own inheritance, like Lady Anne Clifford. Lady Wilbraham (1632–1705), who built and may well have designed her own house at Weston-under-Lizard, Staffordshire, as well as improving her husband's house at Woodhey in Cheshire, used both her paternal inheritance and funds of her husband's.

Women were particularly active in restoration and interior decoration. The Countess of Rutland was not the only woman to restore a castle. Lady Anne Clifford (1590–1676) had a great passion for castles and, having spent much of her life engaged in litigation to recover the Clifford estates, proceeded to restore its castles, some of which had been in ruins for generations. Brough, Brougham, Appleby and Pendragon castles in Westmorland and Skipton castle in Yorkshire were all repaired, and in some cases rebuilt, in the 1650s and 1660s. Lady Wilbraham advised her son-in-law and daughter, Sir Thomas and Lady Middleton, on their restoration of Chirk Castle in the 1670s. In each case, a medieval castle was being restored after the Civil War as an act of family pride, a much stronger motive in women's building commissions than displays of learned taste. By the eighteenth century, there were more opportunities for small building projects with women occupying smaller town houses. A large number of the commissions to Sir John Soane in the late eighteenth century, for decorative work on houses in London, came from women.

During the sixteenth century, important changes took place in domestic architecture and these changes influenced the way women used houses. Previously, the houses of yeomen and their superiors consisted of a hall, in which communal male activities took place, and private chambers occupied by women and children. Segregation was more by sex than by status. From the seventeenth century, houses were organized in a series of separate rooms with increasingly differentiated functions. Great houses still had public or state rooms, not least because in the reigns of Elizabeth and James I it was expected that noblemen would entertain the monarch. But the rooms used by the owners were separate from the main business of the house, and while men and women were less segregated, the classes were more so.

Great houses were also increasingly separated from the economic activity which provided the income to support the establishment. Farms, quarries, brickfields and the like were kept at a distance, as was the community with which the house had a relationship. An example of the great house in transition is Wollaton Hall in Nottinghamshire. Built in the 1580s, it retained a great hall and the rooms appropriate to ancient customs of hospitality, but it was situated in the middle of a park, at some distance from the farm which supported the estate. The employees on the estate no longer appeared in the house, and with this separation came a greater division between indoor and outdoor life, and the increasing specialization of estate management and record keeping.

Women in great houses became more isolated. Higher-class women had strictly regulated contacts with the outside world; their male relations were more likely to travel and to have contact with other people. Women servants in great houses also had more circumscribed lives than their sisters in the fields. They lived some way from other households, and the higher the status of the household, the more strictly defined was their work. The fashion for spending part of the year in London or at a resort like Bath became important: it gave women a social life outside their own households. Spas had much to offer the healthy as well as the ailing.

Other internal features affected the way in which women used houses. The great houses which superseded hall houses had galleries in which women might exercise when the weather was inclement. At Chirk Castle, where Lady Wilbraham was advising her daughter and son-in-law on restoration work in the 1670s, a long gallery was installed, something which new houses of the period, including Lady Wilbraham's own house, Weston Park, rarely had. As symmetry and correct classicism became increasingly important features of great house building in the later seventeenth and eighteenth centuries, long galleries tended to be built only for the display of serious art collections. Some builders preferred to display their learning in the form of books, and libraries became commoner in new buildings in the seventeenth century. In 1634 the Countess of Leicester had to keep her books in a trunk by her bed. Queen Caroline, noted for her interest in books and intellectual company, commissioned William Kent in 1736 to build a library at St James's Palace.

Galleries were not just utilitarian exercise rooms, they were an important part of owners' display. It was here that owners showed off their taste and cultivation in paintings, usually portraits, but also sculpture. Bess of Hardwick had a gallery; its function was to celebrate her family. Of seventy-six pictures in Hardwick Hall in 1601, twenty-six were of people related to her and most of the rest were kings and queens of England. Bess's granddaughter, Alatheia Countess of Arundel (d. 1654), shared the love of collecting of her husband, Thomas Howard, Earl of Arundel. They were part of the court circle around Prince Henry and developed their connoisseurship by travelling in Italy. She supervised building activities at her husband's various houses, as he was often abroad on embassies for the king. In 1638 she paid the sculptor Nicholas Stone over £500 for work on their house in St James's Park, London. She is shown in a painting by Daniel Mytens of about 1618 in front of the ground-floor picture gallery of one of their houses.

Other forms of architectural patronage were open to women. Large numbers of funerary monuments were commissioned by women, from the most grandiose, like the Duchess of Marlborough's monument of 1733 to the duke in the chapel at Blenheim, to modest commemorations of family and friends in parish churches. A brief inspection of almost any parish church will yield a monument erected by a woman. There are also many monuments to women, and not just rich and noble women. In the late seventeenth century, there was a statue of an old weeding woman at Woburn Abbey.

Women also commemorated their families in repairs and alterations to churches. In the early seventeenth century, Lady Sherard rebuilt the south aisle of Stapleford church, Leicestershire, and added a family vault. She also erected a fine monument to her husband and repaired the chancel roof in the neighbouring church at Whissendine. Mrs Elizabeth Parkin commissioned a Gothic church from John Carr of York at Ravenfield, West Yorkshire, in 1756. Women endowed almshouses, hospitals, schools and colleges. Since many of these works were bequests, however, the benefactors often had no influence over the design.

In building and gardens, women found a form of expression in which they were not bound by the conventions of learned taste or by the requirement to display their wealth. It is clear that this element of choice is important in women's commissions and that, while there may not be any evidence of a 'feminine' taste, there is evidence of a refusal to be restricted by the conventions which dominated men's buildings. Whether it can be argued that women had a particular affinity for Gothic architecture is uncertain, but it is clear that women were happy to commission Gothic buildings in periods when they were unfashionable, like Stapleford Park in the 1630s and Mrs Parkin's Gothic church of the 1750s.

Gardens

Gardens offered women the scope for engaging in projects which required only modest expenditure, and where they might indulge in more fanciful concepts than was possible in building. Lucy Harington, Countess of Bedford (d.1628), may have been responsible for the grotto at Woburn, which was designed by Isaac de Caus in the 1620s; he certainly designed a magnificent garden for her at Moor Park, Hertfordshire. John Evelyn wrote disparagingly in 1682 of Lady Fox's plans for her house and garden at Chiswick on the grounds of the unsuitability of the site: 'I wonder at the expense; but women will have their will.' In the 1730s Queen Caroline (1683–1737), consort of George II, built a hermitage at Kew, which was lined with busts of philosophers and where Stephen Duck the 'thresher poet' lived as hermit. She commissioned from William Kent designs for Merlin's cave, containing waxworks of Merlin and his secretary; Queen Elizabeth and her muse; Elizabeth, queen of Henry VII; and the goddess Minerva. These figures were modelled on members of the queen's court. Not everyone thought this an admirable venture. The Duchess of Marlborough wrote that she had heard that it was '10,000 times more ridiculous than what was done before for the philosophers'.

There are other examples of follies and grottoes built for women, such as the Marchioness de Grey's pagan altar of 1748 at Wrest Park, Bedfordshire, and the grotto designed by Mrs Delany (1700–88) in the 1760s for the Duchess of Portland at Bulstrode, Buckinghamshire.

Just as gardens were places for recreation, so gardening was an aspect of recreation, as the title of the manual of 1717 *The Lady's Recreation: or The Art of Gardening Improved* illustrates. Gardens were a part of the domestic world in which women were expected to have an interest, through growing plants for medicinal and culinary purposes. It is not, therefore, surprising to find that botany was the science in which women were allowed to take a serious interest. This is particularly noticeable in the eighteenth century. Queen Caroline initiated the royal interest in gardens at Kew, and her daughter-in-law Augusta, Princess of Wales (d.1772), laid the foundations in the 1750s and 1760s of what was to become the Royal Botanic Gardens. The Duchess of Portland used her garden at Bulstrode, Buckinghamshire, for furthering her interest in botany, where, according to a visitor in the mid-eighteenth century, she 'has every English plant in a separate garden by themselves'.

Painting and Decoration

In early modern England the distinction between 'art' and decoration was not a clear one. Many painters did decorative painting to earn a living. Women who earned their living as painters were usually related to men in the same kind of work. The Widow Stanhopp (*fl.*1625–6) was head of the firm of painters which worked at the king's house at Theobalds, gilding the weather vane and painting wood grain on the panelling. Margaret Pearce (*fl.*1670–80) was a widow, probably of one of the Pearce family who did painted work in number of the Wren city churches. She painted an altarpiece at St Bartholomew Exchange, consisting of the Ten Commandments surmounted by 'a spacious Glory painted on the figure of a sacrificed lamb-skin' and flanked by the figures of Moses and Aaron. Mary Grimes (*fl.*1679) did similar work at St Michael Bassishaw, but unlike Margaret Pearce, was not related to a family of painters. There must have been a great shortage of skilled workers in the building boom accompanying the rebuilding of London after the great fire of 1666, which may account for the visibility of Mary Grimes and Margaret Pearce.

One of the few women who made a living from painting was Mary Beale (1633–97). She supported her family by painting portraits in the style of Lely, and many of her portraits have been misattributed to her contemporary, William Wissing. Through her family she was connected with intellectual circles and she did much of her work with clergymen and members of the universities. Two foreign women who made a living as painters in England were Artemesia Gentileschi (1593–1653) and Angelica Kauffman (1741–1807). Gentileschi, the daughter of a painter, probably came to England for a short period in the late 1630s, at the invitation of Charles I. Kauffman came to England in 1766 and lived there until 1781, though she continued to send commissions to England after leaving for Italy. She was particularly unusual in that she made a successful career as a painter of historical subjects as well as the more usual feminine portraits and pictures to be incorporated into decorative schemes.

It was slightly more usual for women to work as miniaturists than as painters of larger works. Samuel Cooper's follower (it is not clear if she was actually his pupil), Susan Penelope Rosse (1652–1700), was the daughter of a painter. She studied and copied Cooper's works, and many of her copies have been attributed to Cooper. Mrs Carwadine (1730?–1800?), a friend of Sir Joshua Reynolds, worked as a miniaturist in London in the 1760s, taking commissions. Boswell reported that she took three sittings to produce a portrait, and that he found her an agreeable woman, unmarried 'but I imagine virtuous'. Women were more evident in applied arts and became more so during the eighteenth century. There were a number of well-known women silversmiths, sometimes working in association with a male relation. Alice Sheene, Eliza Godfrey and Anne and Hester Bateman all produced silver, their best-known surviving work being Communion chalices, though they also produced various domestic articles.

Painting was one of those accomplishments which women of a certain social status were expected to acquire. From the middle of the seventeenth century, painting and drawing were taught to young ladies. Mrs Elizabeth Creed (1642–1728) painted decorations as well as pictures. She was related to the Dryden family of Canons Ashby, Northamptonshire, where she painted a panelled room with *trompe-l'oeil* architectural devices: capitals, pilasters and a frieze. Similar devices may be seen in Barnwell and Tichmarsh parish churches, where she painted wooden monuments to emulate stone. She was, like so many of the women who put up monuments to their relations, intensely concerned with establishing her own claims to noble and ancient descent. Her monumental inscriptions refer extensively to her lineage, and the only portrait she is known to have painted was of her ennobled relation, the Earl of Sandwich. Her daughter, Elizabeth Steward (1672–1743) of Cotterstock Hall, Northamptonshire, painted her own hall in what was described as 'a very masterly style', and may have helped her mother with the work at Canons Ashby, Mrs Creed being nearly seventy at the time she did it.

Fashions in painting and a concept of suitability influenced what women painted: they concentrated upon portraits; they developed landscape painting; and they were also encouraged to copy old master paintings. Mrs Delany painted copies of pictures by Corregio and Raphael, as well as landscapes, and her interest in plants began in her youth when she studied them and drew them for patterns for needlework. On his visits to country houses in the 1760s and 1770s, Horace Walpole noted pictures by noblewomen like Lady Burlington, who had painted her daughters in oils, and crayon drawings by Gertrude Duchess of Bedford, Miss Reade and Lady Anson. Mrs Humphrey Weld engraved her own house and gardens at Lulworth, Dorset, in 1721. Sarah Bridgeman published in 1739 a series of views of the house and park at Stowe engraved by Bernard Baron from Rigaud's paintings.

Painting and drawing were among the accomplishments of a young lady, but connoisseurship was not. Indeed, any pretensions women might have had were mocked rather than encouraged. Few women collectors were taken seriously. The Countess of Arundel in the 1620s and 1630s travelled extensively on the continent both with her husband and alone (which gave rise to some scandal), commissioning and buying pictures and furniture, many of a kind never before seen in England. She commissioned a portrait from Rubens and was involved in Charles 1's purchase of the Duke of Mantua's collection. She had a long association with the art dealer, Daniel Nys, but the only things she is known to have brought back to England were a black servant and a gondola (which she proposed to use on the Thames). Lady Betty Germaine (1680–1769) and the Duchess of Portland (1715–85), both wealthy widows, built up important collections of paintings, but women's interest in painting was usually seen as either an expression of pride in their family or simply as interior decoration.

Sculpture

Many people who called themselves sculptors worked chiefly on funerary monuments and on architectural details like fireplaces, capitals and coats of arms. Until the late eighteenth century, it was extremely unusual to find women actually working in stone or wood. However, being a sculptor also involved running a business, and there are instances of sculptors' widows running their husbands' workshops after their deaths. Rebecca Burman, widow of Thomas Burman (who had been commissioned by the painter Mary Beale to make a monument for her parents-in-law at Walton, Buckinghamshire), took on an apprentice in 1679, five years after her husband's death. Mary Deane, widow of the City Mason John Deane, received £400 in 1708 for work on the Guildhall, only part of which had been owing at the time of her husband's death. Women were also involved in trades associated with sculpture and masonry. Mrs Long, wife of an Essex stonecutter, was reported in 1747 to have revived the art of staining marble, presumably for interior decoration.

The most remarkable woman associated with masonry was Mrs Eleanor Coade, at the very end of the period, a business woman whose trade owed nothing to her male relations. Mrs Coade had, in the 1750s, been a linen draper, but in the 1760s she bought a business making artificial stone architectural details by a ceramic process, such stone details being much in demand for the neo-classical architecture made so fashionable by the Adam brothers. Mrs Coade's works produced plaques, balusters, capitals, urns, figures, coats of arms, friezes, quoins, keystones and a host of other items for such architects as Robert Adam, Sir John Soane, William Chambers and James Wyatt. The firm later branched out into Gothic pieces mainly for churches, but also for such patrons as Horace Walpole, with whom Mrs Coade engaged in an acrimonious dispute over the cost of her work for him. She not only conducted the business, commissioning sculptures to be cast in Coade stone and selling them, but made some of the sculptures herself, which she exhibited at the Society of Artists' exhibitions in the 1770s. Coade stone products were widely used in such places as Buckingham Palace; several squares in Bloomsbury, London; Merrion Square, Dublin; and Arundel Castle, Sussex. But the best example of her work is her own house, Belmont, in Lyme Regis, on which she advertised her wares.

Anne Seymour Damer (1749–1828), protégée and heir of Horace Walpole, was a sculptor. The daughter of Lady Caroline Conway, whose needlework pictures Walpole admired, she studied in the 1760s under the sculptors Ceracchi and John Bacon, and exhibited various works at the Royal Academy in the 1780s. Her usual subjects were animals and portrait busts, but she did the heads of Thames and Isis which decorated the bridge that her father built at Henley-on-Thames. Mrs Damer was a wealthy woman who chose to practise sculpture rather than trying to make a living from it. Other women who are known to have produced sculpture did so occasionally and were closely related to male sculptors, like John Flaxman's sister-in-law Maria Denman (1779–1859), who exhibited a cupid's head at the Society of Artists.

PART FOUR

Women's Mental Worlds

CHAPTER ELEVEN

Literacy and Learning

For much of the period it was believed that the purpose of educating women was to prepare them for marriage by inculcating the practical skills and moral values which would enable them to be good and dutiful wives. Religious education was the most important element in what was taught to girls. They were expected to be devout, to provide spiritual leadership in the household, and to know how to conduct themselves in a moral fashion. They might also receive some instruction in housewifery. Academic learning was of secondary importance, and girls were often taught to read without being taught to write as well.

Literacy

It is difficult to assess how many people were literate, and there are many stages between being functionally literate and being completely illiterate. It is not sufficient to take the ability to sign one's name as evidence of the ability to read and write, though this may be a useful indicator of change over time. Evidence from wills is unclear because only a small number of women made wills (about 15 per cent of wills in the diocese of Norwich between 1633 and 1637). Old age or ill-health might affect writing, especially as most wills were made on deathbeds. Depositions in the church courts in the diocese of Norwich in the 1630s illustrate the extent to which women will-makers were unusual. Of the women will-makers, 12 per cent could sign their names; of the deponents, only 6 per cent (compared with 56 and 47 per cent of men respectively.)

We do not know whether it was customary for women to do book-keeping. In a business based on a household, it is quite possible that the accounts were kept by a woman, but we have no direct evidence of who actually did this kind of work, nor of whether it customarily fell to a particular member of the household. Women might, too, have a different standard of literacy from their male relations. Lady Twysden and her husband, Sir Roger, both kept diaries in the seventeenth century. Her spelling and general expression suggest that, though she was a fluent writer, she did not read much. He, on the other hand, was obviously well educated. Many of the female members of Henry Walker's London sectarian congregation in the 1650s could read, and they refer to reading the Bible, the works of William Perkins and other pious books. They were probably the wives of artisans and skilled tradesmen. The usual age for children to have learned to read was about seven, though there were precocious children of both sexes like Oliver Heywood's wife, a minister's daughter, who could read a chapter of the Bible when she was four and at six could take down passages from a sermon she had heard.

The possession of reading matter is not necessarily a good indicator of literacy, as books could fall into the category of heirlooms – precious possessions which people continued to own even if they had no particular use for them. Women's inventories in the late seventeenth and early eighteenth centuries show that women were as likely to own books as men, and more so in the more economically advanced areas of the country. On the other hand, only women who made wills had inventories, and only a minority of women made wills. Four-fifths of the women were widows, so it is possible that the books had been their husbands'.

In the early Middle Ages it was more usual for women to be able to read and write than men, except for clergy, but by the sixteenth century fewer than 10 per cent of women were literate. During the seventeenth century, the proportion rose above 10 per cent and reached about 25 per cent by the 1720s. There were marked variations in women's literacy between both regions and classes. In the early seventeenth century, a much higher proportion of the female population of London was literate, possibly as much as a quarter, than in rural areas. In the diocese of Durham, only 2 per cent of women were literate, a level lower than that of all but the most humble men. In the course of the seventeenth century, women became considerably more literate: by the later years of the century, nearly half of London women were literate and the proportion increased further in the eighteenth century. In East Anglia the numbers of women who were at least able to write their names rose. In other parts of the country, female literacy increased very considerably from the 1640s (7–14 per cent) to the 1720s (26 per cent), but there were higher levels of literacy in the south-east of England than the north until the later eighteenth century, when the north overtook the south. The marked change in London could reflect a change in the kinds of women who were recruited to work in London: women who were not literate stood little chance in a competitive labour market, which suggests an improvement in provincial education for girls. It is also likely that more schooling was available to women in London.

Schooling

For much of the period, the majority of literate women had not been to school, but had learned to read and write at home. It is very striking that many women who had academic accomplishments, like a knowledge of mathematics or classical languages, were the daughters of learned men or of rich men who employed tutors.

Daughters of noblemen were sent, like their brothers, to the households of other noblemen and noblewomen. In the mid-sixteenth century, Lady Neville's household contained her own three daughters and four other gentlewomen. The young Lady Jane Grey was sent away at the age of nine to live in the household of Queen Catherine Parr. The custom of sending girls away to other households became less common as schools for girls developed, but it did not die out. In 1708 the eight-year-old Mary Granville, better known as Mrs Delany, having spent three years in the charge of Mlle Puelle with nineteen other girls, was sent to join her uncle and aunt at Whitehall to learn the ways of the court.

Before the Reformation, girls, the daughters of noblemen and wealthy merchants, might be sent to live in a convent. The education that convents provided was very limited, and few can be said to have been running schools in the sense in which we understand them. Girls might learn to read, but not necessarily to write. Young novices were educated, but it is very uncertain how much convents actually took on the education of girls not intended for a vocation, since most English orders were strictly enclosed. St Clement's nunnery, outside the city walls of York, may have provided some kind of education for girls in the fourteenth century, but this is the only evidence in a city well provided with nunneries.

The dissolution of the convents meant that there was no longer any institution to which girls might be sent away, and the interests of girls were largely overlooked in the new grammar school foundations set up to replace the monastic schools for boys. The founders of the grammar school in Canterbury believed that 'it seems very unfit [that] girls should be taught in a school within the precincts of the church, especially seeing they may have instruction by women in the town'. But girls were not completely ignored. Bunbury grammar school, Cheshire, in 1594 was supposed to take girls up to the age of nine. Uppingham and Oakham schools founded in the 1580s in Rutland have seals depicting four boys and two girls. At Polesworth free school in Warwickshire, founded in the early seventeenth century by Sir Francis Nethersole at the instigation of his wife, there was provision for both sexes, with an emphasis on needlework, reading and religious instruction for the girls.

Schools of various kinds were provided throughout the seventeenth century, sometimes exclusively for girls. In the 1660s Alice Horwood gave a school for twenty poor girls to the town of Barnstaple, Devon, and in the 1670s Sir Marwood William Turner, Lord Mayor of London, provided a school for ten girls and ten boys at Kirkleatham, Cleveland. Lady Catherine Herbert, childless widow of the 4th Lord Herbert of Cherbury, in 1716 left £6,000 to build and endow almshouses at Preston-upon-the-Weald, Shropshire, for twelve poor women and twelve poor girls, who were to be taught reading, writing and sewing. Some years later the number of girls increased; they were admitted at the age of seven and trained as servants. William Law saw his responsibilities in a slightly different light. He established a school in 1746 at King's Cliffe, Northamptonshire, for the village girls and gave the parish a library of pious books. Foundations intended for both boys and girls often neglected the girls. In 1640 Foster's school in Sherborne, Dorset, was established for ten poor boys and ten poor girls. There is plenty of evidence for the boys being taught, but none until the early eighteenth century for the girls.

David Busby's detailed study of the educational provision for early-eighteenth-century Bedfordshire shows what kind of schooling was available for girls. Fifty-five parishes had no school, while fifty-six had something for 'children' – usually no sex is specified. A number of parishes had endowed schools. Sarah Emery, who died in 1692, left money to endow schools in Ampthill and Mepershall. The school at Ampthill in 1717 had twenty-six pupils of both sexes, who were taught reading, writing, casting accounts and the principles of religion by a master and two dames. Boys paid 6d. a week for lessons in reading and writing, and 4d. for reading alone. Girls paid 3d. a week to be taught reading by the mistress or 6d. to include further lessons in reading and writing from the master.

At Mepershall, under the terms of the endowment of 1698, six poor boys were taught to read, write and cast accounts, and six poor girls were taught to read and to sew. The school was open from Michaelmas until midsummer, so that the children might work 'in country labour' during the summer, but for three hours after the service on Sunday evening they were to learn the catechism and read the scriptures for the period that the school was closed. In the 1720s, the children were instructed in the principles of Christian religion, in reading and in plaiting straw, and girls were taught to sew. The school provided them with books and spinning wheels, but the pupils had to provide their own material to spin. Girls progressed through various kinds of craft until they were able to knit stockings. Two of the Bedfordshire schools were principally for girls. Dame Constance Burgoyne left £100 in 1711 for a charity school at Sutton where sixteen poor children were to be taught to read by two schoolmistresses. The children, chosen by the church-wardens and overseers, were chiefly girls.

Private schools, set up by individuals, were rather more ephemeral and might also have a particular religious affiliation. In 1717 a Quaker came from another parish to Barton, Bedfordshire, to teach elementary literacy, but he refused to teach the catechism. Other schools were run by local clergymen. The woman who ran the school at Great Barford in 1720 had a regular arrangement to teach children to read and to catechize them. Elsewhere, there were informal arrangements for dame schools – usually run by one or more poor women in the parish who could teach basic reading and the catechism. Sometimes these women were unable to write themselves.

Many girls' schools were founded as part of the attempt to solve the problem of the poor, and in that respect they resemble parish apprenticeships more closely than the modern idea of a school. Girls might be taught to read and write, but the schools' main purpose was to train girls to work, chiefly in domestic service. Once pupils could be placed in a position as a servant, they were no longer the responsibility of the parish. Reading was an asset for a servant, but it was also an aid to piety. Christ's Hospital, visited by John Evelyn in 1687, had 800 pupils, boys and girls. The girls were 'instructed in all such work as becomes their sex and may fit them for good wives, mistresses, and to be a blessing to their generation'; unlike the boys they did not learn mathematics.

Parish apprenticeships were a product of the Elizabethan Poor Law and were an attempt to provide pauper children with training of a kind which would enable them to earn their livings. Masters were not always keen to take parish apprentices unless the premium paid by the parish was increased by some local benefaction; the most skilled trades rarely took parish apprentices. Most girls were apprenticed as housewives, and only occasionally were they taken on in trades like stay-making or weaving. Pauper children were often apprenticed younger than normal apprentices, and illegitimate children still younger. The period of the apprenticeship was about seven years, but the termination of the apprenticeship might be expressed in a variety of ways. Often girls passed out of their apprenticeships at the age of twenty-one, and sometimes they were released earlier if they got married. The arrangements became much slacker after 1660 when formal apprenticeship regulations began to fall into desuetude, though when an Act of 1662 gave apprentices the right to remain in the parish in which they had been indentured, greater care began to be taken about them. By the eighteenth century, however, changes in the organization of work meant that formal indentures were hardly ever made.

Schools for the daughters of the gentry were more concerned with polite accomplishments than were endowed and parish schools. Dancing, playing musical instruments, singing and foreign languages appeared on the curriculum of the schools which were set up in increasing numbers after the Restoration in the outer suburbs of London or in healthy places like Bath. The numerous schools that were established in rural Islington and Hackney in the late seventeenth century concentrated on the kinds of accomplishment considered necessary to secure a husband; some also taught housewifery and accounts. It is possible that the amount of academic learning available to women in schools declined as scholarship made way for polite accomplishment. The more serious schools often had an overtly religious function. There were Catholic schools in London in the early seventeenth century, and after the Restoration there were nonconformist academies for girls, all of which had to operate more or less clandestinely.

Academic subjects – mathematics, theology and classical languages – were rarely taught in girls' schools. Those girls who did learn these things either were the daughters of learned men, usually clergymen, who were taught by their fathers, or had parents rich enough to employ a tutor, though often the tutor was chiefly there to teach the sons of the house. The daughters of Sir Thomas More were celebrated for their learning, as was Damaris Masham (1658–1708), friend of John Locke and daughter of Ralph Cudworth, divine and Cambridge Platonist. She educated her son

Francis herself and published several works of theology. Elizabeth Singer Rowe (1674–1737) was the daughter of a nonconformist divine and was taken up by Lord Weymouth, who taught her French and Italian and introduced her to his chaplain, the non-juring Bishop Ken. Thomas Pitt wrote to his son Robert Pitt in 1721 concerning his granddaughter's desire to learn geography; he had sent her money to pay the master 'and have promised her books to fit her for it'. The teaching of girls was a more haphazard affair than that of boys, even in households where academic learning was valued for women. In the 1620s Mr Hill was paid 11s. for teaching the gentlewomen of the Newdigate family for only a week, and it was common for tutors to come and go without much regard for continuity of teaching. This certainly seems to have been the case for the daughters of the 1st Earl of Cork, two of whom, Catherine Lady Ranelagh (1614–91) and Mary Countess of Warwick (1624–78), were noted for their intellectual interests.

A school where academic learning was prized, and where the tradition descended from one generation of women to the next, was the Bar Convent school, York. This school, founded in 1686 by the nuns of the order of the Institute of the Blessed Virgin Mary, aimed to foster faith in Catholic women by education as much as by spiritual training. The nuns themselves were learned in classical and modern languages and in the new sciences of the seventeenth century. But poverty and isolation seem to have ossified the curriculum; the convent could not afford to buy new books in the eighteenth century, and the need to be discreet discouraged participation in Catholic controversy. The teaching was not, however, restricted to academic learning; dancing remained on the curriculum until the nineteenth century.

Although teaching was not the career for women that it became in the nineteenth century, it did provide some women with an occupation. From the mid-seventeenth century, private schools for young ladies began to open and many of them were run by women. Katherine Philips, the poet, had attended a school in Hackney run by Mrs Salmon, and nearby was the school run by Mrs Perwich. In Bath in the 1720s, Mrs Emblon and Mrs Pullen ran a school for young ladies. There were some opportunities for women as governesses. Margaret Duchess of Newcastle (1624?–74) was taught reading and writing by 'an ancient decayed gentlewoman'. The 1st Earl of Cork employed two gentlewomen and a French woman in some kind of capacity as governesses to his daughters. We know nothing about the gentlewoman who taught Mrs Delany's six-year-old niece needlework and manners.

Women's Writing

Much work has been done in recent years on women writers, especially by those who are interested in feminist literary criticism and in the first-person narrative. We are concerned here not so much with the content of what women wrote as with the part which writing played in women's lives. Given that for much of the period few women were able to write, what did they write when they could do so? They produced little public material until the later seventeenth century, but there is a good deal of private writing, especially letters, diaries and spiritual autobiographies, as well as pious meditations and poetry. For many women, writing had two functions: contact with family and friends, and as an aid to piety.

Letters for much of this period had both a public and a private function; they were often circulated round a number of people and copies taken if they contained matters of public interest. Women's letters were more likely to be private. Many of the women's letters that survive are addressed to their husbands during periods of separation, often when the husband was in London and the wife at home in the country, and the letters relate to business and family affairs at home. The correspondence between Joan Thynne and her husband John in the 1570s covered their children's health, her estates in Shropshire and the lengthy legal disputes which these had generated. Such subjects recur in most wives' letters. Although it was common for families to exist in only two generations, in noble families with long-lived matriarchs, letters were an extremely important means of keeping in touch. Lady Anne Clifford corresponded with her daughters and granddaughters. Sarah Duchess of Marlborough corresponded weekly with her granddaughter Diana Spencer after her marriage to Lord John Russell. The duchess had brought up Diana Spencer after the death of her mother, and her letters are full of the duchess's doings and opinions.

Women were considerable producers of confessional writing, some of it in the form of diaries, some of it more self-conscious spiritual autobiography. Much writing of this sort had a religious function. Puritan ministers stressed the value of spiritual accounting, of believers weighing up their lives and examining their actions and motives as a guide to the action of God's spirit.

Some of this writing found its way into print for its exemplary value, not unlike the sermons preached at the funerals of pious ladies that were published afterwards. There was, for example, *A Narrative of God's Gracious Dealings with that Choice Christian, Mrs*

Hannah Allen, published in 1683, and *The Holy Life of Mrs Elizabeth Walker*, published in 1690, both of which incorporated passages of autobiographical writing. Spiritual autobiographies did nothing to make the reputation of the author as a writer, but much to promote her reputation for spirituality. The person actually responsible for the publication was not always the woman herself, but was often a male publishing entrepreneur (though printing was a trade in which there were a good many women). For example, Arise Evans, a Welsh visionary, was responsible for discovering and publishing the prophecy of the dumb Elinor Channel in 1655. Spiritual writing was not confined to women from the higher levels of society. Katherine Chidley (*fl*.1641–53) was the wife of a tailor. Many of the women prophets and autobiographers were from the middling sort, having come to radical religion through the itinerant missionaries of the 1650s.

Personal narratives had an oral as well as a written form, since many of the sects of the 1640s and 1650s required as a condition of church membership that postulants should give a public account of their conversion to the gathered congregation. In some cases the postulants were questioned, an experience which could be disconcerting. One young woman answered so fearfully and uncertainly that the congregation was doubtful about accepting her, 'but when she heard this, she burst out into tears bitterly, before the church'. John Rogers, minister of the congregation where this incident took place in the 1650s, identified as a problem the inability of 'maids, and others that are bashful' to speak in public, and arranged for such people to give their testimonies in private.

The motive for publishing autobiographies, prophecies and spiritual reflections was religious and related to the message contained therein. Other women's writings which resemble these are polemical works concerned with politics, with education or with marriage, for example Elinor James's *Advice to the Citizens of London* (1688), Bathsua Makin's *An Essay to Revive the Ancient Education of Gentlewomen* (1673) and Mary Astell's *Some Reflections upon Marriage* (1700). The force of the message was what motivated the authors to seek publication, and they rarely earned anything but execration for their excursions into print. It is, however, noticeable that several of the women who published on these subjects in the later seventeenth century were connected with the printing or bookselling trades. Mary Astell was connected with a bookseller, Mrs Manley had a liaison with a London printer, and Elinor James was married to a printer.

Much of the poetry which was written in the early seventeenth century circulated in manuscript. A few women, like Mary Sidney (1561–1621), had poems published during their lifetime. Others, like Anne Killigrew (1660–85), had their work published after their death. Publication probably became easier as the market for printed matter grew in the eighteenth century. Mary Lady Chudleigh (1656–1710) published her work during her lifetime. More women's work was published as the eighteenth century progressed. Some poets, like Mary Barber (1690?–1757), a friend of Swift, published their work by subscription, and this became a popular method from the 1730s.

Women did not necessarily write for other women. In the late sixteenth and early seventeenth centuries, very few of the books produced for women were by women. What is very striking from the 1580s, however, is the growth in the volume of literature for women, chiefly plays and works of fiction. This suggests less that publishers had identified women as a specific target for sales than that recreational reading had become much more popular, and that previous strictures against it, especially for women, had ceased to be observed.

During the eighteenth century, journalism for women developed. Early periodicals tried to attract women readers (evidence of the increasing literacy of the middle-class women who had access to such reading matter). But these periodicals, both those like the *Athenian Mercury* (1691–97) and the *Spectator* (1711–13), edited by John Dunton, Joseph Addison and Richard Steele, and those like *Female Spectator* (1744–6) and the *Lady's Museum* (1760–1), edited by Eliza Haywood (1693?–1756) and Charlotte Lennox (1720–1804), sought to separate women from the 'men's world' of politics and the professions, into a group with their own exclusive interests. These journals were very clearly aimed at a middle- and upper-class readership. The kinds of topic covered were love and the subjects needed for informed conversation. The *Lady's Museum* had articles on such topics as Sir Anthony Van Dyck, the history of Ceylon and the original inhabitants of Great Britain, as well as poems. It was assumed that women would organize their households rather than do the work themselves. The *Female Tatler* of 1706 spoke up on behalf of women:

> The French nation have so complaisant a regard for the fair sex that they always mix with 'em in conversation. . . . But English ladies, the moment they rise from dinner, are packed off to their tea tables, where they spend half their lives times in talking of fans and tea-cups, sugar tongs, salt shovels and gloves made up in walnut shells.[1]

[1] *The Female Tatler*, 3, 11–13 July 1706.

The *Ladies Journal*, published in Dublin in 1727, argued against 'men's pretended prerogative of learning peculiar to themselves', citing as models of learned ladies Sir Thomas More's daughter, Margaret Roper, the translator; Elizabeth Carew, the patron of poets; Anne Askew, the martyr; Elizabeth Weston, Latin poet; Queen Elizabeth; Katherine Philips, the poet; Aphra Behn, the writer; Mrs Cemliver (Centlivre?), the actress and playwright; and Mrs Haywood and Mrs Manley, writers and journalists.

Literature and Livelihoods

To make a living from writing implied access to education of a kind which we know was not available to many women, but the increasing number of women who published writings testifies to the spread of education among women. Evidence of women who supported themselves by writing is fragmentary, partly because so much printed ephemera and so many pamphlets, broadsides and newsbooks, were published anonymously. Aphra Behn (1649?–89) is always cited as the first woman to make her living by writing, though the only evidence for this seems to arise from the circumstance that when she left the debtors' prison in about 1670 her only means of livelihood was her pen. She was certainly writing at the period when writers first began to make a living without aristocratic patrons, and there were other women, such as Frances Boothby (*fl.*1669) and Elizabeth Polwhele (*fl.*1670), who wrote for the theatre.

By the eighteenth century, it was possible for women to support themselves by writing, chiefly in journalism. Elizabeth Carter (1717–1806), a member of the Bluestocking circle, supported herself writing for the *Gentleman's Magazine* from 1734 to 1739. Mrs Manley (1663–1724) wrote plays, romances and a variety of other works, and a series of newspapers for women, of which probably the best known was the *Female Tatler*. This she produced in 1706 in the guise of Mrs Crackenthorpe, 'a Lady that knows every thing'. She claimed, in this persona, that she did not write the paper for profit, 'having an estate of £300 per annum and always kept two maids and a footman'. She certainly had a patrimony of about £200. She was associated with Richard Steele, and in 1711, after being prosecuted for slander, she succeeded Swift as editor of *The Examiner*. Her biographer wrote of her,

I have often heard her say, If she had been a man, she had been without fault, but the charter of that sex being much more confined than ours, what is not a crime in men is scandalous and unpardonable in women.[1]

Eliza Haywood (1693?–1756) was driven to seek a livelihood on the stage when her husband deserted her and their two children. She then started to write. She produced novels and plays, but is best known for the *Female Spectator* (1744–6), a serious journal for ladies which dwelt much on metaphysical matters.

While it might be difficult for women to make a living from writing, there were a good many women who made a living as printers. There were women printers in the sixteenth century, the majority of them related to male printers and a number of them related to French emigrés. Rather more is known about Jane Yetsweirt than can usually be found about such women. She was the widow of Charles Yetsweirt, whose father had been granted by Queen Elizabeth a patent to print English common law books. Charles was not a printer by trade, and his right, and later his widow's, was challenged by the Company of Stationers, the gild of printers. As their challenges became more forceful, so did Mrs Yetsweirt's resistance, in order to protect 'the patent of printing the laws which is mine only stay of maintenance'. She carried on the business from her husband's death in 1595 until 1598, when she married Sir Philip Botellor and surrendered the patent.

In the period 1641–60, when printing flourished thanks to the relaxation of censorship, thirty-four women, mainly wives and daughters of printers and booksellers, are known to have traded in London and the provinces. Their numbers diminished in the eighteenth century. Some of them ran businesses for only a short time, immediately following the death of their husband or father. Hannah Sawbridge's husband George died in 1681, and she continued his Ludgate Hill business for five years. Others obviously made the business their life, like Mrs Harford who ran her late husband's bookshop in Portsmouth for fifteen years after his death in 1695, and Grace White, who not only took over her late husband's printing business in Coffee Yard, York, but in 1719 founded a newspaper, *The York Mercury*, and passed on the business to her husband's grandson. Elizabeth Adams of Chester took over her late husband's business as printer in 1733 and produced the *Weekly Courant* for twenty years, when she was joined by her son. In 1756 she diversified and was selling patent medicines.

---

[1] *Mrs Manley's History of her Own Life and Times*, 4th edn, 1725, E. Curll, London, p. 7.

Teresia Lady Shirley (1593–1668) was a Circassian who married Sir Robert Shirley, envoy of the Shah of Persia. Van Dyck painted her in Persian dress in Rome in 1622.

Simon de Passe's engraving of Pocahontas was engraved during Pocahontas's visit to London in 1616–17.

Portrait of Jane Ebbrell, spider brusher at Erdigg in Denbighshire in 1793, where she had worked for nearly seventy years. She started as a housemaid and had married the coachman.

Mrs Mary Honeywood (1527–1620) had 16 children. During her lifetime 114 grandchildren, 228 great-grandchildren and 9 great-great-grandchildren were born.

Below *Women harvesters around 1730 at Dixton, Gloucestershire, are shown raking the hay after it has been mown by men.*

Dairymaids at Charlton Park in Gloucestershire c. 1740, working outside but close to the house and farm.

Weston Park in Shropshire, designed in the 1670s, probably by Lady Wilbraham herself.

Peter Lely's portrait of Elizabeth Wilbraham (1632–1705), a substantial heiress, who used her patrimony for many building projects as well as commissioning paintings.

The Countess of Arundel, grand-daughter of Bess of Hardwick, shared her husband's love of collecting and supervised many of his building projects. She is shown in this portrait of 1618 by Mytens in the ground-floor gallery of their London house, which was conceived almost as a museum.

Mary Beale (1633–99) made her living in the later seventeenth century as a portrait painter, charging £10 for a three-quarter-length portrait. This self-portrait dates from earlier in her career, c. 1665.

Frontispiece of the sale catalogue of the Duchess of Portland's collection in 1786. This sale of the collection of botanical and mineral specimens, shells, fossils, birds' eggs, china and curiosities made by the Duchess of Portland (1715–85) lasted for 38 days.

Mrs Delany (1700–88) made such a reputation from her collage pictures of plants that she was commissioned to record new specimens brought from abroad to Kew Gardens and the Chelsea Physick Garden.

Mary Ward (1585–1645), founder of the Institute of the Blessed Virgin Mary, was the woman most responsible for bringing Counter Reformation Catholicism to England.

Scholarship

Both men and women thought that learning inhibited a women's chances of marriage. A few women inveighed against these prejudices and restrictions. Bathsua Makin (*fl.*1673), wrote fiercely of the 'debauched sots' of men who thought that women were endowed with fewer powers of reason and were less capable of improvement by education than men. 'Had God intended women only as a finer sort of cattle, he would not have made them reasonable.' She had been taught by Comenius, she was tutor to Charles I's daughter Princess Elizabeth, and she ran a school in Tottenham where students might learn the usual accomplishments – music, dancing and French – together with Latin, Hebrew, botany, geology, experimental philosophy, painting, cooking and astronomy, at a cost of £20 a year. Later Mary Astell (1666–1731) wrote in her *Serious Proposal* of the need for higher education for women to prepare them better for the world.

Women feature little in the ideas of the reformers of the Renaissance and Reformation, whose work had such an impact upon the education of men. Women were discouraged from taking a serious interest in theology, the principal medium of intellectual exchange for men. They were not discouraged from pious pursuits, but rather from the kind of technical theological debates which required knowledge of classical authors as well of the early church fathers' writings and of the great medieval schoolmen like Thomas Aquinas and Marsilius of Padua. Though there were both learned women and women rulers in the sixteenth century, humanist educational reformers did not address themselves to the subject of women's education in general, or the need to give princesses a political education.

Erasmus was initially sceptical about whether Christian humanism might benefit women. He was respectful of the erudition of Queen Catherine of Aragon, though he was primarily interested in learned noblewomen as prospective patrons. He corresponded with Thomas More's daughter Margaret Roper (1505–44) (who translated into English his treatise on the Lord's Prayer), and referred to More's household as 'a veritable home of the muses'. It was More's household which persuaded him to change his mind. He wrote in 1521, 'It was not always believed that letters are of value to the virtue and general reputation of women. I myself once held this opinion: but More completely converted me.' But Erasmus did not see women's learning as something which might contribute to intellectual life in general. Rather, he saw it as a way of protecting women's virtue: 'there is nothing that more occupies the attention of a young girl than study', which keeps her from 'idleness and lascivious games'. Later in life, the woman's learning might contribute to the strength of her marriage: 'they are bound by much stronger chains who are linked in the devotion of their minds'. This was not an argument for intellectual independence, because Erasmus adds, 'A wife will respect a husband more whom she recognizes as her teacher.' This limited vision of the purpose of education for women persisted virtually throughout our period.

Translation was one of those scholarly activities which were felt to be within women's capacities. We have seen that Margaret Roper did translations. Her contemporary, Joanna Lumley (c.1537–77) was the first translator of a Greek drama into English. She translated a play with a strong feminine subject, Euripides's *Iphegenia at Aulis*. The demand for translations such as Mary Arundell's (d.1691) *Sayings and Doings of the Emperor Severus* increased with the growing reading public, and many popular editions of the classics appeared during the seventeenth century.

Collecting was an important way for women to develop a learned interest in various subjects. It combined aspects of connoisseurship and interior decoration with what one might call the museum impulse. Oriental porcelain began to arrive in England in the late sixteenth century, but it was collected only by a few people at court and by merchants with Far Eastern connections. Its popularity increased during the seventeenth century, and by the 1660s it was fashionable to make porcelain collections. The China-mania which swept the country in the 1690s is credited to Queen Mary, but what she actually brought from Holland was the fashion for a massed display of porcelain. She also brought with her the fashion for women to have cabinets of curiosities.

One of the great collectors was the dowager Duchess of Portland (1715–85), a considerable heiress in her own right, who during her twenty years of widowhood devoted herself to establishing a museum. She was the daughter of Edward Harley, 2nd Earl of Oxford, whose own collections formed the basis of the British Museum. Her mother, too, had an important collection of family pictures. At her home in Whitehall, the duchess accumulated possessions whose sale in 1786 took thirty-eight days and which numbered over 4,000 items in the auction catalogue. She left large collections of such artefacts as snuff-boxes, clothing from the aboriginal inhabitants of New Zealand and North America, china, crystal and an important collection of books, one of which was

Queen Elizabeth's prayer book, as well as the Portland vase. She had a great interest in scientific subjects, and much of her collection consisted of specimens, especially shells, corals and minerals. She employed the eminent botanist and pupil of Linnaeus, Daniel Solander, to catalogue the collection, and Georg Ehret, the botanical illustrator, to draw plant specimens for her.

The Duchess of Portland was omnivorous in her scientific interests. She was eccentric and extremely rich. But her collection does reflect a scientific interest which a number of other women shared, in botany, the one science which they might legitimately study. Women were able to pursue their study of plants beyond the permissible female concerns of food, medicine and the garden. Mary Somerset, Duchess of Beaufort (d.1714), daughter of Arthur Capel (who was well known for his interest in gardens), was associated with the Temple Coffee House botanical club, another of whose members was the curator of the Chelsea Physick Garden, Samuel Doody. The Duchess of Beaufort did extensive work on the gardens of the family's houses at Badminton and Chelsea (which was next door to the Physick Garden) and in the 1690s built glass houses for growing plants obtained from abroad, especially from Virginia and the Netherlands. She employed an artist to make a record of her botanical specimens. Queen Mary encouraged the introduction of new species and began a substantial collection of plants from the islands of the Atlantic in the gardens of Hampton Court. It is likely that her interest had been fostered by her tutor Henry Compton, Bishop of London, himself the collector of plants in the gardens of Fulham Palace.

Women were largely excluded from the world of scientific exploration and experiment: there was no place for them in the universities or in bodies like Gresham College, the Oxford Philosophical Society and the Royal Society. But for those interested in the physical world, collecting was an important activity. These private collections aided the classification of the natural world, helped to establish taxonomies for animals, birds, plants and minerals, and subsequently formed the basis of several museum collections.

The most important women in this respect were Queen Caroline, consort of George II, and her daughter-in-law Augusta Princess of Wales, whose combined work initiated the Royal Botanic Gardens at Kew. Queen Caroline was interested in gardens for recreation and built a number of grottoes and other fanciful buildings, but she had a serious interest in many subjects and especially in gardening, of which she said, 'I think I may say that I have introduced that, in helping nature, not losing it in art.' Elizabeth Blackwell (*fl*.1737) used her interest in botany to support her family in the 1730s. Encouraged by Sir Hans Sloane and the then curator of the Chelsea Physick Garden, Mr Rand, she made a living by making botanical illustrations of plants supplied by Mr Rand. She drew, engraved and coloured her pictures, producing in 1737 her two-volume *Curious Herbal*. This was not simply a work of botany, but was concerned with the medical applications of plants. Mrs Delany (1700–88) illustrated flowers by means of paper mosaics, or collages, and was so highly thought of that new plants were sent to her from Kew Gardens and from the Chelsea Physick Garden to copy. She was on friendly terms with Sir Joseph Banks and Daniel Solander, who had accompanied Cook on his voyage round the world.

For men, who controlled the means to education, its chief function for women was to train them to be good wives. Women were required to be devout, and to subordinate their intellects to those of men. A few women spoke out against this, but it is striking how a few women developed intellectual interests of their own outside the conventional academy.

CHAPTER TWELVE

Women's Religious Communities

Throughout the period 1500–1760 there were religious communities for women; some were of fully professed nuns, others were of devout women who sought a refuge from the world or to prepare themselves better for the world. These communities provided an environment in which learning could be fostered and where women might develop both intellectual and spiritual lives outside the formal supervision of the established church and other male-dominated institutions.

Nuns and the Dissolution

In the decades before England's final break with Rome in the 1530s, monastic vocations had been declining and the numbers of monks and nuns were much reduced. In 1500 there were about 2,000 nuns as well as various supernumeraries: lay sisters, pensioners and devout laywomen who chose to live in or near a convent. By 1534 the number of nuns had fallen to about 1,600, living in 136 communities. The four largest nunneries in the country rarely contained more than thirty nuns. The majority of nuns lived in very small communities, often of fewer than ten, in small rural settlements. By the early sixteenth century, many such communities had only two or three nuns. At the time of the Reformation there were fourteen nunneries in Yorkshire and twenty-five monasteries, while Northamptonshire had six nunneries and Middlesex five. The Middlesex houses included some of the largest and richest in country; even so, only one had more than twenty nuns. The small size of most convents made them particularly vulnerable to catstrophes. The house of the Poor Clares (female Franciscans) at Aldgate in London was eliminated in 1515 when twenty-seven nuns died in an epidemic and the buildings were destroyed by fire.

Over half of all convents followed the Benedictine rule. Many of the other orders based their rule upon that of St Benedict but added variations. Women were not allowed to operate as mendicants (male friars, peripatetic preachers living under vows of poverty, chastity and obedience), although the chief mendicant orders, the Franciscans and the Dominicans, did have female houses which were enclosed, keeping vows of strict poverty and seclusion. Indeed, the Dominican nunnery at Dartford was considerably more strictly enclosed than many other orders, and the nuns devoted themselves entirely to prayer and contemplation. In addition, there were Augustinian canonesses. Canons lived in a religious community but worked as parish priests; canonesses generally lived a less austere life than nuns and taught girls, embroidered vestments and transcribed liturgical works.

Conventual life offered women education and considerable scope as administrators of people, lands and finances, apart from prayer and contemplation. The majority of nuns were of gentle or noble birth. Thomas Aquinas had written of nuns in the thirteenth century that they 'are promoted to the dignity of men whereby they are liberated from the subjection of men', and this had practical consequences. The abbess of Syon had charge in 1539 of fifty-two choir nuns, four lay sisters, twelve brothers, and five lay brothers (originally the abbey had been founded for sixty nuns), as well as a small community of devout laypeople who lived in the neighbourhood and attached themselves unofficially to the abbey. The abbess was responsible for the abbey's business affairs, which she delegated to a treasurer, and she was advised by laymen on the administration of the abbey's property, which in 1509–10 produced an income of £1,635. The chief steward of the abbey was a lawyer, a position held by men of the eminence of Thomas More and Thomas Cromwell. The nuns were noted for their learning, and the abbey had an important library. After the invention of printing the convent became a publisher of devotional works in English. The prioress of the Benedictine convent at Shoreditch had charge of thirteen nuns and four novices as well as lay brothers. She was responsible for very considerable property in London – endowments left by devout city merchants, producing an income of £300 a year, the rents being collected by male agents.

As all the orders of nuns were enclosed, teaching, nursing and other work in the world were not formally allowed. Schools, hospitals and orphanages were associated with convents, but they were generally run by lay sisters not by the nuns themselves. Conventual hospitality for travellers and pilgrims was an important part of their contact with the outside world, and the male Benedictine orders were particularly noted for this, not least because their houses were richer, but the convents at Polesworth in Warwickshire and Catesby in Northamptonshire were well known for their hospitality. Life in the poorer convents, on the other hand, must have been very hard. Nuns were permitted to beg for alms, and it is evidence of the increasing poverty of many convents that the number of royal licences to beg increased during the early sixteenth century. Three of the six Northamptonshire convents had such licences. Most of the nuns in poor rural convents which had only three or four members were able to scratch a living from the land around the convent, did their own domestic work, and probably lived as poor countrywomen did anywhere.

In 1536 the closure of convents and monasteries worth less than £200 a year was ordered. Some pleaded special circumstances and were exempted, but about 400 of the smaller convents and monasteries were closed down, their revenues were sequestered by the crown, and the nuns and monks dispersed, some to larger houses of the same order, some to secular life. A disproportionate number of the closures were of convents because they tended to be smaller and poorer than monasteries. In 1539–40 the main dissolution of the monasteries took place and was finally ratified by statute in 1540. As a result, all convents, monasteries, priories, abbeys and friaries were closed and their property taken by the crown. Some of it was used to endow schools and hospitals which had formerly been administered by monasteries or convents, but most of it was used as crown revenue.

It is sometimes claimed that the history of the Reformation in England has been dominated to an unjustified extent by the history of the dissolution. This complaint has less justice for the female orders than for the male orders. The male orders, especially the Benedictines, Franciscans and Dominicans, have been assiduous chroniclers of their own histories. The female orders have been much less so, possibly because more orders of monks survived than of nuns. But the sheer quantity of remains, especially of buildings, place names and street names, keeps reminding us of the effects of the dissolution. The great abbeys are the most obvious, especially the Cistercian abbeys, such as Fountains, which have survived as romantic ruins sometimes 'improved' by eighteenth-century landscape gardeners. Other great abbeys, such as Peterborough, became cathedrals when new dioceses were created or, like

Tewkesbury, important parish churches. It was the religious houses that were less architecturally spectacular, or that were in more out-of-the-way places, which became private houses or quarries for other buildings. Many of the great houses of England like Woburn and Stoneleigh were adapted from monastic buildings or were built on the site of a monastery.

Most of the buildings occupied by nuns were dismantled for building materials or converted into private houses. The buildings of the convent at Chertsey were dismantled to provide stone for building Hampton Court; the Benedictine nunnery at Wilton in Wiltshire, with eighty nuns one of the largest in England, disappeared into the house built by the first Earl of Pembroke in 1544. The nunnery of the order of Fontevrault at Amesbury, which had had a hundred nuns at its height and which still had thirty-three and an equal number of supernumeraries at its dissolution, was granted to the Duke of Somerset and converted into a house by his son, the Earl of Hertford. The duke also received the Brigettine convent at Syon in Middlesex and the neighbouring Hospital of the Virgin Mary and Nine Orders of Holy Angels at Brentford, which subsequently disappeared into the buildings of the Earls of Northumberland. The Benedictine convent at Shaftesbury, one of the richest in the country with fifty-six nuns at its dissolution, was absorbed into the town. Lacock Abbey, which had housed Augustinian canonesses, became a private house and largely retains the nuns' domestic quarters to this day.

Convents often disappeared because many of them were no more than small private houses or farms to begin with. There were fewer nuns than monks, they lived in smaller communities and their communities were poorer, so there was much less to be plundered from convent buildings and estates than there was from monasteries. Often the only evidence of the former existence of a nunnery is in place names, such as Nunburnholme and Nunkeeling, Yorkshire (Benedictine nuns), Canonsleigh, Devon (Augustinian canonesses), and Minories, Aldgate, London (Poor Clares); or in references to hospitals and leper houses run by lay sisters, as in Maiden Bradley, Wiltshire. Sometimes these female houses had closed down long before the dissolution.

Nuns left fewer traces in other respects than monks. Even abbesses were rarely commemorated by monuments after their death. The abbots of the great collegiate churches like Westminster and Peterborough were commemorated by fine monuments and by the singing of Masses for their souls by the monks of the foundation. Few nunnery churches remain, so it may be that there were monuments to abbesses which did not survive the dispersal of monastic property. However, nunneries were rarely rich enough to commission monuments, and abbesses were probably commemorated simply by Masses said or sung for their souls. A few nuns' monuments survive, like the brass of 1400 at Baldock, Hertfordshire, but they are very uncommon and usually very modest. Three date from after the Reformation, and were put up at the expense of the nuns' families to whom they turned for support after their convents had been dissolved. Elizabeth Throckmorton, abbess of the Benedictine abbey at Denny, Cambridge, one of the largest and most important nunneries in the country, is commemorated by a small brass plate in the parish church near her family home at Coughton, Warwickshire. She retired there with two other nuns when Denny was dissolved in 1539. At Denham, Buckinghamshire, is a monument to Agnes Jordan, last abbess of the great Brigettine convent of Syon, who died in 1544. She had retired to Denham with eight nuns and a pension of £200 per annum after the dissolution. At a less exalted level, there survives a brass at Dingley, Northamptonshire, to Agnes Boroeghe, a former nun from a convent in Clerkenwell who settled there and died in 1577, 'to the great loss of the poor who [in] divers ways were by her relieved'.

But what became of the nuns? After the dissolutions of 1536 nuns were offered the choice of transferring to another house of the same order, or of leaving the religious life altogether and being released from their vows of poverty, chastity and obedience. A number were released from their vows and took husbands. In 1539 an Act was passed declaring that, though nuns might be released from their vows of poverty and obedience, they could not be released from their vow of chastity. Thus nuns from convents dissolved after the Act, in the later months of the dissolution of 1539–40, were prohibited from marrying. Nuns from the dissolutions of 1536 and the early months of 1539 who had married were prosecuted in the church courts for incest and their husbands were allowed to divorce them. The Act was set aside in 1549 and by 1554 about 15–20 per cent of former nuns had married, though inevitably it was the younger and more junior women who did so. Few abbesses or prioresses married; two who did were the heads of the Lincolnshire Cistercian nunneries of Legbourne and Gokewell.

Under the Acts which dissolved the religious houses, former members of the orders were granted pensions. These were intended to keep them, but many of the pensioners must have been in considerable financial straits. Those who had less than £5 a year were in difficulties from the outset, and with the inflation of the 1540s their position can only have worsened. Most nuns had pensions of £2–3 a year, while most monks had £5–6. It might just have been possible to live on £2 10s. in 1542, but by 1552 £7 10s would have been necessary to maintain the same standard of living. Only 12 per cent of former nuns had pensions of more than £5 a year, and only 2 per cent of more than £10. A number of abbots and priors had pensions of £200 or £300 a year, but very few abbesses or prioresses received similar amounts. Abbess Bodenham of Wilton received £100 a year and Abbess Zouch of Shaftesbury £133 6s. 8d. After 1552 the payment of all pensions over £10 stopped and other payments fell into arrears, increasing the financial hardship of the pensioners. Pensions were paid as of right; even the prioress of Littlemore near Oxford got a pension of £6 13s. 4d., despite it being known that she had an illegitimate daughter whose dowry she had supplied out of the nunnery's property.

Women were more dependent upon pensions than men because of the lack of alternative employment for ex-nuns. Though English nuns had traditionally been recruited from the daughters of the rich and well connected, not all had families to whom they could turn for protection. Many men were successful in finding ecclesiastical positions, often as parish priests, sometimes as higher ecclesiastical officers, like bishops to the newly created dioceses, but there was no such place for women in the reformed church. In 1554 a census was taken of ex-religious to whom pensions were paid. In Lincoln, the diocese which had been most densely populated with religious houses, there were 160 former monks and 101 former nuns. Many of these nuns were too old, ill or poor to go to the census places and had to send someone else in their stead.

A few nuns found patrons. Joan Dean, a nun from Syon abbey, where the nuns had a reputation for their learning, became governess in the household of Sir George Gifford. Lady Catherine Bulkeley, abbess of Godstow abbey near Oxford, returned to her family home at Cheadle in Cheshire, and was able to afford to set up her own household. She lived in the parsonage and was responsible for rebuilding and glazing the chancel of the church there. Presumably she had some financial support from her family as well as her pension of £50 a year. Gabrielle Shelton, a nun from the fashionable convent at Barking, lived with her father in his new house of Carrow Priory in Norfolk, which he had bought from the crown.

Many members of dissolved religious orders stayed in the vicinity of their convents, sometimes setting up house with other sisters, or being taken in by their families or by philanthropically minded laypeople. Sempringham, the headquarters of the Gilbertine order, which had linked male and female houses, still had ten former monks and ten former nuns living in the parish in 1553. Two former Dominican nuns lived together at Walsingham, and a number of the nuns from the convent at Elstow settled nearby in Bedford. Some nuns joined sister houses on the continent, and a group of Brigettine sisters from Syon set up a house in Flanders, returning to England in 1557 under Queen Mary and going back to Flanders at her death in 1558.

Nunneries after the Reformation

Monasticism, both male and female, has always been subject to reform and reorganization; the variety of religious orders at the time of the Reformation was the result of a continuing process of seeking a holier rule by which to live. The Cluniacs were reformed Benedictines and the Cistercians were reformed Cluniacs, and the orders of friars were founded in response to irreligion in the cities. The Protestant Reformation caused a tremendous upheaval in western European monasticism: England was not the only country where it effectively came to an end, though in Germany there were a number of successful transitions to Protestant monasticism, with some Lutheran orders. But this upheaval did not interrupt the process of reform and renewal within the Roman Catholic regular orders. Furthermore, the Counter-Reformation, or Catholic Reformation (as distinct from the Protestant Reformation), gave rise to new ideas about monasticism. From these ideas arose the Jesuit order, founded by Ignatius Loyola in 1540, Francis de Sales's Order of the Visitation, founded in 1610, and Vincent de Paul's Sisters of Charity, founded in 1633.

Despite the fact that England was cut off from these movements by the proscription of Roman Catholicism, English monasticism was not. Some English monks and nuns joined other houses of their orders in France and the Spanish Netherlands (Belgium). Only the Brigettines and the Carthusians were able to retain a corporate identity. Indeed, the Brigettine house from Syon abbey survived intact, to return to England in 1861, having settled first in Flanders and then in Portugal. In 1622 it was pilloried in a pamphlet written by a sailor who claimed to have been a lay brother there for two and a half years. He said that there were forty or fifty nuns in the convent, of whom all but five were English, as well as three friars and a drunk. He remarked that the nuns were less noble than they had been, being mainly 'recusants' daughters of the meaner sort, and silly tender-hearted chamber maids'. He claimed that the convent had a fortune amounting to £10,000 which was lent out at interest in Antwerp, and that their chastity was as 'scarce and penurious as their poverty is plenteous'.

By the 1590s the Brigettine convent was the only English house for women, so in 1596 Lady Mary Percy decided to establish a Benedictine congregation in Brussels. So successful was this that further houses were established in Ghent (1624), Boulogne (1652), Dunkirk (1662) and Ypres (1665). These houses were organized on pre-Reformation lines, but under the influence of Counter-Reformation spirituality. A powerful inspiration was the fate of the Roman Catholics who had been executed for their faith in England, especially the three women executed during Queen Elizabeth's reign. During the seventeenth century, twenty-one new foundations for English women were established on the continent and English nuns outnumbered English monks, which had never been the case before 1539, the number of nuns peaking in the late seventeenth century.

By the mid-seventeenth century, there were more English convents of Poor Clares (female Franciscans and one of the foremost contemplative orders for women) on the continent than there ever had been in England. This was in part due to the work of Mary Ward (1585–1645), of whom we shall hear more later, who joined a Poor Clare convent at St Omer in 1606 and decided to found a house for English women. In 1607, a gift of land at Gravelines having been secured, the convent was opened. By 1611 it was too small and a new building was erected partly with the nuns' own labour. By 1619 there were so many nuns that it was decided to found another house near Artois; and during the 1620s three more houses were founded, two of them in Ireland. During the mid-eighteenth century the order declined somewhat, but in the 1740s it had thirteen novices from England and Ireland. Houses of Franciscan and Dominican nuns were founded on the continent and survived until the French Revolution, when they transferred to England.

English women were attracted not only to the old, pre-Reformation orders, but to the reformed orders which were founded in response to the Catholic Reformation. There had been no Carmelite nuns in England before the Reformation. In 1562 the order was reformed by Teresa of Avila, and several English houses of Discalced Carmelites, as the new order was known, were established abroad in the early years of the seventeenth century.

The most remarkable of the women who preserved English conventual life was Mary Ward. Originally a member of the Poor Clares, in 1609 she founded her own order, the Institute of Mary (later the Institute of the Blessed Virgin Mary), modelled on the Jesuits and based upon the idea of mobility, flexibility and female leadership. Other women on the continent modelled communities on aspects of the Jesuit rule, but this was the only missionary order for women. The nuns were not required, as in closed orders, to hear the offices (the daily religious services), and their superior was a woman, without, as in most continental orders, having to come under the jurisdiction of a bishop. The order centred its activities on household religion, and the nuns wore no habits and carried money, most unusual among Roman Catholic orders. One James Wadsworth, who claimed to have been sold as a slave to the Moors and had various other adventures, wrote in 1629 that there were then 200 'Jesuitesses', as they were known, in colleges in St Omer, Liège and Cologne. He said that, despite the disapproval of the Pope, Mary Ward was trying to establish new houses in Rome and Vienna, and that the nuns were daily expected in England.

Mary Ward was superior of the order from its foundation in 1609 until her death in 1645. The nuns were highly educated women who were dedicated to preserving Roman Catholicism through learning, often working as teachers. Many of them had studied classical languages and the new sciences. They aroused much opposition from the Catholic hierarchy, especially from the English Jesuits, and in 1631 the Institute, then consisting of 300 nuns, was suppressed. Thanks to Mary Ward's personal efforts it was refounded on a less ambitious scale, placing less emphasis on the independence of the nuns. Mary Ward's own interest was in preserving Roman Catholicism in England, and nuns had been travelling there from 1615. She herself returned to England and in 1643 was living with a few companions at Heworth, outside York. She died there in 1645, but the small community survived until 1650.

One of Mary Ward's companions, Frances Bedingfield (1616–1704), established a school at Hammersmith, just west of London, in 1669, and another near York not long after. The anti-Catholic fury of the Popish Plot in 1679 led to the closure of the Yorkshire school and convent and the imprisonment of some of the nuns, but enough of them survived to be able to take advantage of James II's dispensation for members of the regular orders. In 1686 Frances Bedingfield bought a house in York and there established the Bar Convent. The convent was always small, with often only ten nuns and about thirty or forty girls in the school, from whom most of the nuns were recruited. Apart from running the school, the nuns acted as spiritual directors to the local Catholic population and dispensed medicines and provided nursing care for poor Catholics. They also had contacts with the local business community, lending out money at interest, though the declining number of professions in the later eighteenth century meant that the convent fell into financial difficulties. These, and political problems on the continent, meant that the Bar Convent more or less lost contact with its continental sister houses.

Catholic conversions in England began to increase and there was even a small community of Catholic convert gentlewomen in Islington in the early eighteenth century. But on the continent the total number of recruits to the English orders in France and Belgium began to decline in number in the eighteenth century. The decline is usually attributed to the effects of the Enlightenment. However, it was almost entirely confined to the male religious orders and to the contemplative female orders such as the Benedictines and the Carmelites. Recruits to the active female orders which ran orphanages, schools, hospitals and homes for fallen women and the old increased in number. The final irony came with the French Revolution when the religious orders were expelled from France and sought refuge in England. Only the convent of the Brigettines from Syon could be said to be actually returning to England because all the others had been founded abroad after the dissolution.

Protestant Communities

It was not only Catholic women who were attracted by the idea of separating from the world to live in a community with other like-minded women. But the idea required careful implementation in order that it be not confused with the Roman Catholic religious orders in a period of vigorous antagonism to Roman Catholicism. Even as late as 1694, Mary Astell's *Serious Proposal to the Ladies* was treated with some suspicion on the grounds that it resembled a proposal for a Popish convent. Her scheme for a community of women so attracted 'a certain great lady' that she volunteered £10,000 toward its implementation. The lady was supposed by some to be Princess Anne (later Queen Anne) and by others to be Lady Elizabeth Hastings (1682–1739), both firm Protestants. Bishop Burnet remonstrated against the project because it looked like an attempt to reintroduce Catholic orders. Mary Astell's scheme was an attempt not to create a life apart from the world, but rather to provide an education for women which would better equip them within the world.

Mary Astell's serious proposal came to nothing, but there were a number of women's communities which did actually exist. Perhaps the best known of these was the community at Little Gidding, where the Farrar family, numbering over thirty people in the 1620s and 1630s, most of whom were women, dedicated themselves to Anglican religious devotions and charitable works among the poor. They followed the Prayer Book services, at a time when the authority of such ceremonies was being challenged, and engaged in theological discussion. The community was satirized as an Arminian nunnery, and for rewarding the poor with money and dinners after they had been catechized. It nevertheless impressed many contemporaries as an example of practical devotion. The community was broken up in the Civil War because of its association with the unpopular religious policies of Archbishop Laud.

Lettuce Viscountess Falkland (*c.* 1611–47) spent her four years of widowhood in the 1640s at her late husband's home at Great Tew, Oxfordshire, in pious meditation and charitable works. The house was described as 'a university bound in a lesser volume'. Before the war Great Tew had been a centre for intellectual life through the interests of Lord Falkland. The Misses Kemeys at Naish Court, near Bristol, kept a devout communal life in the 1690s and gave asylum to the non-juring Bishop Ken. It was not only rich women who might congregate in this way. In 1738 Mary Wandesford left money for ten poor Church of England spinsters of York to 'retire from the hurry and bustle of the world into a religious house of Protestant retirement', wording which suggests an order rather than an invitation.

One eighteenth-century development in religious communities was the arrival in England of the Moravian brethren in 1728. They managed their churches through committees which had both male and female members. They established communities in various places in the 1740s. At Fulneck, Yorkshire, land was made over to them, and in 1742 they erected three buildings in a line – a house for men, a chapel and a house for women. Later a widows' house, a school and two family houses were added. Mrs Lybbe Powys visited the community in 1757 and described how men and women were segregated in church and different clothes were worn by married and unmarried women. They were not a women's community like those we have already looked at, but they were a community in which separation of the sexes was a fundamental principle and where women both lived and worked away from men. They visited sick women, tended poor women and ran a school for girls, and women travelled around preaching in the 1740s.

There is a distinction between the communities of women who gathered for devotional purposes and those formed or proposed primarily to promote education. Many opponents of Roman Catholicism found it difficult to dissociate religious communities from Catholic convents, as can be seen in the very similar criticisms of Mary Astell's proposal and of the community at Little Gidding. Nevertheless, the existence of communities of devout women, not necessarily tied by formal vows, but with an understanding that they were dedicating themselves to a life of the spirit, does indicate that the absence of nunneries in the period between the dissolution in 1539 and the appearance of the first Anglican communities in the 1840s was a real lack in women's lives.

CHAPTER THIRTEEN

The Practice of Christianity

Women in early modern society had a certain amount of independence as to their religion. Most denominations debated the extent to which a wife or daughter was obliged to obey her conscience rather than her husband or father in matters of faith. There is plenty of evidence of women who followed their own consciences even where it meant challenging the authority of a husband or father. In the 1670s Agnes Beaumont (1652–1720) was cast out of her house by her father for her religious activities and Anne Wentworth (*fl.* 1670s) by her husband for hers. Anne Wentworth wrote of her willingness to return to her husband, 'provided I may have my just and necessary liberty to attend a more than ordinary call of God'. The consequences could be tragic. At about the same time Susannah Slater, wife of a Spitalfields weaver, petitioned to be released from the mad-house in Lambeth where she had been incarcerated for seven years without being able to see her children, friends or relations. She had been committed there by her husband at the instigation of his relations when she refused to leave the Church of England for the Baptists.

During the period 1500–1760 western Christendom was transformed from a single universal church, dissidence from which was equatable with treason, into a group of pluralistic societies in which the state defined the limits of religious practice within a broadly Christian framework (with exceptions to include Jews in some European states). This transformation accompanied a revolution in European thought and society and had a radical effect upon the lives of men. Here we consider how far the Reformation and the upheavals of the 1640s and 1650s made a difference to women's lives and the practice of their religion.

Women and the Reformation

The Reformation was a series of fundamental challenges to the spiritual, intellectual and temporal authority of the Roman Catholic church, resulting in the creation of a variety of alternative Christian theologies, known collectively as Protestantism. In those countries where Protestantism was adopted, the practice of religion was transformed, though we do not know what proportion of the population actually understood and adoped the new theology. There was also a fundamental intellectual shift towards a whole set of individualistic values, elevating the individual's own relationship with God above the institutions of the church.

The effects of Protestantization upon local communities have been better studied for Germany than for England, and it is clear that there were markedly different responses in different parts of Germany. In the Lutheran town of Zwickau in Saxony, a series of reforms was enacted by the town council, aimed at creating a godly society in the town by eliminating sources of moral ill. A girls' school was established in 1526 in a former friary, though it taught little more than reading, writing and housewifely arts. The two vocations which women might enter independently – prostitution and the convent – were eliminated. The city brothel was closed down and the building sold, and the women were ordered to be instructed in the new faith by the pastor. Prostitution was driven underground. Most of the nuns were Beguines, semi-professed sisters who engaged in good works. The sisters, the majority of whom were elderly, continued to live together on the proceeds of the sale of the beguinage, and worked as seamstresses. Prostitutes and nuns made up only a small fraction of the total number of women in Zwickau, and the changes which took place in the lives of other women have less to do with the Reformation than with contemporary economic changes. The Reformation reduced women's opportunities for communal participation. Female gilds and religious organizations were suppressed and cults of female saints were prohibited. But the women of Zwickau did not receive all this passively, for the town was one of those where radical Anabaptist beliefs gained support. The suppression of the Anabaptists in 1529 left women's lives considerably more restricted than they had been before the Lutheran Reformation.

The evidence for England suggests similar devlopments in the early stages of the Reformation. Urban areas took to the new religion with greater zest than rural areas, and younger people adopted the new ways with more enthusiasm than their elders.

There was no marked association of class or gender with either the old or the new religion. In 1536 women were prominent in a riot at St Nicholas's priory at Exeter against the demolition of the rood loft. In Devon and Cornwall in 1548–9 the rioters in favour of traditional practices were chiefly men, and so were the most active Protestants, but women were to be found among both groups. Agnes Priest, a poor woman from Boyton, Cornwall, in 1558 attacked oral confession, pardons and purchased prayers, denied purgatory and declared holy bread and water to be abominations.

By Edward vi's reign there was relatively little support for traditional Roman Catholic practice. There was no great popular resurgence of enthusiasm for the old ways with the reintroduction of Roman Catholicism in Queen Mary's reign, nor much sign of any hankering after them during the protracted negotiations of the Elizabethan settlement. Nevertheless, many people were in a state of great spiritual uncertainty. Father John Gerard, a Roman Catholic missionary priest, who spent a great deal of time in England in Elizabeth's reign, wrote in 1588,

> During the time I moved about freely, I reconciled to the church many fathers and mothers of families, more than twenty in all. . . . In addition I received a large number of servants and poorer people . . . and, through the grace of God, I steadied many tottering souls in their allegiance, and heard numerous general confessions.[1]

His task may have been made easier by virtue of the fact that it took a long time for Protestantism to be widely assimilated into people's private beliefs (as opposed to their practices). As late as 1569, for example, Isabel Ward of Micklegate, York, asked for prayers for our Lady to be said at her funeral.

Before the Reformation there were many communal religious activities for women, often concerned with the cults of saints. Between 1529 and 1531 the shrine of St Sidewell at Morebath, Devon, attracted gifts of all shapes and sizes, from Eleanor Nichol's gift of a wedding ring, to Alison Sayer's girdle and beads, and Margaret Holcombe's 5s. towards gilding. Women were often custodians of chapels and responsible for the appearance in public of the image of the saint to whom the chapel was dedicated. Pre-Reformation churches had large quantities of textiles, the care of which fell to laywomen. In the 1490s a woman was paid by the churchwardens of Ashburton, Devon, for washing and mending the linen used in the church and for making surplices, and such

---

[1] *The Hunted Priest: the Autobiography of John Gerard*, Philip Caraman (transl.), Fontana, 1959, p. 41.

activities must have been going on all over the country. A survey of the goods held by churches in the northern counties in 1552 shows what large quantities of vestments, ceremonial clothing for the clergy, altar cloths and textiles associated with the administration of the Mass were required in even humble churches.

Richer women were often benefactresses of religious institutions, and they endowed male monasteries as well as convents. Chantries (endowments for the commemoration of the dead) allowed endless opportunities for spending by the devout, and at more or less any level, from a chapel with a priest to say Mass in perpetuity, to a sacrament lamp or a single Mass at a charge of a few pence. Though their heyday was the fourteenth and fifteenth centuries, they were still being founded right up to the Reformation and they were very numerous: there were over a hundred in London alone. There were many in the countryside too – most of the more important parishes in Buckinghamshire had chantries, for example. Women might tend chantry chapels, but they could not say Masses, though nuns sometimes took part in Masses for the dead. Sir Thomas Lovell, an early-sixteenth-century Chancellor of the Exchequer and a benefactor of the Augustinian canonesses at Haliwell in Shoreditch, gave the priory a chapel where he was buried and where the nuns were to pray for his soul.

There were also religious gilds, associations of laypeople, men or women, who dedicated themselves to serve a particular saint by means of their devotions and charitable work. In the late fifteenth century, Mrs Jane Wyat founded a gild to maintain a school and almshouse in Oundle, Northamptonshire. Women might also work as lay sisters (women who were under less strict vows than those of fully professed nuns), running hospitals and leper-houses, as well as doing domestic work in the larger and better-endowed convents.

Once the new religion was established, women might go to hear different preachers in different churches, but otherwise there was a marked reduction in the range of public activities open to them. Increasingly, their religious duties were restricted to the household, to the maintenance of godliness at home, and to the education of children and servants in the true religion. But if Protestantism reduced women's opportunities for communal religious activity, why did so many of them adopt the new religion? The evidence of France – where the spread of Protestantism owed much to the influence of French noblewomen, who espoused the new religion and acted as patrons to Protestant pastors – prompts the question: did Protestantism have a particular appeal to women of the leisured classes?

Certainly the Protestant women whose careers are charted in Foxe's *Book of Martyrs* achieved a very considerable degree of spiritual advance from the new religion, though this was also a consequence of the testing circumstances in which they had to practise their faith. Were the spiritual rewards of being able to establish a personal, private and direct relationship with God sufficient to compensate for lack of the old communal, public worship, in which women had access to confessors and a multiplicity of activities that were specifically feminine, not to mention the intercession of the Virgin Mary and the female saints? Educated women certainly found satisfaction in charting the progress of their spiritual lives under the new regime. Confessors might be replaced by close friendships with ministers who acted as spiritual mentors. Many women recorded their debt to particular preachers and to the authors of religious works. Protestant ministers themselves often shied away from the kind of dependent relationship which had existed between confessors and devout women, a relationship particularly accessible to the high-status woman who might be patron to a priest or even have a private chaplain. But this did not stop ministers from having close friendships with women; friendships in which women were able to explore and expand their spiritual lives. The new religion encouraged women to think for themselves not only about the nature of God, but also about the nature of their own faith.

Both major reforming movements and smaller radical congregations re-examined the institution of marriage. The reformers removed marriage from the list of sacraments, thus eliminating the principal obstacle to its dissolution. The Church of England was, in the end, the only major European Protestant church not to allow divorce. To ensure the maintenance of morality, even though marriage was no longer a sacrament, the church used its own discipline, the church courts, to punish offenders, and matrimonial and sexual offences remained the chief concerns of the church courts.

Clerical marriage was another vexed subject. The continental reformers all rejected clerical celibacy, but Henry VIII never allowed clerical marriage. Indeed, it became a felony in 1539 and remained so until 1549 when priests were allowed to take wives. The predicament of the wives discarded by clergymen in this period was described in a pamphlet defending the marriage of the clergy:

For when they had thus separated the wife from her own husband, then were there no small married men of birth (whom I could name) that fell to wooing of some priests' wives and would have made them their whores if the poor women had not resisted their devilish enticements.[1]

During Edward vi's reign members of the clergy did marry, but not to a uniform extent: in Essex a high proportion of clergymen took wives, in York a low proportion (only four of the ministers in the city, which had forty-two parishes). When Queen Mary came to the throne in 1553, the Act allowing clerical marriage was revoked and members of the clergy who had taken wives were deprived of their posts. Eighteen of the sixty-four ex-monks in the diocese of Norwich had taken wives and all but two shed them during Mary's reign. If the clergy divorced and did penance they might remain priests, but they were not allowed to return to their old positions, having to move to new parishes. It proved to be difficult to prevent such people from keeping contact with their wives and families, and at Elizabeth's accession most were reunited with their wives.

At Elizabeth's accession there was no formal declaration that the clergy might marry, and whether they were allowed to do so remained in some doubt, especially after it was revealed how much the queen herself objected to clerical marriage in her famous remark to Mrs Parker, wife of the Archbishop of Canterbury: 'Madam I may not call you; mistress I am ashamed to call you; and so I know not what to call you.' Nevertheless, many members of the clergy did marry, and in 1553 an Act was passed legitimizing the children of married clergy and recognizing the right of the wives of clergymen to a dower. The 39 Articles of 1571 actually declared that it was lawful for the clergy to marry. Despite this recognition, clerical wives were a group of women who went even more unnoticed than most other wives. Unlike other women they did not acquire their husbands' status; in the case of bishops who were peers, this put them in a particularly anomalous position. To be the child of a clergyman continued to carry stigma into the seventeenth century, and daughters of clergymen often married members of the clergy. There was, especially in the early years of clerical marriage, some concern that the clergy should have suitable wives, and in 1559 a royal injunction ordered that, because of 'the lack of discreet and sober behaviour in many ministers of the church, both in choosing their wives and in indiscreet living with them', no minister or deacon might marry 'without the advice and allowance first had upon good examination by the bishop of the same diocese and the justices of the peace of the same shire'.

[1] James Sawtry, *The Defence of the Mariage of Preistes*, London, 1541.

The Reformation, then, was not on the surface of great advantage to ordinary women. It substituted a varied communal religious life for one whose public activities were much more restricted. It did offer the chance of a greater spiritual autonomy, but it created a group of women, both former nuns and wives of clergymen, who were treated most cruelly under the legislation concerning the marriage of the clergy and former members of the regular orders.

Women and the Church Establishment

In the Church of England women were excluded from all positions of power, both clerical and lay. Very occasionally they held positions as churchwardens or sextons. Members of the laity had the power to appoint clergymen to particular parishes, though this had always been theologically somewhat dubious. This right was transferable in just the same way as manorial rights or other forms of property, so a female sole heir to an estate might inherit the power to appoint clergy to one or more parishes. Women might exercise some power, or at least some choice, over a small number of ecclesiastical appointments (though queens had power over a great many). Women were perfectly entitled to appoint vicars to benefices if they were patrons, but it became extremely unusual for them to do so. Maud de Rochechouart and Margaret le Despenser made presentations to benefices in Yorkshire in their own right in the thirteenth and fourteenth centuries, but by the sixteenth the only women to do so did it in association with a man. One such was Isabelle Tunstall, who made an appointment with Brian Tunstall to Fosten-in-the-Wolds. Lady Rachel Russell in the late seventeenth century took a serious interest in the patronage of the churches on her family's Hampshire estates, and there is a letter of hers discussing the suitability of Mr Swayne to be rector of Kingsworthy and vicar of Micheldever. Given the number of benefices in lay hands and the likelihood of an inheritance passing to a woman, there were potentially 1,000 ecclesiastical benefices in the hands of women in the eighteenth century. We do not know how far these women exercised their rights to make appointments. Wealthy noblewomen also had private chaplains and tutors for their children; these appointments were often a way of sheltering men whose views were unacceptable to the church at large.

The possession of the patronage of a benefice also conferred the responsibility for the repair of the chancel of the church, for failure to do which the patron could be presented in the church courts.

How many of the women who expressed their piety by building or refurbishing churches were actually doing so because the responsibility fell on them as patrons is impossible to estimate, but devout churchwomen were considerable benefactresses. Alice Dudley gave £250 for rebuilding the church of St Giles-in-the-Fields in London in 1631, and paid for the paving of the church and chancel. She also provided altar rails, luxurious hangings, Communion plate and a Turkey carpet to be spread over the altar on weekdays. These gifts made a very clear doctrinal statement of support for the Laudians who were trying to raise the standards of ceremony in the Church of England. With the reaction against Laudian innovations and the arrival of a new rector in the parish in 1642, the costly hangings were sold and the money used for poor relief. She also gave sets of Communion plate to numerous Warwickshire churches near her family home at Stoneleigh. By the eighteenth century it had become less fashionable to express piety by church building, though in the 1730s Lady Foley completed the church at Great Witley, Worcestershire, which her husband had planned. But women continued to give plate to churches in large quantities.

For many rich women, devotion might be advertised by various kinds of charitable endowment: almshouses, hospitals and schools. They also commemorated their families and friends with fine funerary monuments which recognized both the virtues of the deceased and the piety and beneficence of the donor. Even grander than a monument was to build or refurbish a family chapel. Often these had been chantry chapels before the Reformation, and afterwards were converted into chapels to contain the monuments to a particular family with vaults beneath for the bodies. Bridget Morrison of Cassiobury built the Morrison chapel in the church of St Mary, Watford, in 1595. Lady Sherard rebuilt the south aisle of the church at Stapleford, Leicestershire, in the 1640s to house the monument to her husband, and to serve as a family chapel to later generations.

After the Reformation the opportunities for all but rich women to contribute to activities connected with the church were reduced, and the level of participation in worship that they were permitted remained much the same. Women might not conduct ceremonies in the Roman Catholic, Anglican and most nonconformist churches. They might *in extremis* administer baptism in those churches which believed in infant baptism. They participated in many church services on much the same terms as laymen: in Communion, in confirmation, in marriage, and in baptism as sponsor or godparent. They were excluded from the ceremonies for ordaining priests or clergymen. Only in the ceremony of churching were women unequivocally the centre. Some twenty-eight days after the birth of a child, a woman went to church with a number of female companions and often the midwife for a service conducted by the minister.

Had women more to gain from participating in the established church or from following their consciences into churches which were not tolerated? Before looking at women's participation in these other churches, we might consider what advantages integration in the established church could confer. It allowed women access to ministers and to scripture learning. It probably exposed their lives to view in the community in which they lived, and thus gave them access to the help and support of the community if it was needed. It gave them access to the schools, almshouses and outdoor relief administered in the parish. It also exposed them to the censure of the church, the churchwardens' inspection and the risk of being brought before the ecclesiastical courts.

It is sometimes argued that Puritanism (by which I mean the wing of the established church in which preaching was emphasized at the expense of ceremony and the sacraments) offered women symbols of emotional gratification by giving their role in the family a greater significance through the emphasis on conversion and personal influence over others. However, it is hard to associate this with Puritanism alone. By the end of the seventeenth century, these values had permeated much of English society. It was only the very rich, the very poor and those strongly committed to other religious denominations who lived outside these values.

Early Puritans

From the very earliest days of the Reformation there were people in the established church who felt that the process of reform had not gone far enough, and that the established church was insufficiently Protestant in its theology and practice. These people came to be known as Puritans. In the 1560s women took part in the riots over attempts to enforce uniformity in ceremonial, especially the wearing of vestments by the clergy, something to which many Puritans objected deeply. Under Queen Elizabeth there were meetings of like-minded people, both laity and ministers, apart from the usual church services. These meetings, for prayer and preaching, were for those who felt that the orthodox services of the church provided insufficient spiritual food for the godly, and women were very active in them. At Dedham in Essex, one such meeting debated the question of whether a woman might pray publicly when she had greater spiritual gifts than her husband.

During the first half of the seventeenth century, there was a continuous stream of objections to the established church. Sometimes resistance amounted to no more than failing to attend the local parish church, or objecting to particular ceremonies. In 1617 thirty-six people were cited at Manchester for failing to kneel to receive the Eucharist, and fourteen of them were women. In 1626 Katherine Chidley refused to be churched. Sometimes it amounted to conducting alternative services, something which was taken very seriously as evidence of a challenge to the authority of both church and state. In Ormskirk, Lancashire, in 1630, twelve parishioners were charged with frequenting a conventicle, and five of these were women; in 1637 the same charge was brought against fifteen parishioners, and this time twelve were women. In 1632 forty-one members of John Lathrop's Independent congregation in London were imprisoned, and many of them remained in gaol for eighteen months. Sara Jones was one of these and there may have been other women members.

By the early seventeenth century, some of these groups had come to the view that their position was incompatible with continued membership of the established church and they took the radical step of separation. Initially, such separatist churches existed clandestinely, until finally they were driven abroad. Women were important in founding several such congregations, like the Independent congregation formed in 1638 in Rotterdam and the Broadmead Baptist church in Bristol. In theory, at least, these congregations offered more scope for female religious gifts, since there was less emphasis on the sacraments, ceremonies and a male priesthood, and more stress upon leading the godly life and its example to others. But there is no record of any woman being allowed a position of authority in any of these churches. The process of persecution had the effect upon radical Protestantism of making it a more interior religion. As the prospect of securing Puritan reform within the church receded in the 1620s and 1630s, radical Protestants turned away from organizational structures to their own souls.

Puritans and Sectaries in the 1640s and 1650s

In 1640 England was a society in which religious observance impinged on everyone and belief was an important part of many people's lives. When the Civil War began in 1642, everyone was nominally a member of the Church of England except for a few Catholics, who endured spasmodic persecution, and a few radical Protestants, some of whom left the country for the Netherlands or New England. Church attentance was required by law, and dissidence from the established church could lead to serious punishments. Women were essentially passive members, involved neither in running the church nor in preaching the Word.

During the 1640s and 1650s, with the relaxation of press censorship and the disappearance of the church courts which enforced religious uniformity, the religious life of the country was transformed. For the first time people were able to speak in public and to print views about religion which would previously have led to them being punished by imprisonment or mutilation if detected by the authorities. What is particularly noticeable is how many of those who preached and wrote pamphlets were from groups outside the traditional learned men, who had monopolized public discussion of doctrine and ecclesiastical practice. Artisans, gentlemen, merchants and women preached, prayed and printed their views for a larger audience. The conservative Presbyterian Thomas Edwards listed some of them: 'smiths, tailors, shoemakers, pedlars, weavers etc. There are also some women preachers . . . who keep constant lectures, preaching weekly to many men and women.'

The actual number of prominent women was relatively small and they were much disapproved of. In the 1640s there was the blind London preacher, Mary Lake; the Baptist woman who preached at Brastead in Kent; and the woman in King's Lynn who denied the truth of the Scriptures. Two women in London, a lace-maker from Cheapside and a major's wife from Old Bailey, did a double act, on one occasion preaching to a congregation of 1,000 people. There was a group of women who held it unlawful to hear a man preach. This spirit spread beyond the sectarian fringes. In 1644 the meeting of the French church in London, a Protestant enough institution having fled from Catholic France, passed a motion expressing regret that 'one of our dear sisters should seem to wish to break away from our body to form a separate sect at this time of reformation to which God in his mercy has called us'.

In the 1650s it was public displays by women that were most

noticeable. The woman who stripped naked during a sermon at Whitehall in 1652 by Cromwell's chaplain, Peter Sterry; Martha Simmonds (1624–65), who walked barefoot through Colchester in 1654 in sackcloth and ashes; Elizabeth Fletcher (*c.* 1638–58), who the same year walked naked through the streets of Oxford for a sign; and the women who accompanied James Naylor into Bristol in 1656; all were deliberately making public demonstrations of their faith. In 1652 Sybil Bryant of Inglesham, Wiltshire, was indicted at the Wiltshire quarter sessions for going into the church with an iron cleaver, interrupting the minister while he was reading a psalm, and saying to him, 'Come down false prophet, Baal's priest, out of the idol's temple.' She was in court for other similar interruptions later in the year, and said that she scorned to obey the ink and paper of the charge.

These public displays by women were much disapproved of, even in the sects. There was little male support for women preaching, even though it was a logical extension of the widely held sectarian belief that earthly learning was not needed to give spiritual weight to a person's utterances. Male sectaries did not advocate, as two women did in a pamphlet of 1655, 'we are all one, both male and female, in Jesus Christ.' Men's response to the idea of women preaching was often of the lowest order and provoked the use of terms like 'usurpation'. It was put about that women who had preached, or had heard a woman preaching, gave birth to monsters.

Even in groups which ostensibly admitted equality between male and female members, women's actions were strictly circumscribed. I can find no instance of a church permitting women any authority over men. Among the Baptists and, later, the Quakers, women preached and held meetings (commonly for women only), but there are no cases of women having positions as elders, taking part in the government of the church, or being permitted to administer the sacraments.

Women became braver at challenging male authority in religious matters. A London clergyman, preaching a sermon on sin and the Devil, found himself challenged by a nurse who said there was no such thing as sin, or the Devil, or temptation, or the Holy Ghost, or Scriptures. A Baptist woman asserted that she was as good as Christ. There is also the curious story of the Quaker woman who was taken into the house of a Westminster merchant out of charity and pawned some of his plate. On being questioned she said, 'it was superfluity to him but she did it to relieve the necessities of the poor.'

These public actions were for only a small minority of women. Women were not drawn in the greatest numbers to those congregations which ostensibly offered them most freedom. Much more numerically significant was the solid body of female support for the moderate Presbyterian and Independent ministers who occupied most parishes in the 1640s and 1650s. Such ministers often encouraged women in the exercise of their faith, in the fostering of it in the household and in the idea of their spiritual progress. Women's preaching aroused opposition, but the conduct of devotional exercises was uncontentious, an extension of women's domestic role as preservers of faith. Elizabeth Hapton, an elderly Presbyterian who lived in Oxford, used, during the 1650s, to have meetings of students at her house. She would read prayers herself, and other spiritual exercises were performed before the attenders were fed with gruel.

Women's participation in congregations may be seen in testimonies. These were accounts of their lives, laying particular stress upon their spiritual development and their conversion, which people had to deliver to the congregation as a condition of entry to certain churches. The applicant had to stand up in the church and give an oral autobiography. Some of these testimonies were written down by the minister. In them we can hear the voices of people who may well have been illiterate, many of whom were women. Naturally, they spoke about the things which were most important to them. There were certain recurrent themes, especially their perception of how misfortune was a test sent by God to tempt them and to be resisted as a measure of their faith. There are frequent references to the tribulations brought by their children, though, interestingly enough, women rarely mention their husbands. There are two very moving accounts by women of the effect that the war had upon their lives. One spoke of how she saw the enemy (the royalists) kill her husband and her child before her eyes. Another said that

My husband was killed by the rebels, which I feared was by my sins . . . and then the enemies came upon us, the cannon bullets flew over my head, and in a few days I was turned out of doors, with my child in my arms.[1]

Some women found it easier to write about religion. There are the polemical works of women like Katherine Chidley (*fl.*1641–53) and the prophecies of women like Mary Cary (*fl.*1636–53). But there were also works which had a less contentious purpose, like the

[1] John Rogers, *Ohel or Beth-Shemesh*, London, 1653, chapter 6, p. (11).

writings of Elizabeth Warren (*fl*.1640s) or Dorothy Burch (*fl*.1646), catechisms, collections of prayers, meditations and spiritual advice, often quite orthodox, unlike the women preachers.

The best known of the small number of women who were attracted to the public exercise of new religious beliefs and practices were the Quaker women. Many religious beliefs were tolerated during the 1640s and 1650s, but it was possible to go too far and the Quakers frequently did so. They did not become pacifist good citizens until much later in the century; in the 1650s they raged with religious fury. Ann Blaykling, a Quaker, was imprisoned in 1654 for preaching, and again in 1656 for calling a minister a greedy, dumb dog. Anne Audland was imprisoned in Banbury in 1655 accused of blasphemous words and for causing a tumult in a church. Most women going naked or barefoot for a sign were Quakers, and a third of the Quakers arrested for disrupting church services were women. In 1659, 7,000 Quaker women presented a petition to Parliament. This activity was treated with mixed reactions by the male Quaker leadership, who were sometimes actively hostile to these women.

Nonconformity and Dissent after 1660

At the restoration of the monarchy in 1660 the Church of England was re-established. Attendance at Church of England services became compulsory again and was enforced by the church-wardens until 1689. In Buckinghamshire in 1662 nearly as many women as men were presented for not attending church (not necessarily a sign of nonconformity). Many of the women who did not attend were married to men who also did not, but there are some instances of married women being cited for non-attendance, but not their husbands. The congregations established in the 1640s and 1650s had to meet clandestinely. In Bedfordshire in the 1660s, two women were admitted to the Independent congregation at Keysoe Brook End on saying that they would rather be doorkeepers at the house of God than dwell in the tents of the wicked. In Middlesex 684 people, of whom 350 were women, were prosecuted in 1684 or 1685 for attending conventicles and fined 5s. Widow Lovet was presented for attending private meetings at a house at Burnham, Bedfordshire, and for keeping her child unbaptized: she was a Quaker. Women provided the premises for conventicles – nine in the diocese of Bath and Wells, eleven in Norwich – and Ursula Adman (*fl*. 1654–69), sister of the prophet Anna Trapnel, was apprehended for holding meetings in her house in Middlesex in 1669.

Despite women's activity, many nonconformist ministers, John Bunyan for example, were unhappy about the prospect of enlarging women's participation. The Quakers were really the only group who allowed women a greater role, though even they did not achieve this painlessly. Quaker women established their own meetings during the 1660s, but these were more a vehicle for organizing charitable work than a means of participating in the government of the movement.

Congregations continued to expect postulants to give testimonies to their faith, and shy young women continued to find speaking out in the congregation a problem. At Stevington, Bedfordshire, in 1686 Mary Bell started to declare 'what she had experienced of the gracious work of the Lord', but could not continue and was taken to one side by two or three of the members, who reported back to the congregation. Discipline was strictly enforced in many congregations, perhaps more so because of the need to show total probity. Unruly members were admonished and might be cast out. Members might be excommunicated for proposing to marry unbelievers (people who were not members of an approved congregation). In 1677 Sister Searl was excommunicated from the Baptist congregation at Kensworth, Bedfordshire, for selling drink, marrying a drunkard and marrying according to the rites of the Church of England (the only legally valid form of marriage). In 1693 Sister Fowler was reprimanded in the Stevington congregation for selling light weight.

After the Toleration Act of 1689 nonconformists, with the exception of Unitarians, were allowed to worship freely, though they had to register their meeting houses and chapels. In Wiltshire, twenty-four meeting houses (chiefly dwelling houses or barns) were registered in 1689, of which fourteen were Presbyterian, one Independent, eight Baptist, and one Quaker. Four of these buildings belonged to women. Women continued to be significant as suppliers of premises, but it was only in the registrations of Quaker meeting houses that their names appear as signatories on behalf of the congregations. Catholics were not allowed to have official places of worship until 1791, and some congregations, such as the Moravians, never registered.

It is characteristic of new religious movements that women play an important part at the outset but that, as the movements became institutionalized, their role diminishes. The history of the Quakers shows this clearly, as does that of the early Methodists. The mob riots against the eighteenth-century evangelists accused them of exercising undue influence over simple people, especially 'silly women', to rob them of their savings. John Wesley himself was opposed to women preaching and in 1761 declared that Methodists did not permit them to preach; he was not opposed to them playing an active part in other ways. In 1789 he gave Sarah Mallet advice on how to conduct services, and at the time of his death in 1791 a number of women were publicly active. The need for effective evangelists and the evident talents of women like Mary Bosanquet Fletcher (1739–1815) and Sarah Crosby (1729–1804) softened Wesley's opposition, but in the period after his death, when divisions developed between different factions, opposition to women's public ministry became more prominent and in 1803 a resolution was passed forbidding women to preach.

What prompted women to play an active and public part in the early Methodist evangelization was the strength of their faith. The most famous of them is Selina Countess of Huntingdon (1707–1791), but there were many others who made an important contribution to the Methodist mission. Most of those active among the earliest Methodists were wives of prosperous men, and their role was that of teacher. There were the wives of ministers who ran women's groups for prayer and discussion, and who were encouraged to seek a wider audience for the Word. Mary Bosanquet Fletcher started by teaching her own family, extended her activities to a school or orphanage in Leytonstone, then moved to Yorkshire where she attracted considerable audiences, two or three thousand at open-air meetings. When she spoke in a church she would not occupy the pulpit. Sarah Crosby assisted her and became well known on her own account. These women travelled considerable distances on their own and had great public reputations.

There were also women of humbler origins who lacked the prestigious connections of the women in Wesley's immediate circle, and who sought to find in Methodism a new outlet for female piety. Some of these women evangelized, but because they did not leave journals or letters there is less evidence of their work. These two strands in Methodism – of the values of the prevailing political order and of proletarian activism – existed from its earliest years, but were less in evidence during Wesley's lifetime. Women were associated with both facets of the movement.

It is arguable whether Puritanism and nonconformity offered women real opportunities which they were denied in the established church. The authoritarian and patriarchal theology is at odds with a non-hierarchical church polity, and historians and theologians will always debate the question of whether the doctrine of election implies democracy among believers. It is certainly true that women were unable to establish themselves in a position of authority in any sect. But it is also true that their voices were heard to an unprecedented extent during the years of persecution, as preachers, teachers and members of congregations. In the 1640s and 1650s they entered the public world, and, by defying the requirements to conform after 1660, they remained in it. Early Methodist women were more law abiding, but they entered public life in the same spirit as earlier nonconformist women.

The Preservation of Faith

Women's qualities of spirituality were prized, and women had an important part to play in the inculcation of religious values in the home. The survival of faith under persecution was very much a female responsibility because of the importance of household religion for those who could not worship freely. Necessarily, much of the history of such survival is hidden, because it involved the practice of religion in secret, but from a few examples it is possible to see the kind of role which women played in preserving proscribed faiths. It is interesting to see how similar are the stories of women with radically different beliefs. Protestant women under Henry VIII and Queen Mary; Roman Catholic women under Edward VI and from Queen Elizabeth's reign until Catholic emancipation; and nonconformist women from the reign of Charles I until the Toleration Act of 1689, all had many experiences in common.

During the reign of Mary the survival of Protestantism owed something to the work of such women as those who visited Cranmer, Latimer and Ridley when they were in gaol in Oxford. Rose Hickman, who had learned Protestantism before Henry VIII's break with Rome, in the early months of Queen Mary's reign

did receive into our house in the city of London divers godly and well disposed Christians that were desirous to shelter themselves from the cruel persecution of those times. And we and they did table together in a chamber, keeping the doors close shut . . . as we read in the gospel the disciples of Christ did for fear of the Jews.[1]

---

[1] Joy Shakespeare and Maria Dowling, 'Religion and politics in mid Tudor England through the eyes of an English Protestant woman: the recollections of Rose Hickman', *Bulletin of the Institute of Historical Research*, 55, 1982, p. 99.

Subsequently, her husband, a merchant, fled to Antwerp leaving Rose, who was pregnant, to have her child in England. After it was born she sent to Oxford to ask the Protestant bishops imprisoned there whether she might have the child baptized by a Catholic priest. They replied that baptism was the least offensive of the Romish sacraments. She joined her husband in Antwerp, where, though it was a Catholic city, the cathedral made it much harder to check up on church attendance than in English parish churches. She had another child in Antwerp and, having discovered a secret congregation of Protestants, 'by the help of some godly women there I procured my child to be secretly carried and there to be baptised by a Protestant minister, I not knowing godfather nor godmother'.

The accounts of the women martyrs of Mary's reign given in Foxe's *Book of Martyrs* suggest that there were many women who refused to give up their Protestant beliefs and practices, and who gave one another mutual support and encouragement. Foxe refers to women of humble origins, like Mrs Trencherfield, a brewer's wife, and Elizabeth Driver who worked in the fields. Some defied their families, like the sixty-year-old Elizabeth Lawson who spent three years in gaol before her release at Queen Elizabeth's accession. On her release she found that her husband had sold all her clothes and refused to help her, even though the house and land he occupied had come with her at her marriage. Most significant of all were the forty-eight women Protestant martyrs of Henry VIII and Mary's reigns and the three Roman Catholic women executed in Elizabeth's reign.

Dorothy Hazzard, mainstay of the Baptist congregation at Broadmead in Bristol in the 1630s, spent much of her life supporting not only her own family, but also other Baptists. For example, she allowed women who were about to be confined to use her house for the birth so that they could avoid being churched. Such good women were resorted to for spiritual advice. A member of a London sectarian congregation in 1650 spoke of how, having been tempted with suicide, she sought the advice of a godly woman who lived on the moors near Leeds, 'and she opened to me the troubles of David and Job and gave me sweet comfort, saying, God is by me and I did not see him.'

Just as nonconformist women had offered safe havens in the 1620s and 1630s, Anglican women did the same in the 1640s and 1650s. Mrs Salter, a widow and sister of Bishop Brian Duppa, sheltered a number of Anglican clergymen, men who refused to give up reading the Book of Common Prayer after its proscription in 1645. Among those who came under her protection were John

Hales, fellow of Eton and a celebrated scholar. He lived at her house at Iver, Buckinghamshire, as tutor to her 'blockish' son and chaplain to the household, at a salary of £25 a year. They were joined by Henry King, bishop of Chichester, and his family, forming what was described as 'a sort of college'. This was partially dispersed in the 1650s when Hales left because he felt that a new order against sheltering malignants (royalists) made it too dangerous for Mrs Salter. However, he had no compunction about taking shelter with Hannah Dickenson, the widow of a former servant of his, at a house in Eton. We have already seen something of the part played by women in preserving nonconformity during the penal years of 1660–89, but their importance is emphasized by the large number of women recorded in the lists of members of congregations, such as that at Willingham, Cambridgeshire, where the majority of members were women in the 1670s.

Women were extremely important in the survival of Roman Catholicism, both during the immediate aftermath of the Reformation, and during the seventeenth and eighteenth centuries when they were subject to spasmodic persecution. The fortitude of recusant women is particularly evident in the late sixteenth century. In Roman Catholic households it was common for the man of the house to conform outwardly to the established church, because of the fines and civil disabilities which resulted from not doing so, but Roman Catholic practice was preserved by women and taught to their children. In the 1590s in York, Catholic women outnumbered men by 2:1. Between 1580 and 1594 thirty York women recusants were detained in Kidcotes prison; eleven died there and one, Alice Simpson, a widow, was there for seventeen years. Catholic women were slightly less likely than men to be prosecuted for their beliefs. In the autumn of 1608 Richard Cholmeley and his wife, with various other people, were bound over to appear at the next assizes in north Yorkshire. Mary Cholmeley was sent home, while her husband was taken off to negotiate his composition payments.

In the early days of the proscription of Roman Catholicism, Catholic women were probably rather less well educated than their Puritan sisters. In 1604 the author of a devotional manual on how to hear mass commented, 'It's a shame to hear women that can hardly read the petitions of the Jesus Psalter undertaking to teach priests to wipe their chalices, to make their mementoes and to perform their ceremonies.'[1] Education had a rather different function for Catholic

[1] Quoted in Hugh Aveling, OSB, *Northern Catholics: the Catholic Recusants 1558–1790*, Chapman, 1966, p. 252.

women than for Puritan women. Puritan women required education to read and interrogate the scriptures. For Catholic women the focus of worship was the celebration of the Mass, which could only be performed by a man. Women had to keep up morale by catechizing their children and servants until it was next possible for them all to hear Mass. They also performed corporal works of mercy for their co-religionists.

Mary Ward (1585–1645) worked to sustain the Catholic mission and also to improve Catholic women's education. Her work finally bore fruit in the school of the Bar Convent in York, founded in 1686 and run by the nuns of the Institute of the Blessed Virgin Mary through the period of the proscription of Roman Catholicism. There was a high degree of continuity among the clientele, with sisters, mothers, daughters and cousins attending the school. The boarding school was attended by the daughters of the northern Catholic gentry, and the day school by the daughters of the professional men and tradesmen of York. The boarding school was more socially exclusive than the day school, but was less so than the continental convent schools to which noble Catholic families sent their daughters. In the early eighteenth century, there were between twenty and forty girls being educated at the Bar Convent and the numbers increased during the century. Apart from preserving the faith of the girls who attended the school, the convent was the centre for a good deal of local Catholic activity, and there were many single or widowed Catholic women living in the immediate vicinity.

Persecution of Catholics waxed and waned, often in response to local conditions and to scares like the Gunpowder Plot of 1604 and the Popish Plot of 1679. The governments of the 1640s and 1650s assumed that Catholics were supporters of the king and some lost their estates, but for many families conditions were not substantially different from pre-war days. Gentry families were in general more successful in remaining Catholic than those lower down the social scale because of the financial burden of the fines for not attending church. By the eighteenth century it was unusual for Roman Catholics to be actively persecuted, but it was also necessary for them not to make too public a display of their religion.

In towns like York, where there were a great many small parishes, there was considerable vigilance over recusancy and numbers of Catholics declined in the seventeenth century; but they started to increase in the early eighteenth century. This increase in the numbers of Catholics was not among those who had traditionally maintained the faith during the seventeenth century: rural aristocratic and gentry families. These were conversions among the urban middle and lower classes. Some of these were marriage conversions, but there were also active lay proselytizers, like Mary Shepherd, a tailor's assistant and convert, who in 1708 was working among seamstresses, servants and apprentices in London.

It is sometimes claimed that times of upheaval afford women opportunities for spiritual leadership which more peaceful periods deny them. The Reformation affected women's lives by denying them opportunities for activity in the church, giving them instead an autonomous, but private, spiritual life. The period of the Civil War and Interregnum, the 1640s and 1650s, gave women opportunities for expression, but denied them any religious authority. As long as the practice of some denominations was proscribed, women were important in preserving the faith, protected by their privacy and invisibility to the authorities. Religion provided women with an independent life of the mind and respect among men for their spiritual qualities.

CHAPTER FOURTEEN

Custom, Belief and Popular Culture

Popular Culture and Custom

Popular culture is often associated with secular activities, but as we have already seen, religion provided much of the culture shared by people of all classes in early modern England. However, there was also an area of culture which took place outside the church and which was shared by people of many ranks, for popular culture is not necessarily exclusively plebeian; it may well be shared by people who also participate in elite culture. But this culture is difficult to chart because of the absence of records, and it is an area of life where evidence of women's participation is very elusive.

We have taken it for granted that women were at least as active in religious matters as men, if not more so. It is certainly true that, for most of the period covered by this book, people did go to church in large numbers and that some people had a strong religious faith, as evidenced by their acts and their words. But it is also true that there was much indifference to religion, from which women were no more immune than men. In the remoter parts of the country it was difficult to provide an effective ministry and proper services, and church attendance was not effectively enforced. There were frequent complaints of bad behaviour in church, of the congregation talking, eating, spitting, sleeping and pissing during services, and women seem to have been no less irreverent than men.

There was also a strong strain of popular anti-clericalism which encouraged people to abuse the clergy and to speak irreverently of the church and its ceremonies. Anti-clericalism might be provoked by the character of particular members of the clergy, though few can have been as bad as the heavy-drinking and quarrelsome rector of Hauxwell, Yorkshire, who attacked one of his female parishioners with a battledore and said that he would rather give

Communion to the Devil than to Cicely Hutchinson, another parishioner. He was also charged with adultery and was deprived of his parish in 1639. It was relatively unusual for people to express total disbelief, but the dangers of doing so were highlighted in the fate of Mrs Bowen, who in 1655 was haunted by the ghost of her still-living husband, Lieutenant-Colonel Henry Bowen, a professed atheist.

Canon law required that the Lord's Day be kept holy, but apart from prosecutions for trading and keeping alehouses open, there is little sign that there was much enforcement of the law. On the other hand, in a largely agricultural society there are many activities which cannot be left undone for twenty-four hours, such as milking cows and feeding livestock. The calendar of the church shaped not just the week but the year, and the church's ceremonies and festivals punctuated people's lives.

The church's calendar altered at the Reformation: saints' days were largely abolished and so were days commemorating events in the life of the Virgin Mary. The medieval craft gild ceremonies celebrating a local saint, or the saint who was patron of the gild, were transformed into civic ceremonies. The Corpus Christi day parades in Coventry were adapted to become the commemoration of Lady Godiva's ride through the city. These ceremonies had always had civic pride as their focus and continued to do so. St George's day remained an acceptable feast-day and the Lord of Misrule's activities at Christmas continued in many places. But much civic ceremony, certainly until the late seventeenth century, was tied up with craft gild activities and therefore excluded women. Mystery plays, gild processions and the installation of the mayor were all predominantly male occasions.

After the Reformation there was a marked lack of ceremonies in which a woman was publicly venerated. Queen Elizabeth and Lady Godiva were no substitute for the Virgin or a female saint, though Queen Elizabeth had an important place as the heroine of English Protestantism. (She could conveniently be contrasted with both her sister Mary and Queen Catherine de Medici of France, who were held up as examples of the brutality of Roman Catholicism.) The practice of celebrating the accession of Queen Elizabeth on 17 November endured into James I's reign despite his attempts to have his own accession celebrated. This and the custom of burning the Pope in effigy were revived in the 1670s during the public demonstrations which accompanied the Exclusion struggle. During the period of the Exclusion Crisis (1679–81) a statue of Queen Elizabeth was erected on Temple Bar, and popular pamphlets constantly invoked the spirit of Queen Elizabeth against the Popish menace.

A good deal of popular culture was derived from pre-Christian ceremonies and customs which had more to do with the annual rhythms of nature than with the Christian calendar. These were perhaps more enduring in the country than in the town. Sheepshearing, Plough Monday, May Day, Midsummer, Harvest Home, and a midwinter festival in which the Lord of Misrule governed, shaped the year as did religious festivals, which might or might not include secular festivities as well as church-going. Women had a particular part in May Day festivities, when young men and women were thrust together. In some places there were occasions when older women were important participants. At Coventry the Hock Tuesday celebration re-enacted the vanquishing of the Danes (the city's men) by the English (the city wives). Revels, wakes and ales all incurred censure from moralists for allowing mixed dancing and the free association of the sexes.

Rites of passage – weddings, christenings, churchings and funerals – all provided occasions for entertainment and drinking. Alehouses were important places where casual sexual liaisons might be conducted, and they were a part of communal popular culture, the location for sports and entertainments. Clandestine marriages might be contracted in alehouses, but more important, alehouses were the location for the feasting and celebration following more conventional marriages, as well as baptisms and funerals. It is really very difficult to know how far the alehouse was a place where women might entertain themselves with propriety.

Apart from regular events, there was a whole class of customs which related both to ancient beliefs and to community control, censuring people who had offended against local custom. Public demonstrations, with people in fancy dress, playing trumpets and drums and banging saucepans, were directed against people who had inverted the accepted order in some way. They often featured someone riding a horse facing backwards and wearing horns, widely recognized symbols associated with public shame. These demonstrations were known as skimmingtons, charivaris or rough music. A characteristic demonstration was that against William and Margaret Cripple, newcomers living in Burton-on-Trent in 1619, who were censured for living together as man and wife when not married, though at a later stage they claimed to be brother and sister. They said that one Sunday evening they were dragged from bed by a procession of respectable local inhabitants (including the parish constable) dressed in disguise, armed with swords and pitchforks, banging drums and frying pans, ringing bells and shouting, 'A whore and a knave'. The couple were then left in the stocks, where verbal insults and muck were thrown at them and someone pissed on their heads. When they were finally released they found that their house had been burgled and a considerable sum of money taken. It is not clear whether the aim of this particular episode was to drive the couple away from Burton-on-Trent (which it succeeded in doing) or to make them reform their lives. Skimmingtons were most often directed against men who had married women of bad reputation, cuckolds, men whose wives beat them, or blatantly immoral married couples. These demonstrations were often concerned with enforcing an ideal of patriarchy and, though they took part in them, women rarely led them.

Another kind of custom, to do with the properties of plants and places, owed much to pre-Christian beliefs. The efficacy of certain plants for curing afflictions, charms and amulets against illnesses and spirits, the need to do or not do certain things according to the phases of the moon, were all part of an oral tradition which existed throughout English society. This tradition was not confined to the illiterate. But the distinction between sufficient knowledge and supernatural knowledge was not clear and may have owed more to the regard in which the person was held by the local community than to what they actually did. There were cunning men and women who could charm away warts or cure sick cattle, and there were people who practised witchcraft.

Witchcraft

The widespread belief in witchcraft is often understood to be a relic of pre-Christian belief. It was certainly unchristian, but in its diabolical manifestations it depended upon believing in a dualist universe in which God and good were counterposed by the Devil and evil. Furthermore, witchcraft beliefs were much in evidence in the early modern period. Witchcraft prosecutions did not begin properly in Europe until the fifteenth century, reached a peak in the sixteenth and seventeenth centuries, and more or less died out in the later seventeenth and early eighteenth centuries. Their incidence varied greatly from country to country and, indeed, between regions within countries. It was also a feature of witchcraft prosecutions that they ran in phases rather than at a constant level, hence the discussion by historians of witch-crazes or panics. But to set this in context, it has been estimated that between 1542 and 1736 fewer than 1,000 people were executed for witchcraft in England, while over a similar period Scotland, whose population was a fifth of England's, saw over 4,000 executions. In Essex between 1560 and 1680 there were over 1,200 presentments or prosecutions for witchcraft. Between 1670 and 1700 there were five indictments for witchcraft in Essex and seven in Wiltshire. In the whole of the sixteenth and seventeenth centuries, only one woman was executed for witchcraft in Sussex.

After the Reformation, the penalties which might be exacted by the church courts amounted to little more than public penance or purgation before witnesses. Even the High Commission could only fine and imprison people. Witchcraft entered English common law in 1542 and witches were prosecuted in large numbers, but never to the extent or with the ferocity with which they were pursued in some other European countries. They were rarely tortured and the theology of the demonic pact, which gave some of the continental witch-hunts their real impetus, played little part in the thinking of English theologians and jurists, and virtually none in the popular imagination. English popular witchcraft beliefs in the sixteenth century were generally related to very local circumstances and had little to do with Christian religion, let alone with the extensive continental literature of demonology. The low level of prosecutions had much to do with the attitudes of the local elite, upon whom the pursuing of court cases was dependent.

James VI was the motive force behind the late-sixteenth-century prosecutions in Scotland, but he lost his concern with witchcraft on coming to England as James I in 1603. A small number of panics, like those in Lancashire in 1612 and in Essex in 1645, may conceal the fact that the level of witchcraft prosecutions declined from the late sixteenth century. The more severe Witchcraft Act of 1604 which superseded the Elizabethan Act of 1563 may have had the reverse effect of that which was intended: by imposing harsher penalties it may have resulted in fewer successful prosecutions. The panic of 1645 was very largely the result of the work of the witchfinder Matthew Hopkins. It resulted in nineteen women being hanged, the largest number ever executed at one time in England.

It is as difficult to explain the ending of prosecutions for witchcraft as their start. Numbers began to decline from the 1650s and the witchcraft statutes were finally repealed in 1736. The rise and decline in prosecutions for scolding and defamation follow a similar pattern to those for witchcraft.

Scolding, defamation and the accusation of witchcraft may all be seen as forms of verbal violence giving expression to tensions within a small community. An accusation of witchcraft might have been women's substitute for physical violence in a period when the poor felt particularly vulnerable. Another explanation attributes the rise in witchcraft accusations to changing economic circumstances. Declining prosperity made the poor much more vulnerable, and those who were responsible for relieving poverty more threatened. Growing prosperity made the poor feel less as if they were living on a knife-edge, and alleviated the tensions between individuals in the community. Certainly the period when witch prosecutions were at their height was one in which the poverty and the literacy gaps were greater than they had been earlier and were later to be.

The deepest division is between those who see witchcraft accusations as a form of elite control (by men over women, by one class over another, by a 'rational' Christian culture over an irrational pre-Christian culture) and those who see them as the expression of local antagonisms and aggressions. Bewitching was an act by an under-class against an over-class at a period when transgression was very likely to take the form of verbal violence: cursing, scolding or defamation.

These explanations all try to take into account the observable characteristics of accusations for witchcraft in the English courts. The majority of accusations were against women (80–90 per cent), and women were often linked in accusations against men. The majority of accusers were women and of a slightly higher socio-economic status than the accused. Most accusations of witchcraft amounted to disputes within the local community. Many cases never came to trial or were resolved by informal means. The mayor and chief magistrate of Coventry recorded how, in April 1656, Goody Naylor complained that Goody Wilding had called her a witch: 'Upon hearing both sides I advised them to be friends or to bring better proof of the words.' In this kind of case we do not know how far anyone believed in the substance of witchcraft, or whether this was simply name calling in a local dispute.

Nearly all the evidence of witchcraft in England comes from material relating to trials. Belief in witches and the power of sorcery are, therefore, most evident where they conflict with accepted norms rather than as part of a wider and acceptable system of beliefs. The majority of accusations were made by people outside the elite, and the elite itself expressed scepticism at the idea of diabolic possession. It is possible that trials under-represent the incidence of belief in witchcraft because they required someone to feel strongly enough about someone's actions to accuse them of witchcraft: that is to say, they felt personally injured in some way.

More than any other crime, that of witchcraft was socially constructed. People might disagree fundamentally about whether a particular act or episode constituted witchcraft. Accusations might be brought against people against whom grudges were harboured, or whose appearance or behaviour did not conform to accepted standards. The idea of witches as marginal people was common even among those who, following the late-sixteenth-century writings of Johan Weyer, believed that witches were deluded rather than possessed. However, attempts to link cases of witchcraft or possession with specific psychological conditions are bound to be unsatisfactory when the whole basis upon which the condition is described is so far from modern psychological terminology and values. Much of the work on witchcraft in the early modern period has been inspired by the concept of the witch-craze, rather than the straightforward belief in witches. England was much less subject to the force of witch-crazes than many other European countries. Indeed, it has been argued that it was only the personal crusade of Matthew Hopkins in Essex in the 1640s which amounted to anything like a witch-craze.

Accusations of witchcraft were based upon different kinds of behaviour or phenomenon – divining, charming or bewitching, and diabolic possession – and other charges, such as deceiving, might be associated with these. In the early seventeenth century, a woman was found guilty at the Devon assizes of deceiving and fortune-telling, but she had also 'laid with great scandal' with the vicar. The English authorities did not distinguish between black magic (maleficium) and white magic. Divining was foretelling the future or seeing something which could not be known. In 1650 Christina Weekes of Cliffe Pypard, Wiltshire, was indicted for using witchcraft and charms to find lost goods, in particular to find two lost flitches of bacon. It could give rise to charges of theft when the accused found by divination a lost object, because only by theft could he or she know where the object was. It could also give rise to defamation cases where the future of someone absent was read from signs. Charming or bewitching could give rise to the prosecution of clients who had engaged the services of a charmer. Diviners and charmers could be prosecuted for taking money for providing these services. Accusations of diabolic possession were unusual.

What did these accusations really amount to? The majority of accusations of bewitching were for causing illness or death in an individual, generally a young person and often a girl. The kinds of illness were different from those defined as medical complaints and were disturbances of the mind, fits, swoonings, lameness, wasting and unspecific pain. Animals might be bewitched, the symptoms usually being unspecific illness or death. Things might be bewitched to disappear, or be moved or altered: blades might lose their cutting edge, for example. People saw spirits, fairies and witches' familiars, and received mysterious instructions.

Apart from charges for acts construed as witchcraft, to call someone a witch in public could lead to a defamation case. Indeed, people appearing in court complaining of the slander of being called a witch were more numerous than people prosecuted for witchcraft. Elizabeth Stile, who had been acquitted of witchcraft at the Chard assizes, sought to bring an action against her prosecutors in 1636.

Allegations of witchcraft produced an unusual degree of contact between ordinary people and professional men. The law was considered to be an effective weapon against witchcraft and was used by a wide range of people for that purpose. A case of bewitching or diabolic possession could produce examinations by clergymen and physicians, both groups increasingly inclined to scepticism about magical practices, as well as by magistrates. Theologians had difficulty explaining why it was that the Devil, the Prince of Darkness, should choose as his earthly instrument the meek rather than the powerful, though it was generally agreed that women, because of their nature, were more susceptible to the Devil's blandishments. The one group, other than the professionals, who might be brought in for an expert judgement were juries of matrons, summoned to search women for witches' marks, extra nipples or other signs of tangling with the Devil.

Witches

So far we have looked at witchcraft, a disembodied concept about which learned treatises were written by lawyers and theologians, which may have influenced deliberations in the higher courts, but which had little impact upon popular beliefs and the conduct of the lower courts. But what about the people accused of witchcraft and, more specifically, women whom it was believed were witches? It is difficult to find accusations of witchcraft against wealthy or powerful men or women, and accusers were nearly always the social and economic superiors of those they accused. Witchcraft

accusations are closely connected with certain acts and antagonisms which upset the stability of a small community, with feuds
between and within families, and with misfortune and natural
disaster. The sense of community extended not simply to preventing dissension within the community, but to preventing community disruptions from harming the community in relation to the
rest of the world.

Historians have spent a great deal of time trying to produce
rational explanations for the existence of witchcraft beliefs, but as J.
A. Sharpe has rightly observed, people who believed that they or
their children or animals had been betwitched were frightened and
felt that real harm had been done them. They complained of real
deaths, real illnesses and real losses. Often accusers were, in taking
a case of bewitching to court, seeking official backing for long-
standing local accusations against a particular individual. Accusations of bewitching made up the vast majority of cases brought, and
there was little concern with people having made diabolic pacts, or
having had marriages or sexual relations with the Devil, or having
borne the Devil's child. Not only did people believe that real harm
had been done them, they also believed that people might *be*
witches and that witches were able to cause real harm.

But who were the women who were accused of witchcraft? They
functioned in a small society and reflected understandable local
tensions. Over 90 per cent of the accusations made in Essex were
against women, and women were associated with most of the men
accused. In the north of England, women were 80 per cent of the
accused. A high proportion were widows or spinsters, women
without obvious male protectors. Some 42 per cent of the accusations against women in Essex were against widows, a much higher
proportion than their incidence in the population, and fewer than
half of the women accused were married at the time of their
accusation. It is clear from work which is now being done that Essex
is far from typical of the pattern of witchcraft in other parts of the
country, but lack of equivalent material is making it difficult to
produce systematic studies. It is also clear that the bulk of the
people accused of witchcraft were women who were old, lived
alone without men, and at the time of their accusation in the courts
had long-standing reputations at least for being troublesome, and
at most for witchcraft.

The relationship between the accused and the accusers is
complicated. Sometimes the accused were dependent upon their
accusers for money or gifts, and there seems to have been an
element of resentment or a feeling of ingratitude in the accusation.

In 1567 in Kelvedon in Essex, Joan Cocke being refused butter, bewitched three cows, one of which died and the others gave 'milk of all colours'. Many of the accusations appear to be altercations between women, though the subject of bewitching might be a woman or a child in the charge of a woman. Mary Cutford of Rainham, Essex wished herself to be a witch 'so that she might be revenged of her adversary', Anne Dawdrie, in 1632. Very few accusations were against women who were midwives or healers of people, though it was not uncommon for the accused to have a reputation for healing animals. Margery Skelton of Little Wakering, Essex, charged with sorcery, admitted in 1566 to healing people by praying and such cures as nut-tree leaves and sage leaves. The particular power attributed to the curses and maledictions of the poor and injured, often older women, might also be significant. Cursing might be used where other action was impossible or had failed, as in the case of the woman who cursed the mayor of York after common land had been enclosed in 1536.

The reasons why witchcraft was gender specific or gender related have been much debated. Feminist historians have argued that witchcraft accusations were a means of reinforcing male dominance by exercising the social control of women by a regime of terror. The sanctioning by the upper classes of the control of women allowed the law to be used against lower-class women, especially at times of economic hardship when women were in competition with men for livelihoods. Witchcraft accusations thus allowed women to be controlled by men by the threat of institutionalized violence, and the nebulous nature of witchcraft and sorcery allowed accusations to be tailored to fit the threat. That women were more often than men the subjects of witchcraft accusations, and more often complained of bewitching, is not seen as an objection to the thesis that the witch-craze was the manifestation of the underlying structural antagonism of men to women.

What makes the thesis that witchcraft was a weapon of male domination harder to sustain is that the local male elite was often unwilling to co-operate with this particular form of social control, as evidenced by the small number of prosecutions compared to the number of accusations, and the even smaller number of guilty verdicts. The thesis also takes little account of the nature of the local community in which both accusers and accused lived. Although accusers were usually the social and economic superiors of the accused, they were part of a village society, a small community in which to bring in the law from outside the community was a serious step. The criminalization of witchcraft from 1542 can be construed as a way of trying to make more women punishable under the common law, since the church courts had largely lost any powers they had had to enforce corporal punishment. It was effective in that it brought a group of women, generally old and disadvantaged, under the view of the law. But it was applied only to a limited extent at different times and in different places. It legitimized control over certain kinds of behaviour. But we know very little about whether people felt that the existence of witchcraft legislation acted as a deterrent.

Witches and witchcraft accusations, almost more than any other phenomenon in early modern England, perplex us. We can comprehend persecution, scapegoating, community tensions and feuds. It requires a real act of imagination to try to understand a society in which beliefs in magic, sorcery and the supernatural coexisted with orthodox Christian belief, with no sense of inconsistency. Modern discussions about witchcraft seek to provide rational explanations in terms of structural tensions in society or community scapegoats. We understand that people felt that there were people in their community who could exercise unseen power over people, animals and things. We do not know how far people believed that they possessed this power themselves.

PART FIVE

Women and Men's Worlds

CHAPTER FIFTEEN

Women, the Law and Property

Women under the Law

The anonymous author of *The Lawes Resolutions of Womens Rights*, a 400-page guide to the provisions of the law affecting women, published in 1632, put women's position succinctly: 'Women have no voice in Parliament, they make no laws, they consent to none, they abrogate none.' Women played no part in making or changing the law, and the common law did not normally acknowledge the existence of any woman who was not under the protection of a man: father, husband, brother or guardian. A digest of the law for magistrates, published in 1653, has a lengthy entry under 'wife', but no entry for women of any other status and no entry for 'husband'. It opens with the words, 'After marriage, all the will of the wife in judgement of the law is subject to the will of the husband; and it is commonly said a *feme coverte* hath no will.' *Feme coverte* was the common law term for a wife, a woman under the protection of her husband. In order to exercise that protection, husbands had to live with their wives and might be prosecuted in the church courts for not doing so.

The logical consequence of this was that women were not responsible under the law, though to what extent was a vexed and much debated question. They were deemed responsible as far as they were able to exercise their reason; and there were also some specified areas of the law where they had particular responsibility. The fact that women might be punished also indicates that they were held accountable for their own actions. Women might be executed for committing a felony, as in 1649 when twenty-three men and one woman, Mary Jones, were executed for robbery and burglary. A married woman caught committing a crime with her husband might be found guilty if it was clear she had instigated it,

227

though she might be acquitted if it could be demonstrated that she had not acted of her own free will. Husbands were responsible when married women were bound over to keep the peace on the payment of a recognizance, and were responsible for paying fines for their wives.

Women had certain responsibilities for their own actions in regard to property. Women operating as merchants in certain cities might buy and sell without their husbands' agreement, though in other property transactions this was required. Women might be wards for minors; most often widows were wards for their own children. Women might pursue their own inheritances in the courts, as did Margaret Countess of Cumberland (1560?–1616) and her daughter, Lady Anne Clifford. They attempted to reverse the will of the Earl of Cumberland, who had left his estates to his brother, inheritor of the title, instead of to his only child, Anne. In the 1620s the two women conducted a lengthy Chancery action, ultimately without success. 'Many did condemn me for standing out so in this business', wrote Lady Anne. Lady Katherine Paston directed a Chancery action for her husband when he became ill in 1618. Women were involved as principal plaintiffs in 16 per cent of all cases in Chancery in the sixteenth century, and in 26 per cent in the seventeenth century.

Property

In English common law, wives could hold no freehold land (real property) except through their husbands; nor could they alter or dispose of property without their husbands' consent, even if it was their own inheritance. Women could not make wills or appoint executors without their husbands' agreement, under the principle 'the wife shines in her husband's beams'. All their personal goods at the time of the marriage, or acquired subsequently, became their husbands' (though, by custom, household goods were usually regarded as the woman's own). In recognition of this, husbands were required to protect their wives, so if the wife wronged someone who required satisfaction, 'either her husband must do it, or by imprisonment of her person it must be done.'

Apart from land and buildings, women owned all sorts of property. Much of the interior equipment of a house was regarded as the woman's own, and many of the dispositions in women's wills concerned household effects and personal property like books and clothing. Widows were more likely than spinsters to have valuable possessions like gold and silver, but their estates were often not worth very much, possibly because their husbands' goods would have been partially distributed at his death. Women who were economically active usually left larger estates than those who were not, and might leave livestock or the tools of their trade.

Only widowed and single women might own freehold land, but all women might take on tenancies, though with some restrictions. Many tenancies were held by right of patrimony or widowright. A survey of the lands of the bishop of Durham for the mid-seventeenth century shows that the majority of women who held land from the bishop did so by 'widowright': that is, by right of their husbands having been the previous tenant; some husbands and wives held joint tenancies; other women held land by surrender from a father or brother. Margaret Gibson, spinster, held half a cottage with a garden by surrender of her brother Robert, and Anne Punshon, heir of Thomas Punshon (presumably her husband), held a tenement in Chester-le-Street by right of being heir to her father, Thomas Chapman.

The settlement of property upon women was regulated by custom, and changes in this custom have given rise to a debate over the extent to which women's control of their property increased or decreased in the early modern period. At marriage, all the woman's property became her husband's. At his death, the normal disposition was a third of the total estate to his widow, a third to his children, and a third to dispose of as he wished. If there were no children, half the estate went to the widow, and if there was no wife, half the estate went to the children, the other half in each case being the testator's to dispose of as he wished. The courts which were responsible for proving wills and ensuring that their provisions were carried out did so in accordance with this formula. It was not until 1692 that the province of York admitted that a testator might dispose of the whole of his estate as he wished.

There were various ways of setting aside custom, of which perhaps the most commonly used was the marriage settlement, though various forms of trust became increasingly popular in the seventeenth century. These enabled women to be left freehold land, whose income they might have and which they might themselves bequeath, without being able to dispose of the land itself. An increasing number of Chancery cases concerning women's property were to do with their trusts. During the period 1500–1760 much case law was made concerning women and their property, and probably the most substantial changes took place in respect of marriage settlements.

Women were not immune to more immediate events like the Civil War. The decline in the incomes of gentry families, caused in part by the impossibility of collecting rents in full, forced many families to live on capital. This meant that they had to borrow or to sell land in order to meet ordinary expenditure as well as exceptional payments, such as the payment of a daughter's dowry. Sir Ralph Verney, neutral during the war, was hard pressed to find the funds to pay the annuities due on his estate, let alone helping his aunt, Mrs Isham, whose house had been ransacked. Unpaid debts and interest compounded the problem. Despite his neutrality, attempts were made by Parliament to sequester Sir Ralph's estates while he was abroad, and he sent his wife to England to try to get the sequestration lifted, which she succeeded in doing in 1648. By the late 1640s incomes from land were rising and harvests were recovering, but there was a great deal of land for sale to meet aristocratic and gentry indebtedness, so land prices were low, being then perhaps three-quarters of their pre-war price.

Marriage Settlements

Women were an essential link in the transmission of property between men, and property transactions were commonly brought about by means of different kinds of marriage settlement. But this transmission was not just between a woman's family and her husband's, it was also between different generations and branches of the same family: so there were two, or more, sets of family interest to reconcile. In particular, families were concerned that their widowed members should be looked after and that children should receive their patrimonies. With the average length of marriage being less than twenty years, the prospect of the remarriage of a surviving spouse and of further children had also to be considered.

The likelihood of a substantial estate having no direct male heir varied during the period, but property rarely passed in a direct line from father to son for more than a hundred years. More precisely, when the population was constant, 60 per cent of married men at their deaths would leave at least one son, 20 per cent only a daughter or daughters, and 20 per cent no children. When the population was declining, more women inherited because families had fewer children and therefore a smaller supply of sons. Marriage settlements thus had two purposes for women. They were designed to safeguard the interests of a woman after her marriage, and they were designed to provide for the succession to the wife's family of their property if the normal line should fail. Step-children and the distant relatives of a childless widower – who, in the event of a wife dying without children, would have been entitled to inherit property which had come from her family – were usually excluded in such settlements.

The third of a deceased husband's estate due to the widow by custom, the dower, was a charge upon the husband's estate and did not in any way represent a return for the property which she had brought with her on her marriage. The widow was entitled to the dower for her lifetime, and it was enforceable upon the heir to the property. The portion, the property which passed from the bride's father to her prospective husband, was separate. It was not technically the wife's property. But in return for the payment of a portion the father of the bride expected that provision be made for the bride upon her husband's death. The traditional dower might be exchanged for a jointure, an annuity or occasionally an agreed part of the whole estate, which was hers absolutely on the death of her husband, to will as she wished. Jointures are found in the sixteenth century, but became a more common device during the succeeding two centuries. Sometimes land which a wife brought with her at her marriage had attached to it the condition that, if she died childless, it should revert to her own family, as happened with the Buckinghamshire lands brought by Mary Abell to her marriage with Edmund Verney.

Jointures were the most common form of settlement of property upon a wife at her marriage. They were often linked with strict settlement, the system by which estates, land in particular, were attached to any title, even if the title was due to pass to a comparatively distant relative. A necessary part of strict settlement was the substitution of a jointure for the dower. This kind of settlement started to come in around 1650, but there is still much uncertainty about how widespread its use became and how quickly.

Historians have been debating at length the effects of strict settlement upon the fortunes of the aristocracy in general and on women in particular. Lawrence Stone has argued that it was a demonstrable part of the shift from the patriarchal to the affective family. The father had to agree to the distribution of legacies to all his unborn children, which gave more financial independence and greater freedom in the choice of a marriage partner to the younger children, and improved the status of women. Since some settlements included clauses by which the father could redistribute between individuals the sum allowed for his children, it is not clear that this was necessarily an egalitarian arrangement or that it promoted the financial independence of younger children.

Eileen Spring has argued that widows were worse off under the terms of strict settlements; that although portions rose in value, jointures fell and rarely amounted to the value of a third of the estate (the proportion to which widows had been entitled under the custom of dower). However, it is likely that the increase in the size of portions owed more to an increase in the price of land than to a change in the regard in which a wife was held. The rise in the value of portions was largely confined to the aristocracy, who expected to buy land with a portion. The assignment of a jointure deprived a widow of any legal rights over her late husband's estate and allowed the main real property (land) to be left to a male heir. Jointures might be worth considerably less than a dower, but they became more common during the eighteenth century partly because of the difficulty of valuing estates as more people accumulated wealth in forms other than land. Needless to say, dowers and jointures were paid sometimes not in full, and sometimes not at all.

Strict settlements have also featured in the discussion about how far aristocratic wealth was consolidated by ensuring that land passed to a single male heir, sometimes a distant relation in the absence of a son. Ostensibly, this aim contradicted that of better providing for the widow and younger children. Estates are characterized as 'burdened' by financial obligations to younger children and widows, though the settlement maintained the integrity of the land while distributing income. It has also been suggested that, under the terms of strict settlements, heiresses, where there was no male heir, fared worse than they would have done under the earlier arrangements. Instead of inheriting a high proportion of the estate, arrangements were often made to reduce the amount of the estate which went to an heiress.

All these arrangements were made by men for women. Women did not play any part in the negotiations themselves. Perceptions of whether women were better off with jointures or dowers have depended, on the one hand, on characterizing the dower as a great drain on an estate, a burden to be borne by the long-suffering heir, depriving him of the use of land during the widow's lifetime; and, on the other, on characterizing the jointure as a drain of a different sort, since the payment of an annuity used up income and the payment of a lump sum used up capital.

Much of this discussion would be concluded if more were known about the actual sums of money involved. We do not know whether widows were better or worse off, whether younger sons and daughters received more or less than they would have done under customary law, or whether daughters and, in particular, heiresses were discriminated against. Since strict settlements were individually negotiated contracts, there was a wide variation in the terms which might be set to deal with the particular circumstances of the two families involved. Without this information it is premature to make judgements about the quality of affection within the family, based solely on the fact of the strict settlement. Strict settlement was only one among a number of different kinds of disposition of property, but it has been given great prominence because it was enforceable in common law, the records of which have been most used by historians studying marriage settlements. Research into marriage settlements in the records of other jurisdictions will provide much more information.

Marriage settlements were regulated in the common law courts by the rules of *feme coverte*. But marriage settlements and the regulation of property fell also under the jurisdiction of the ecclesiastical courts, which dealt with all probate matters, under the traditional system of English customary law administered through the manorial courts (not operative over the whole country, and to a large extent concerned with tenancies and land rights), and under the equitable jurisdiction of the court of Chancery.

In none of these other jurisdictions did the doctrine of *feme coverte* operate as it did in common law. Common law did not recognize pre-nuptial contracts; all contracts made by a woman were annulled by her marriage (just as today marriage annuls all wills made before the marriage). But the church courts and Chancery had no such doctrine. The church courts were concerned with property only in so far as it was the subject of disputed wills; their jurisdiction over matrimonial matters related to persons rather than property. The court of Chancery recognized the legal right of women to separate property and would uphold the right of a woman to her jointure and to the payment of 'pin money', an allowance paid by the husband during his lifetime to his wife.

Much of the evidence about the enforcement of marriage contracts comes from disputes, in which the cupidity of each side is often painted in the blackest terms. But there is no doubt that the purpose of marriage settlements was to protect the interests of the widow. Jointures were not solely a device for protecting the estate for a male heir; nor were marriage settlements usually designed to protect the woman's property during the husband's lifetime. Settlements were not a device for the very rich alone. Most people had some property, even if it was not land. The disputes whose resolution was sought in the court of Chancery tended to be those worth larger sums of money, but even so, many of the disputes concerned portions of less than £300 or jointures of less than £40 per annum, and involved the widows of lesser gentry and yeomen. Probate accounts suggest that marriage settlements were not unusual among yeomen and even labourers. The rich were most likely to make settlements because there was more at stake financially. Remarrying widows who might well have property or children from their previous marriage also used them as a device recognized and enforceable in law, so as to protect their interests.

The more that we actually look at the disposition of women's property, the more it is evident that the legal doctrine of *feme coverte* was not a single blanket provision imposed upon all women and their property at all times. But it is also clear that, while the notion of married women's separate property existed when it came to providing for her widowhood, her property was not separate for the duration of her marriage, and if her husband chose to squander the family's property, there was little she could do to stop him.

Women's Wills

Further recognition of the significance of women's separate property can be seen in their wills. Given the restrictions which officially governed women's capacity to dispose of property, one might have expected that women could not make wills. But there are substantial numbers of women's wills; of the wills made in Leeds and Hull between 1520 and 1650, women's wills account for about a fifth.

The majority of these wills were made by unmarried or widowed women, but a few wives also made wills. Some of the married women who left wills had been married before and had, as a condition of their second marriages, retained the disposal of some of their property: for example, to children from the earlier marriage. Married women also made wills when there was a debt or legacy outstanding to them at the time of their death. It was common for wills to be made on the deathbed, so there are a number from women in childbed, often making dispositions for their young children, and widows often died leaving young children too. Older widows commonly left bequests for their grandchildren.

Female testators were of all ages, and many of them had comparatively modest estates, like the inmate of the Trinity

Hospital in Hull who in 1611 left goods worth scarcely £5. Many of the wills are for goods and money rather than land or buildings. The goods mentioned in wills tend to be the wife's personal property: linen, jewellery, clothes and books. It was possible for women to leave their businesses; in 1603 Katherine Power of Hull left an interest in a Humber ferry, and in 1643 Elizabeth Casson of Leeds left fulling mills.

Testators could attempt to govern their beneficiaries from the grave, and it was not uncommon for bequests to be made with conditions preventing an unsatisfactory son-in-law or profligate son from squandering an inheritance. The majority of bequests were to close relatives, usually children or parents, then brothers, sisters and nephews and nieces, but occasionally women either outlived their relatives or had none. A number of servants' wills exist and bequests were often made to the employer and his or her family, as well as to the servant's own family. Equally, employers, even of the most modest numbers of servants, frequently made bequests to their employees.

Apart from being testators, women were also frequently named as executors of wills. Husbands most commonly appointed their wives their executors, and if a man died intestate, his widow was almost always appointed the administrator of his estate. Professional help was used by women both in making wills and in carrying out testamentary business, and it was regarded as perfectly usual for women to do these things.

It is true that the legal disabilities under which women laboured were very great and prevented women from amassing great fortunes on their own accounts. On the other hand, women had access to legal process and were able to use the fruits of their property and to protect them. How far women's access to the law changed over the period is uncertain with the current state of knowledge, though changes in marriage settlement arrangements made greater access to the courts necessary, as can be seen in the growing number of Chancery cases involving women. Between 1500 and 1760 the universal system of the wife's portion and the widow's dower was replaced by a general type of settlement in which details were negotiated to suit individual circumstances. Communal protection by custom gave way to free competition in which women might need to go to law to enforce a contract.

CHAPTER SIXTEEN

Women and Men's Worlds

Women, the Family and the Political Theorists

The father's role in the family is clearly recognized in the analogy between the state and the family. It was implied by James I in 1610: 'Kings are . . . compared to the fathers of families for a king is truly Parens Patriae [father of his country], the politic father of his people.' The father is seen here as someone who could dispose of his inheritance, his favour and his punishment to his children at his pleasure. The arch-exponent of patriarchy was Sir Robert Filmer. Filmer believed that the unlimited powers of God the Father passed to kings as fathers of their people. Writing in 1648, he declared that the subject's obedience was to the supreme fatherly power of the monarch, which must necessarily be unlimited, 'for if it be limited it cannot be supreme'.

The early Stuarts celebrated a form of fatherhood which owed much more to the Fatherhood of God than to the father of any earthly family. As we have seen, fathers of families did not exercise untrammelled authority, and the notion of companionate marriage was also changing the idea of the role of the father. So the analogy of the state to the family described not just an idealized notion of the state, but also an idealized notion of the family.

The father of the country was the king, but the mother had no equivalent. The king's consort was not expected to play this role, and while a queen reigning in her own right might be regarded as the parent of her country, no attribute specific to motherhood was attached to this. Indeed, Queen Elizabeth's virginity and distance from motherhood were celebrated. Some theorists referred to children and *parents* rather than simply father and child, but no special role for the mother was implied in this.

The only institution which might be said to have had the

attributes of a mother was the church, but the questions of authority raised by the Reformation and, later, by the spread of nonconformity were rather more patriarchal than matriarchal in spirit. The concept of the mother church owes more to abstract ideas about the qualities a mother is supposed to possess (nurturing, welcoming, all-forgiving) than to any notion about a mother's relationship with her children.

A wife's obedience to her husband was both upheld and subverted by religion. In 1500 religious uniformity was regarded as the essential pillar of political stability; by 1760 religious pluralism was a fact of life and political loyalty was defined in a different way, in secular terms. A wife was bound to follow her conscience, but she was also bound to obedience to her husband. A husband had to do his best to ensure that his conscience and his wife's were not at odds, and his authority was impaired by his wife having a different religion. A late-sixteenth-century mayor of York, whose wife was a recusant, was told that he was unfitted to govern a city who could not govern his own household. Men with Catholic wives were suspected of being in sympathy with their wives' beliefs while themselves conforming out of policy. This suspicion extended to the highest in the land: the Catholic wives of Charles I and II were objects of suspicion because of their supposed influence over their husbands.

If the family provided an analogy for the state, the state also provided an analogy for family relationships, especially in relation to a wife's obedience to her husband. In 1700 Mary Astell wrote that neither law nor custom afforded women redress from the misuse of a husband's power:

> He who has sovereign power does not value the provocation of a rebellious subject, but knows how to subdue him with ease, and will make himself obeyed; but patience and submission are the only comforts that are left to a poor people, who groan under tyranny, unless they are strong enough to break the yoke, to depose and abdicate, which I doubt would not be allowed of here.[1]

She also said, 'If absolute sovereignty be not necessary in a state, how comes it be so in a family?'

From the late seventeenth century, contract increasingly displaced the family as the model for the relations between the state and the subject. The theoretical significance of the family diminished, but this made little difference to the way in which

[1] Mary Astell, *Some Reflections upon Marriage*, 1700, quoted in Bridget Hill (ed.), *Eighteenth Century Women: an Anthology*, George Allen and Unwin, 1984, p. 113.

women were perceived in relation to political processes. Locke attacked Filmer's divine right patriarchalism and expressly repudiated any connection between the magistrate and the father/master/husband. Eighteenth-century theorists turned their attention to the nature of the contract and to more individualistic concerns than the corporatism of seventeenth-century theorists. But the prevalence of contract theories marked the end of any vestiges of feudal obligation, obligation which derived from hierarchy and inheritance, and which had included women; contracts, on the other hand, were made between powerful individuals.

Women, Office-Holding and the Political Nation

Women were not a single category of people in law or in custom, and there were few places where women were explicitly prevented from participating in political processes. Many laws did not specify the sex of those to whom they applied, and in the later Middle Ages custom commonly admitted women to a variety of offices. They held a number of positions by right, usually by hereditary descent or as substantial property owners. In towns, women gild members and householders also might have civic voting rights, though they rarely held office.

The use of custom diminished during the seventeenth and eighteenth centuries, and so correspondingly did the opportunities for women to hold office by this means. Two developments contributed to this. The first was the decline in customary jurisdictions (manorial courts and feudal dues), which transferred a large area of local administration to the common law. Nevertheless, the common law courts generally upheld women's right to hold local offices when this right was challenged. When challenges were made, it was usually on the basis that there was something wrong with a particular woman holding a particular office rather than a general belief that women were disabled by their sex from occupying public positions. The second development was the increasing unacceptability of women's appearance in public. Women were increasingly prevented from taking on positions which would require them to play a public role. They occupied fewer local offices in person from the later seventeenth century as the influence of gilds and church courts declined, and entry into the urban elite and to parish offices was increasingly controlled by other means.

In theory, women property owners, who were a small proportion of the total number of those who owned property, were
entitled to stand as and vote for such local offices as churchwardens, constables, surveyors of the highways and overseers of
the poor. Eligibility for office and for voting was subject to local
variation; usually it was attached to the ownership of a particular
piece of property. The actual choice of some officers was by the leet
or manorial court, the vestry, or occasionally the vicar or JP
(depending upon the office). People who were personally exempt
might be ordered to provide a deputy. In the later Middle Ages,
women occasionally held office in wards and parishes.

After the Reformation, parishes became divisions of civil
government, and churchwardens acquired greater responsibility
over fellow parishioners, disbursing substantial sums of money in
the parish. In parishes in the diocese of Chester in the sixteenth and
early seventeenth centuries, the parish poor were paid for such jobs
as washing linen, sweeping the church and the street, hanging up
holly at Christmas and whipping dogs out of church. There are a
number of cases of women holding the position of churchwarden.
At St Budeaux, Devon, one of the two wardens was normally a
woman in the early seventeenth century, and in 1645 two widows
were elected at Staplegrove, Somerset, as they were at Otterton,
Devon, in 1737. At East Budleigh, Devon, twenty-one women held
the position of churchwarden between 1663 and 1836, one of them,
Sarah Birch, three times in the 1630s. But it is also evident that
women, especially in the eighteenth century, often got a man to
deputize for them. In the 1740s there are two instances of Devon
women getting their servants to act for them as churchwardens.

Women might be nominated as parish constables but usually
appointed a deputy, though there were a few women constables in
rural Derbyshire in the seventeenth century. Overseers of the poor
were usually men, responsible for collecting the poor-rates, settling
the parish accounts, and providing work for the poor, but
occasionally women held the position, most commonly in poor
country parishes, and there are a number of examples in
Staffordshire. Occasionally, women served as parish clerks, a more
humble job than it sounds, mainly concerned with washing the
church linen and the vicar's surplice, cleaning the plate and
supplying the Communion bread. A rare example of a woman
sexton, the official who was responsible for maintaining the
churchyard and graves, was Hester Hammerton, sexton of
Kingston upon Thames in the early eighteenth century.

Technically, women might hold positions as JPs and sheriffs; the last woman known to have done so in early modern times was Lady Anne Clifford, high sheriffess of Westmorland in the 1660s and 1670s. Positions of this kind passed by descent and there was no prohibition on descent to a woman. Lordships of manors could pass to women and might have associated with them the right to make election returns: in other words, to nominate and declare elected Members of Parliament. There are two instances of this right being exercised by women in the sixteenth century. In 1553 and 1554 Dame Elizabeth Copley, widow of Sir Roger Copley, made the returns for the MPs for the borough of Galton in Surrey, even then a rotten borough; and in 1572 Dame Dorothy Packington returned the two burgesses for the borough of Aylesbury, one of them being her son-in-law.

Peeresses were not summoned to sit in the House of Lords after the fourteenth century, though in the eighteenth century there were forty-nine peeresses in their own right, a slightly smaller number than that of Roman Catholic peers who were disabled by their religion from taking their seats. Charles II made two of his mistresses peeresses: Barbara Villiers (1641–1709) was created Duchess of Cleveland, Countess of Southampton and Baroness Nonsuch in 1670, and Louise de Keroualle (1649–1734) was created Duchess of Portsmouth, Countess of Fareham and Lady Petersfield in 1673. Other peeresses received their titles by virtue of a defect in a title or line, like Alice Duchess Dudley. There was evidently no intention that they should take seats in the House of Lords. Queen Anne permitted one of the Duke of Marlborough's daughters to take the title of Duchess of Marlborough in the absence of male heirs in direct line, but again without any political rights.

These examples do not demonstrate that women exercised political power, but they do indicate that women were not excluded by their sex alone, though between 1500 and 1760 their exclusion became more systematic. There was complete equality for men and women property owners as subjects of state policy. Death and taxes were just as certain for women as they were for men. Women were obliged to pay taxes, but were unable to influence decisions to levy taxes or the level of assessment. The notion of representation being tied to taxation was foreign to early modern England: even those who, before the Civil War, objected to the king's arbitrary taxes, did not demand that all those taxed should be represented. Parish officers collected taxes and might distrain upon defaulting taxpayers' possessions. Women defaulters were more likely than men to pay up at the eleventh hour rather than allow their goods to be seized.

Taxation was levied upon householders, male and female. However, the largest group of women heading households were widows, and widows were often too poor to be liable for tax. In 1522 a muster roll was called as a covert way of preparing a tax assessment for the coming war with France. In one Berkshire hundred, twenty-four women householders were listed; fifteen were widows and some of the others may have been. Only one is identified as a single woman apart from four women who were only just old enough to be assessed and appear as daughters. There were also better-off widows like Widow Collingridge of Wendover in Buckinghamshire, who was assessed for a payment of £35 Ship Money in 1635 and who volunteered 2s. when voluntary contributions were solicited for the relief of the Protestants in Ireland in 1642. Widow Bampton from Great Kimble paid £10 Ship Money in 1635 and subscribed a shilling to the relief of Protestants in Ireland. Women were assessed for the Hearth Tax in 1663 and for virtually all the taxes for which returns survive.

Between the sixteenth and eighteenth centuries, the opportunities for women to serve in various offices and to exercise limited political rights diminished, but at no time had many women actually done these things. Positions which might give women authority over men, especially men of their own social status, became less accessible to women as prejudices against their appearance in public developed.

These changes are particularly to be contrasted with the extension of political rights to a higher proportion of the adult male population. In part this was the consequence of two centuries of price rises, which meant that a 40s. freehold, the minimum property qualification for voting in a parliamentary election outside a borough, was a relatively smaller piece of property by the middle of the eighteenth century than it had been at the beginning of the sixteenth. In boroughs the situation was slightly different and there is some debate about the extent to which they became more or less oligarchic in the early modern period. Perhaps as many as three-quarters of adult men in London in the later sixteenth century were freemen of the city, while it became increasingly uncommon for women to be admitted as freemen.

Women and Political Action

So far we have considered what opportunities there were for women within traditional political institutions, but plenty of political action takes place outside Parliament or civic government. During the seventeenth century, the courts were used to test royal power, especially when Parliament was not sitting. The participants in such test cases as Hampden's Ship Money case of 1637–8 were men, but there was no technical objection to women pursuing such suits. In 1632 Lady Grenville used the court of Star Chamber to secure alimony from her husband by accusing him of slandering the Earl of Suffolk. A number of women took part in the riots that followed Charles 1's attempts to drain the fens in 1633, and were named in the Star Chamber proceedings. 'They had a signal to assemble themselves by sometimes a bell, sometimes by a horn, they threatened to kill the workmen if they came thither to work again' and they had done this fourteen times. Widow Smith was ordered to pay a fine of £500, though she was later let off on marrying a minister; several other women were fined 500 marks each and had to pay damages to the engineer, Sir Cornelius Vermuyden.

The most common forms of political action for women were speaking in public and participating in riots, demonstrations and processions. Riots motivated by grain shortages, enclosure and fen drainage often had a political component, as in fen drainage riots of 1633, but as the authorities treated them as breaches of the peace, we shall look at them in more detail in the next chapter.

Women certainly felt able to express political opinions. A Roman Catholic Wiltshire gentlewoman appeared at the quarter sessions in 1603 for describing Queen Elizabeth as a 'bloody queen' and her lord chief justice as 'a bloodsucker'. She expressed the belief that James 1 would restore Catholics to their rights, but in 1605 appeared again for expressing too strongly her disappointment with the new king. In 1652 in Bedfordshire a woman was fined 5s. for opprobrious words against the government, and in 1648 a London woman was prosecuted for selling unlawful pamphlets.

It was not uncommon for women to petition Parliament: wives and widows of seamen or soldiers seeking relief, wives of prisoners and sometimes women with other grievances. Women presented many petitions during the Civil War. On October 1645, 2,000 'maimed and wounded soldiers and widows' presented a petition to the House of Commons protesting their hardship. Parliament agreed that there should be a special church collection for them. Later that month the widow of one Major Backhouse was granted £100 on her petition to the House of Commons for the payment of his arrears. In January 1646 widows of soldiers and creditors of Parliament presented a petition 'crying and importuning for satisfaction of moneys due to them'. An MP commented on seeing them that it was strange, at this time of the Parliament's prosperous condition, to see

> how rude and impetuous [especially some of the women were] crying out, as the Members passed through the crowd of them, Pay us our money, we are ready to starve, and seeming ready to tear their clothes from their backs.[1]

The persistence of the demands for the payment of pensions and arrears suggests that Parliament had not made sufficient provision for the welfare of wounded troops and the families of wounded and dead soldiers.

Before the Civil War a number of more political petitions were presented. In January 1642 'city dames' presented a petition against the bishops' votes in the House of Lords. In February 1642 gentlewomen, the wives of citizens, tradesmen and other inhabitants of the cities of London and Westminster, petitioned Queen Henrietta Maria not to leave the country because her presence was 'the comfort of their loyal hearts' and, probably the point of the petition, 'the spring and fountain of their prosperity'. The petition had no effect, for on 23 February 1642 the queen set sail with one of her daughters and the crown jewels, which she tried to pawn in Amsterdam. Perhaps the most eloquent statement of what one group of women thought about the war is to be found in another petition of February 1642:

> Women are sharers in the common calamities that accompany both church and commonwealth, when oppression is exercised over the church or kingdom wherein they live; and an unlimited power have [sic] been given to prelates to exercise over the consciences of women as well as men; witness Newgate, Smithfield and other places of persecution wherein women as well as men have felt the smart of their fury.

To which John Pym replied, 'We entreat you to repair to your houses, and turn your petition into prayers at home for us': in other words, this is no place for a woman.[2]

Between 1646 and 1649 Leveller women presented several petitions, ostensibly for the release of their husbands from gaol, but also making a case on their own behalf. No one knows who was the author of these petitions. 'We have an equal share and interest with men in the commonwealth', they claimed in 1649, a share recognized in no document appearing under the names of the male

---

[1] Bulstrode Whitelock, *Memorials of the English Affairs*, London, 1682, p. 193.
[2] Quoted in E. A. McArthur, 'Women petitioners and the Long Parliament', *English Historical Review*, 24, 1909, pp. 700–1.

Leveller leadership. The Leveller women were much mocked for their activities. Newsbooks called them 'lusty lasses', 'Levelling she-saints' and 'the meek-hearted congregation of oyster-wives'. They were told by Parliament that they were involved in a matter 'of an higher concernment than you can understand' and advised to return home to wash their dishes, to which one woman replied, 'Sir, we have scarce any dishes left to wash.' Parliament did them the final indignity of declining to record the presentation of the petition in its journals.

Women participated in demonstrations against the Civil War in the 1640s, but it would be anachronistic to regard these demonstrations as expressions of pacifism. The Quakers did not adopt non-violence as a policy until after the Restoration. It is more appropriate to see women's objections to the war in the context of local politics and rivalries. In the affray following a military exercise at Rayleigh in Essex in 1642, men and women fought the military volunteers because they supported Parliament. A royalist newsbook reported in September 1643 on the interception of letters from London from the wives of men serving in the trained bands trying to recall their militant husbands.

Some women actively tooks sides in the war. Loyal noblewomen defended their husbands' homes. Brilliana Harley at Brampton Bryan, Lady Blanche Arundell at Wardour Castle, and the Countess of Derby at Lathom House all endured sieges of weeks in defence of their husbands' homes. The royalist newsbook, *Mercurius Aulicus*, rejoiced in the heroism of the Countess of Derby, running regular stories about the siege as it entered its tenth, its thirteenth and finally its eighteenth week, describing her as 'the incomparable Countess of Derby' and keeping a tally of the artillery and colours her men had captured from the enemy. Newsbooks used women's participation as a way of indicating that the other side was so enfeebled that they could only get by with women. 'How many ladies may we hear of that will hold out a siege as long as my Lady Fitzgerald hath done at Trecrohan? Of late, her men made a sally, as desperate men usually do when commanded by a woman.'

Many of the stories which circulated about women in military engagements were scandalous rather than complimentary. They were part of the propaganda war which was devoted to exalting the valour of one side and to emphasizing the cowardice of the other. Civil War newsbooks – weekly newspapers produced not only by each side, but by different factions within the two sides – took a great delight in satirizing the activities of women of the other side. A characteristic type of story is this:

Lady Norton, mother to that most noble colonel . . . and governess for the present of the town of Portsmouth . . . was very busily employed in making some new works about Portsea bridge: and was not only every day in person amongst the workmen (whom she encouraged by her goodly presence) but brought also with her every day 30 or 40 maids and women in a cart . . . to dig and labour in the trenches. To the great honour of the sex, of her person more, who in short time will grow as able to command in chief as the good Lady Waller to possess the pulpit.[1]

Women acted as spies for both sides. Sir Thomas Fairfax ordered the payment of £10 to 'Mary the scout' for 'special service done by her at Taunton' in 1645. In 1646 the House of Commons ordered Mrs Endymion Porter to leave London within the next four days and the kingdom within seven lest she be proceeded against as a spy. Women worked as fund-raisers too. A committee of gentle-women was formed in 1643, meeting two or three times a week in London to procure money, plate and jewels for the use of the two houses of Parliament. A second committee was set up in Coventry, 'consisting of Mistress Mayoress and some 9 more blue stomachers, so full of zeal and reformation that they dare commit anything'.

People who had had soldiers quartered on them, and their livestock seized by the army, petitioned Parliament for compensation. In 1644 Widow Leadham, a prisoner in the debtors' prison, petitioned the committee of the Eastern Association for payment for quartering two soldiers. She must have been very poor, for the sum due to her was only 6s. and she employed a professional scribe to write out her petition. In January 1645, twenty-four men from Kilsby, Northamptonshire, two hundred cattle and sixty horses were taken by Banbury garrison, after the villagers had refused to pay their contributions for the support of the garrison. Three days later the women of the village went to Banbury and arranged with the governor, Sir William Compton, the restitution of men and property on condition that the contributions were paid. The men refused to co-operate, 'till at last the sisterhood began to lecture them (for others can preach as well as ladies) and they submitted'.

During the period of the Civil War, women had more opportunity to assert their views than before or after. However, this was not necessarily part of the revolutionary ethos, rather the reverse. The reason for women's greater prominence was the breakdown of conventional mechanisms of control and organization. Both women and lower-class men had the opportunity to assert themselves over certain political and religious issues, but with one

---

[1] *Mercurius Aulicus*, 16 August 1642.

important difference. Radicals like Gerrard Winstanley and the Levellers argued for political rights for lower-class men, but did no such thing for women. Just as religious radicals argued only for men's right to be called to the ministry, regardless of education and class, as long as they had the gift of the spirit, political radicals argued only for the extension of political rights to more men. Neither group could accept the possibility of women's jurisdiction over men. Women's political activity during the 1640s and 1650s has to be seen in this context. These were euphoric times, but much more so for middling and lower-class men than for women.

At the Restoration one group of London women took a position on what was happening and presented *A Declaration of Several Maydens*, in which they declared that 'the only means . . . to bring these nations out of bondage' was to set the crown on the head of Charles II. There is little evidence of women taking part in the political demonstrations of the later part of Charles II's reign, during the Exclusion Crisis. Of forty-eight people arrested in London for making speeches for exclusion, only four were women. Individual women were involved in clandestine activities, in spying and plotting. Mrs Huddleston was paid £10 for intelligence in 1660, and Aphra Behn (1649?–89) went on an intelligence mission to Antwerp in 1666. Elizabeth Cellier (*fl.*1680), a Roman Catholic midwife, was tried and acquitted in 1680 for her supposed involvement in the Meal Tub plot, and was tried again later the same year for libel on account of the vindication which she had published after her first trial. Lady Rachel Russell (1636–1723) was accused of running her husband's political career, and in 1683 he was executed for supposed involvement in the Rye House plot.

Women were actively involved in Monmouth's rebellion of 1685. There is a story of how the young women at an academy for the daughters of the more prosperous families of Taunton embroidered banners for the rebel army. The girls, escorted by their mistresses, marched to Monmouth's camp and presented their work. The headmistress died in Dorchester gaol and the girls were ransomed. In the trials following the suppression of the rising, Judge Jeffreys made himself notorious for his savage sentencing. Dame Alice Lisle was accused of high treason for sheltering two nonconformist clergymen. She was unsure of whether she even knew the men, but Jeffreys advised the jury that 'the evidence was as full and plain as could be, and if I had been among you, and she had been my own mother, I should have found her guilty'. She petitioned the king for mercy and won the concession of being beheaded rather than burned at the stake. The less well-connected Elizabeth Gaunt was burned for harbouring a rebel in her chimney.

Women's authority was highlighted when a son was born to James II's queen in June 1688 and the authenticity of the birth was questioned. But the nature of the bloodless revolution, plotted by men of the political nation, offered women little scope for involvement beyond taking part in the demonstrations that welcomed William at Torbay and on his arrival in London. One of the first women's petitions to William and Mary was from a group of women whose husbands had been hanged by Judge Jeffreys. Elinor James (*fl.*1715), Anne Docwra (*fl.*1682–1700) and other women produced pamphlets on public affairs, often with a religious subject, but rarely dealing specifically with the position of women.

A particular issue might politicize a group of women. In 1739 ten aristocratic and gentlewomen, many of them the wives and daughters of peers, forced their entrance to the House of Lords. The House was debating the war with Spain and these women were determined to attend, though the Lord Chancellor ordered that they be not admitted. The Duchess of Queensberry demanded admission on behalf of the group, and they stood outside the House until the late afternoon 'with neither sustenance or evacuation, every now and then plying volleys of thumps, kicks, and raps against the door, with so much violence that the speeches in the house were scarce heard'. They then remained perfectly silent for half an hour, after which the Lord Chancellor, supposing them to have gone, opened the doors so that the members of the House of Commons might attend the debate as spectators. No sooner were the doors opened than the women rushed through them and pushed their way into the front of the visitors' gallery. They remained there until after 11 o'clock at night when the house rose, applauding the good speeches and deriding those of which they disapproved.

The history of women's political action is very much one of reaction to political issues of concern to women, often through their economic impact. Economic issues moved women at all levels of society to action, from the humblest women in grain riots to Mrs Delany trying in the 1740s to persuade the ladies of Dublin to use Irish cloth for their gowns because of the hardship caused by the new restrictions on its export.

The Women Behind the Men

Ideologically, this is a difficult subject. For those who want to see women in their own terms, the idea that some women were important because of the influence they exercised over a man, usually a husband, is unacceptable. But in the context of early modern society, with its network of family and patronage, marriage and descent could make a great deal of difference to the power it was possible to exercise. Marriage to a prominent political figure was a way of participating in the political nation in a way which was denied to the wives of other men. Women were important purveyors of both patronage and influence by their marriages. They contributed to the creation and extension of networks of kinship and marriage, which had political consequences which were not inadvertent. But the real extent of women's political influence must be conjectural, even in the case of someone as well known as Sarah Duchess of Marlborough.

We shall probably never know how much the kings of England listened to their wives' counsels, though it is likely that the more uxorious they were, the more their wives were solicited for advice. One of the most interesting of these relationships, and one about which it is only possible to speculate, is that between Charles I and his wife Henrietta Maria, sister of Louis XIII of France. She gives the impression of having been bossy, and was probably as poor a judge of character and occasion as her husband. Both were intensely sensitive to slights to their position; indeed, it could be argued that there lay the root of the problem of Charles's relations with Parliament. Her correspondence from the Netherlands, whence she had gone in the early months of 1642, before civil war had actually broken out in England, was full of admonitions to Charles: 'Delays have always ruined you', 'Want of perseverance in your designs hath ruined you' and so on. Exhortations to stiffen his resolve filled her letters. The trust she put in advisers in the later years of her exile also reveals her lack of judgement. The unsavoury schemer Henry Jermyn, in whom she placed considerable confidence in the 1650s, did the exiled Charles II's cause great harm by making him the focus for hopeless plots.

Royal mistresses were rarely able to achieve this kind of influence over English kings' policies, but it was certainly the case that favour with the monarch's favourite could bring considerable patronage. Henrietta Howard, Countess of Suffolk (1681–1767), became mistress of George II while he was still Prince of Wales, and built herself a villa at Marble Hill with two grottoes. After George's accession she was much courted by those who thought she would prevail in the king's counsels, but Queen Caroline (1683–1737) was the stronger. The queen's support of Sir Robert Walpole was critical to his success. She had reached a *modus vivendi* with Lady Suffolk (who had originally been one of her ladies of the bedchamber), and remarked in 1736 of her husband's dalliances that she 'was sorry for the scandal that it gave others, but for herself she minded it no more than his going to the close stool'. The queen was a woman of great character and was patron of Leibnitz, Newton and Halley. While she was dying, the aged surgeon bleeding her set fire to his wig with the candle, whereupon she bade him to stop so that she might laugh.

Wives of noblemen and prominent political figures might find themselves in a position to become involved in matters which fell under their husbands' influence. Catherine Knevet (d. 1633), wife of Thomas Howard, 1st Earl of Suffolk, in 1604 accepted a pension of £1,000 a year from the Spanish government in return for information; her husband had refused one. He was Lord High Treasurer of England between 1614 and 1619, though he was suspended in 1618 when he was accused of having embezzled sums in the order of £250,000 from the Treasury. His wife was charged with having extorted money from people who had business at the Treasury. After a hearing in the Star Chamber in 1619, they were fined £30,000, ordered to restore all money wrongfully obtained, and imprisoned in the Tower, separately, at pleasure, though he was soon released and was partially rehabilitated. She had great ascendancy over him and undoubtedly used his high office to enrich herself. Francis Bacon, who much disliked her, compared her to a shopkeeper.

Lady Rachel Russell (1636–1723), wife of William Lord Russell, has been described as having in her husband 'created the major politician she could not be'. He was a peaceably disposed MP in the parliaments of the Restoration with country party and nonconformist sympathies. From the mid-1670s he allied himself strongly with the anti-French faction and subsequently became a leading advocate of the exclusion of the Roman Catholic Duke of York from the succession to the throne. He was implicated in the Protestant Rye House plot of 1683 and was tried for high treason, found guilty and executed. Lady Russell acted as secretary and note-taker during the trial and, in the short interval between his sentence and execution, worked tirelessly to save her husband's life. After the accession of William and Mary in 1688 his reputation was vindicated. Lady Russell spent her widowhood caring for her children and her very considerable estates, 'taking a particular interest in bestowing the clerical benefices at her disposal in accordance with her own and her husband's principles'. Though she worked on his behalf, it was at least in part her doing that he got into difficulties in the first place.

Some of these women actually influenced political affairs themselves, while some simply acted as brokers of patronage between men, but the opportunities to do either probably varied considerably according to the nature of the royal court. The court of Anne of Denmark provided important opportunities in the early seventeenth century for noblewomen to gain access to the court in their own right, as attendants to the queen. Women assumed a greater importance as clients and brokers of patronage and as patrons themselves than had been the case during the sixteenth century. These extra opportunities were provided by the presence of two courts (the king's and the queen's), but when Anne of Denmark died in 1619 noblewomen's opportunities for court patronage were reduced. The remaining Stuart queen consorts played little part in political life on their own account, except for Henrietta Maria's machinations both as the centre of a pro-French faction in the 1630s and while in exile in the 1650s.

Plainly, some women did influence their male relations and used their position to involve themselves in political affairs. However, women were also blamed for getting men into difficulties and it is often impossible to know how much they were being made scapegoats, and how much they were actually responsible for unpopular or ill-advised decisions. Some of the criticism levelled at Henrietta Maria, for example, was of the same order as the doctrine of the king's evil counsellors, a reluctance to admit that Charles I could have made foolish decisions on his own.

Women Living as Men

Women who challenged men's monopoly of political action were sometimes accused by their detractors of trying to be men, but they made no pretence about their own gender. A few women actually attempted to live as men, sometimes temporarily, sometimes more permanently, and were a popular subject for newspapers and ballads, which tended to dwell on the scandalous characteristics of the story.

Perhaps the best-known group is the Polly Olivers, the women who dressed as soldiers and joined the army. In 1647 in the parliamentary army, 'Women in man's apparel and soldiers' came and listed themselves in Colonel Hammond's regiment; they were discovered and taken into custody.'[1] Some women followed their husbands. In 1655

> A drummer belonging to the regiment in the Tower proves to be a woman, and hath been brought to bed of a boy, and lies-in near East Smithfield, she was of good report, and her comrade was her husband, but it was not known until now.[2]

There are a number of other accounts of Civil War soldiers on both sides who were unmasked as women: Jane Ingleby is supposed to have fought at Marston Moor, and Anne Dymoke appeared at the parliamentary garrison at Ayr in 1657.

Christian Davies (1667–1739) set out to follow her husband, having discovered that he had joined the army in Flanders. She left her business and children to the care of friends and enlisted in the army. She was wounded and taken prisoner by the French, was exchanged and then returned to the army, fighting in several of Marlborough's campaigns. She was finally revealed as a woman after being wounded at the battle of Ramilles (she had by this time found her husband but sworn him to secrecy so that she might continue soldiering). She was discharged from the army, but continued to follow it in the company of her husband. After his death she married another soldier, who was killed in 1710. In 1712 she was granted a government pension of a shilling a day. She married again and her third husband was a pensioner of Chelsea Hospital, where she was buried in 1739.

The pregnant Hannah Snell (1723–92) was deserted by her Dutch seaman husband. She gave birth to a daughter, but the child lived only seven months, whereupon Hannah Snell set off in search of her husband, dressing as a man and using her brother-in-law's name, James Gray. She enlisted first as a soldier and then as a marine and served in the Indian Ocean. Wounded at Pondicherry, she concealed her wound for fear that she would be unmasked. After serving on several ships, she returned to England and went to London to collect her pay. Here she revealed her sex and went on the stage, appearing as Bob Bobstay, a sailor, and Firelock, a soldier. She continued to wear men's clothes even after leaving the theatre. She was granted a government pension, took a pub in Wapping, married (she had discovered that her first husband had

---

1 *The Weekly Account*, no. 7, 10–17 February 1646/7.
2 *The Perfect Proceedings of State Affairs*, 19–26 July 1655.

been executed for murder in Genoa), and died in 1792 in Bedlam, having become insane three years earlier.

These women were not using men's guises simply to achieve the essentially female end of recovering their husbands. They used them as a means of travelling and finding adventure in ways which were normally closed to women. Cross-dressing undermined definitions of gender and thus of relations between the sexes, especially relations concerned with power. It was an unusual thing to do, but it did not put the woman who successfully lived as a man beyond the pale: contemporary accounts emphasized both her strength and her femininity. The husbands of Snell and Davies had, by running away, forfeited their claims to obedience from their wives. Some of these women were also realizing a sexual preference for women. We know nothing of the motives of the Norwich woman who in 1629 was whipped for wearing men's clothes and 'offering to go forth with the soldiers'. The actress Charlotte Cibber Charke (died *c*.1760) played male parts in the theatre and boasted of her conquests of women. Hannah Snell acquired a female friend at Portsmouth to whom she returned after her sea voyages.

A fascination was exercised by this inversion which was exploited in plays, chapbooks, ballads and popular pamphlets. Sixteenth- and seventeenth-century plays commonly featured female characters disguised as men. In the accounts of these female warriors, the line between fact and fiction is ill-defined, especially in ballads and chapbooks. Long Meg of Westminster, a Lancashire woman in London who was a cross between Robin Hood and Mary Frith, was the subject of a late-sixteenth-century chapbook, and accounts of the lives of Christian Davies and Hannah Snell were widely distributed. There were also legendary female smugglers and pirates, like Naomi of Yarmouth who rode with a group of smugglers, and Ann Bonney and Mary Read who were convicted of piracy in 1720. These women provided strong role models of independence to other women, but fighting women were also titillating: there were women boxers in the Bear Garden in London in 1722. It is interesting that a real person provides the model for the majority of these legendary characters, but we do not know how far genuine autobiographies exist. Both Hannah Snell and Christian Davies 'dictated' their accounts.

Early Feminists?

How far were the women we have considered taking self-conscious political action in the cause of women's rights in the broader sense?

Very little, I suspect. There were women who were conscious of those rights, but they were individuals, not part of any political movement. Political radicalism – that is, the political radicalism of men – in the seventeenth and eighteenth centuries concentrated upon different kinds of freedom and did not address the question of political rights for women. In the seventeenth century, the Levellers considered women's rights to be the same as servants': as dependants their interests were to be protected by the man who had assumed this responsibility. Nothing was said about the rights of a woman who had no male protector. In the eighteenth century, the rights of women were similarly disregarded, but this time the rhetoric of the radicals provided women with a language which they might apply to their own situation. It was in this context that Mary Wollstonecraft wrote *Vindication of the Rights of Woman* (1792).

A number of women in early modern England have been considered the mothers of feminism: Margaret Cavendish, Duchess of Newcastle (1624?–74), Bathsua Makin (*fl.*1673), Mary Astell (1666–1731) and Margaret Fell Fox (1614–1702) have been seen as the intellectual forebears of Hannah More (1745–1833) and Mary Wollstonecraft (1759–97). But these earlier women did not address the condition of women in general terms. They did not challenge the nature of marriage or the conduct of gender relations; nor did they contest class divisions or call for political rights for women. They tackled individual issues, such as the need for better education for women or the trials of marriage. Their perspective on the world was different from the women who, at the very end of the period, adopted a fundamentally new approach to women's position in society, one which took them outside the household and into the world as autonomous beings. The earlier women took the place of women to be in the family and household. The later women conceived of extending individualism to women a hundred years after men had started to think of themselves in this way.

CHAPTER SEVENTEEN

Women and Crime

Only recently have historians begun to consider the ways in which the boundaries between sin, crime and madness have moved over time. In early modern England everyone sinned, but not everyone committed crimes in so doing. These boundaries have a gender component: women's supposed sexual voraciousness explained men's being seduced to sin; madness accounted for women who spoke up outside the conventional bounds of their sex. During the early modern period these boundaries moved.

The male and female recorded crime rates in twentieth-century Britain differ widely from each other: only about 10 per cent of criminal prosecutions are of women. In early modern Europe the figure was more like 20 per cent. The underlying reasons for the difference between men and women may not necessarily be the same then as now, and the difference between the two figures for women does not necessarily imply that women have become less criminal in the last 200 years. Certain acts which involved women have been decriminalized. For example, adultery necessarily involves a woman, and if a high proportion of prosecutions are for adultery, there will be a high female crime rate. If, however, most prosecutions are for highway robbery, the proportion of women will be very low. Nevertheless, there is a debate in progress about whether early modern England was a more or less violent society than our own. Much of the discussion hinges upon the technical interpretation of statistics and definitions of criminality.

In early modern England, women were less likely than men to engage in the kinds of criminal activity which attracted the attention of the authorities. The kinds of crime for which they were indicted tended to be different, with fewer felonies and more petty crime. There were also differences in the incidence of prosecution, and the type of charge for the same types of crime: women were four times less likely than men to be charged at the assizes or the quarter sessions with a felony, unless the charge was of infanticide or witchcraft. Location also influenced the incidence of female prosecutions: more women were prosecuted in the town than in the countryside.

Breaking the Law

I have used the concept of breaking the law rather than that of crime alone because the law in early modern England encompassed control over areas of life which we now consider to be the preserve of the individual, like bastardy and church attendance; these were punishable, but were usually dealt with in the ecclesiastical courts. There are also modern crimes for which there is no early modern equivalent: for example, a vast amount of time is taken up nowadays with offences connected with motor cars. In early modern England an equivalent amount of time was not taken up with offences connected with horses and carts because personal transport was not as important then as it is now.

The exact division of responsibility between common law courts and church courts is not at all clear, and many offences might be tried in either. It was a matter of local custom in which court a case of bastardy, for example, was tried. In recent years, church court records have become an increasingly important source of information about women. Women appeared in the church courts considerably more often than in the secular courts, as plaintiffs, defendants and witnesses. Women were not immune to the desire to challenge accepted values, but did so in the moral rather than the criminal arena.

For the earlier part of the period, up to the middle of the seventeenth century, the church courts were important for enforcing moral values. They did this by prosecuting religious dissidents: men and women who refused to go to church or held unacceptable religious views. They also prosecuted sexual and matrimonial offences. Prosecutions usually resulted from presentments by churchwardens at bishop's or archdeacon's visitations. These presentments were made in the context of a community in which everyone knew each other's business and where questions such as 'Are there any people that being lawfully married and not separated or divorced by course of law do not cohabit together?' received detailed answers. In 1662 in the Buckinghamshire parish of Penn, Elizabeth Burridge and Grace Oviatts were cited for being married women not living with their husbands. Elizabeth Burridge replied that her husband lived and worked as a hired servant for someone in another parish, and Grace Oviatts said that her husband worked as a day labourer in Beaconsfield and resorted to her once or twice a week where she lived at her father's house at Penn.

How did people get into the secular courts in an age without a police force? The prosecution of most felonies was the responsibility of the injured party. Only in the prosecution of suspicious deaths was there any official responsibility through the coroner. Prosecution of crimes like larceny, burglary and assault depended upon the victim informing the authorities, identifying the culprit and attending the court. By the eighteenth century, cases were being brought by labourers, but generally cases were brought by those who were better off and by those whose patience had been pressed beyond endurance by the severity of the crime or the frequency with which it was committed. Many petty crimes were dealt with by informal sanctions: the restitution of property, for example, or the sacking or eviction of a difficult or dishonest employee or tenant. Alternatively, offenders might be bound over by the magistrate to keep the peace, rather than having a formal, expensive and protracted suit brought.

A higher standard of behaviour was required of women than of men. When Thomas Mace and his wife were both found by the mayor's court at Norwich to have been drunk on a Sunday night in 1633, it was the wife who was sent to the stocks. Evidence of the operation of the double standard was especially plain in cases of adultery and fornication. Adultery was necessarily an unequal offence; the immediate punishment of women stemmed from the desire of local authorities not to have to support a bastard child on the poor rate.

The number of women appearing in the courts on criminal charges was small in comparison with the number of men. In sixteenth-century Hertfordshire, for example, only 15 per cent of the indictments for theft were of women (a similar proportion to that for England and Wales in 1972). In eighteenth-century Surrey, 24 per cent of the property cases in the courts involved women, not a radically different proportion given that this embraces a larger category of crimes. At the Essex assizes in the period 1559–61, seven cases of murder, two cases of witchcraft, three rapes and numerous burglaries were tried. Of the seven murder trials, two were of women for murdering children, one was of a man who had struck a woman on the head with a hedging bill and then sawn off her arms and legs, and the rest were of men for murdering men. The witchcraft cases consisted of one man and one woman. The rapes were all by men of women; in two cases the accused was the woman's employer.

Evidence for Essex, Sussex and Hertfordshire suggests that the vast majority of homicides in the late sixteenth and early seventeenth centuries were commited as acts of unpremeditated aggression. They draw attention to the prevalence of domestic violence in this period. Wives accounted for three-quarters of the victims of domestic murders. (Figures published for 1989 give wives or lovers as 48 per cent of the total female victims, and husbands or lovers as only 10 per cent of the total of male victims.) Wives were associated with premeditated murders, often choosing poison as their weapon. There were also substantial differences from county to county: for example, there were a large number of killings of children and servants in Essex and also a large number of witchcraft prosecutions, and hardly any such crimes in Sussex and Hertfordshire. Indictments for infanticide and for rape were also few in all three counties, though both crimes were probably much under-reported.

Crimes involving interpersonal violence appear very common in the early modern period, but this is partly because they are prominent in court records. The primary function of law enforcement was to keep the peace, and public brawling was readily detectable and seen as something that needed to be dealt with firmly and promptly. By comparison, property crime, which features largely in modern crime statistics because there is a high level of reporting for insurance claims, was much less visible. Interpersonal violence was not confined to men. In 1574 an Essex woman was sentenced to the cucking stool for having 'brawled and scolded with Roger Veale the lord's bailiff for executing his office and made an assault upon him in the constable's presence with firebrands'. In Coventry in the winter of 1655–6, the mayor, the chief magistrate, recorded a number of incidents of violence involving women. The wife of Nicholas Unit was sent to the house of correction for scolding and fighting in the Bear Inn; and Mrs Neale and Goody Tayler appeared before him for brawling, and 'I advised them to be friends'.

Violence between women was relatively common: there are numerous accounts of brawls in churches about pews. In St Ebbes' church in Oxford in 1584, two women were cited in the archdeacon's court for fighting over a seat and calling each other names. This raises two interesting issues. Many cases of violence between women involved incidents where one felt that her status had been impugned in some way (as, for example, by being required to occupy a pew in a less favourable or prestigious position). The evidence in cases of defamation suggests that the preservation of reputation was an extremely important motive in women's actions, so it is possible that women were prompted to violence, to make a public display, over issues where they felt that they were being denigrated in public.

It is also possible that violence between women was singled out for particular attention at law. The legal profession in general and the judiciary in particular have always been a repository of male values. Violence *between* women offends the male ideal of femininity; it is a denial of all those qualities of gentleness, nurturing, motherliness and passivity which are prized as feminine. Perhaps violence between women was more likely to be presented in the courts because of the offence caused by the sight of women fighting, when many a pub brawl between men might be ignored or passed off with a reprimand. Modern attitudes to female violence are strongly gendered: judges are more likely to consider female offenders pyschologically disturbed than male, and medical explanations are sought in cases involving female violence. But the criteria for mitigation in cases of violence are much less applicable to women than to men: self-defence, provocation and lack of premeditation are all important defences for men which are not available to women. Almost all female violence is directed against someone known well to the perpetrator, and often someone at whose hands the woman has suffered over a long period.

The good reputation of a woman was the one aspect of her presentation to the world which was hers alone. It was also very vulnerable to disparagement, and this almost certainly lay behind the appearance of women in a large number of defamation cases in the church courts. A high proportion of defamation cases were brought by women as well as against women. Characteristic examples may be found in the Durham High Commission, where in 1628 Ralph Green appeared on a charge of calling the widowed Dorothy Hutton a turn-coat in respect of her religious conformity. Thomas Grey, a clerk, brought a charge of defamation in 1629 against Dorothy Proctor, a spinster, for calling him 'a base bastardly rogue' and a 'base rascal'. Dorothy Proctor's mother was a tenant of Grey's. In particular, it was women's sexual reputations which required protection, since it was of little concern to the world if her cooking was bad or her laundry smutty. In the York church courts, 90 per cent of the defamation cases with a female plaintiff involved allegations of sexual impropriety. A number of defamation cases involved one party calling another a witch.

Women were much more in evidence in the lower courts than in the higher courts. The presentments of women made by the constables of Coventry between 1629 and 1742 were chiefly either for breaches of trading regulations or for not fulfilling civic obligations. Breaches of trading regulations included selling goods in short measure, unlicensed ale-selling and unlicensed brewing. Of the forty-one people presented for selling ale without a licence in 1629, three were women, all widows. Women heads of household were presented for failing to mend the paving, and not clearing ditches or the pavement. In the 1650s, when there were no church courts and the religious settlement was in the process of revision, a whole set of new offences appeared in the secular courts. In 1655 the mayor of Coventry sent the male and female servants of Goody Hite, who had had carnal knowledge of each other, one to gaol, the other to the house of correction; he ordered Goody Remington to be bound over for abusing the churchwardens of Stoke; he sent Goody Pywell to the house of correction for 'living idly'; and he bound over Widow Chantry to good behaviour for 'being of an ill fame in entertaining soldiers in her house'. Apart from these offences against morality or public order, there were offences against the Sabbath. Three Quakers, who travelled on the Lord's Day without a licence, were set in the cage. Goody Yardley was convicted of grinding corn on the Lord's Day and there were various convictions for cursing. The greatest commercial fraud by a woman was that of Mrs Rose, who was charged with distributing counterfeit coin. The notebook of an eighteenth-century JP suggests that the two most usual reasons for a woman to appear before him were for travel passes or in connection with the birth of an illegitimate child.

In the Northamptonshire quarter sessions in the mid-seventeenth century, women appeared for keeping unlicensed alehouses, not going to church, being drunk, profane cursing and failing to keep the peace towards another individual, and single women with children were presented for bastardy. The Warwickshire quarter sessions for the 1690s had a case of assault and battery by Mary Flewellen on Edward Mayo. There were also a number of settlement cases involving women.

Women were rarely prosecuted for offences concerned with malpractice of a craft or trade. They were largely excluded from trades liable to the enforcement of regulations about faulty goods. Women featured occasionally in prosecutions for giving short measure, but much of the retailing they did was on too small a scale to be liable to the regulations governing weights and measures. They were prominent among the prosecutions for keeping un-licensed alehouses, and in 1633 Margaret Hayband of Norwich was forbidden to keep an alehouse after a conviction for selling less than a full quart of ale for a penny.

Women prosecuted for theft were most likely to be pickpockets and shoplifters, the less serious thefts. Women involved in smuggling tended to be prosecuted as receivers of smuggled goods of small value. There are some cases of women housebreaking, though usually they were accompanied by a man. In 1598 two spinsters were hanged for breaking into two houses with a man, and stealing some kitchen utensils and food. In the eighteenth century women committed a higher proportion of property offences in towns than in the country, and the number of prosecutions of women for property crimes increased in years of dearth and declined in years of plenty. This suggests that thefts by women were generally in response to need and were opportunistic. They did not always confine their thefts to articles of little value. A Chelmsford spinster was acquitted of stealing £100 from a man's bag in 1590, and Elizabeth Stalinge, spinster, stole £53 from Mary Same of Castle Hedingham, Essex, in 1594. Thefts by servants from their masters or mistresses were taken to be a particular betrayal of trust, though they took place with some frequency. The maid-servant of Henry Sepon of Shenfield, Essex, was indicted in 1563 for the theft of a cassock, a hat and three shirts (worth together £1 9s.) 'contrary to the faith and confidence placed in her by her master'.

Though women tended to commit crimes which needed less daring and initiative than those committed by men, there were a few female highway robbers. There were several cases in the 1590s, a time of great hardship when many people took to the road in search of work. In 1593 six yeoman and a pregnant spinster seized £1 10s., a pack of cloth worth £40 and a horse worth £3 in a highway robbery at Clavering in Essex, and in 1598 a single man and a married couple took 14 shillings-worth of cloth in a robbery at Harlow, Essex. There are fewer instances of women committing highway robberty on their own, though in Essex in 1735 a woman mounted on a side-saddle and brandishing a pistol held up a butcher who had to surrender his watch and 6 guineas.

Moll Cut-Purse, the heroine of the play published in 1611 by Thomas Middleton and Thomas Dekker, *The Roaring Girl*, is one of the better-known dramatic characters of the seventeenth century. She was based loosely upon Mary Frith (born *c.*1589), who was notorious for dressing in men's clothes, smoking a pipe and consorting with criminals. She was said to have run a gang of thieves and been a receiver of stolen goods. Her anonymous biographer wrote in 1662 of how she resisted the conventional restrictions upon women's lives:

> She could not endure their sedentary life of sewing or stitching; a sampler was as grievous as a winding sheet; her needle, bodkin and thimble she could not think on quietly, wishing them changed into sword and dagger for a bout at cudgels.[1]

Broadside ballads featured women highway robbers, women who had gone to sea or joined the army disguised as men, and women smugglers and pirates. Their appeal was that of the challenge to women's traditional roles, but the idea of women making a career in crime also played a part. Exponents of law enforcement have always needed the idea of the professional criminal, or the criminal under-class, and the idea of professional *women* criminals suggests something at once dangerous and exciting.

Work on the periodic fluctuations of crime in the early modern period is still at rather an early stage. However, it is already clear that, at least in the south of England, rising property offences were associated with high grain prices until the Civil War, during which offences declined, partly because the courts were not operating properly. Property offences then stayed low after the Restoration. In the eighteenth century, homicides declined while property crimes increased, though with very marked declines during periods of war and a corresponding rise with the return of peace. According to the very limited evidence available on petty crime, there was a shift in the late sixteenth and early seventeenth centuries away from using the lower courts to prosecute crimes of violence against persons, towards using them to enforce regulations concerning personal conduct and commercial activity. It is difficult to tell whether this marks a change in behaviour or a change of attitude towards court prosecutions, with other means being used to settle disputes that had flared up into violence. Gender divisions in these statistics are highly tentative, often because the samples are very small.

---

[1] Quoted from an anonymous life in Thomas Middleton and Thomas Dekker, *The Roaring Girl*, ed. Andor Gomme, Ernest Benn, 1976, Introduction, p. xiv.

Victims

In east Sussex in the seventeenth century 11 per cent of all victims of crime were women and the number of women victims exceeded the number of women perpetrators. We have already seen that women were likely to be the victims of bewitching and of accusations of witchcraft and sexual misconduct. Many of the victims of burglary were women, often widows. For example, a sixteenth-century Essex shoemaker stole from a widow's house goods worth £2 2s., consisting of a black frieze dress, two red petticoats, a pair of flax sheets, a double rail, a headkerchief, five linen neckerchiefs, a pair of silver gilt buckles, a couple of other small items and 9s. in cash. Petty thefts were also often from women: washing, small sums of money and small household goods all appear in the records as being the property of women. Women were also often the victims of more serious thefts: 17 per cent of those who brought cases of burglary to the East Sussex courts in the seventeenth century were women, all widows. But most startling is the fact that women were 50 per cent of all the East Sussex murder victims. In the eighteenth century there was a noticeable decline in prosecutions for killing servants, but a marked rise in domestic violence, especially by husbands against wives.

Women were the usual victims of rape, a charge rarely brought, and difficult of securing a conviction. Of twenty-six cases brought in late-sixteenth-century Essex, sixteen resulted in acquittals. A good many cases were masters raping servants, and there were surprisingly large numbers of clergymen among the accused. Rape went to the assizes because it was a felony. Cases were generally in this form: John Gouldthwaite of Kelvedon, Essex, was presented in 1590 because he 'hath committed fornication with one Joan Summerson . . . as she hath confessed before the justice and the constable, vehemently against her will'. Indecent assault seems to have come up even more rarely than rape. Indecent conduct was often treated as the result of drink rather than as an attempt to victimize women. In 1581 John Harris of Layer Breton, Essex, 'behaved himself very disorderly by putting forth his privities'. His defence was that he lost 6d. and undid his breeches to show that the coin was not hidden there. In 1590 Henry Abbot of Earls Colne, Essex, 'in his drunkenness said that his privities or prick was longer by 4 inches than one Clerke there'. In Oxfordshire in 1584, Henry White of North Stoke was charged with the misdemeanour of running after maidens in the churchyard. There were also sexual assaults on children by men: in late-sixteenth-century Middlesex, children as young as three years of age were involved.

Accusers, Witnesses and Jurors

Women had a role in the courts other than that of the accused or the defendant: they appeared frequently as accusers and as witnesses. A considerable number of prosecutions were initiated by women, especially in the eighteenth century. The largest numbers of prosecutions initiated by women were in urban areas, and they increased between the mid-seventeenth century and the early eighteenth century. Married women could not by themselves initiate a prosecution, but there seem to have been means by which they could circumvent this restriction, and they were more likely to initiate proceedings if they worked outside the household. The majority of female-initiated prosecutions in eighteenth-century Middlesex were concerned with keeping the peace rather than with theft. It is possible that this form of action was replacing the defamation suit as a way of resolving conflicts between women. Few property prosecutions were initiated by women, especially in the countryside. It is clear that women's familiarity with the courts and their procedures was much greater in the town than in the country; urban women were more independent and there were fewer informal mechanisms for arbitration. However, it is also clear that women were taken less seriously in the courts than men. Many of the cases they brought were thrown out, though this was more likely to happen in the higher courts than in the lower.

Women often appear in cases as witnesses, and as with indictments, they were taken less seriously than men. The testimony of a man was often preferred to that of a woman. Women appeared more as witnesses or deponents in the church courts than in the common law courts, and there was a much higher proportion of women deponents in the church courts in London than in other dioceses. Almost half of the deponents in the London and Middlesex church courts in the period 1560–1700 were women, compared with about 17–20 per cent in other dioceses where the population was predominantly rural. The majority of these women came from the middling ranks of society and were somewhat younger than most of the male deponents, providing further evidence that women were more familiar with the law and its workings in urban areas than in rural.

All lawyers, magistrates, judges and clerks were men, as were nearly all of those who enforced the law: parish constables, sheriffs and churchwardens, none of whom was full-time or professional. Women were never in a position to apply the law to others or to decide upon or carry out punishments. They did not sit on the bench or serve as jurors. However, they were important in the juries of matrons which were called to assess whether a woman under a capital sentence was pregnant (because if she was, the sentence had to be deferred). Such juries also looked for witches' marks, attested whether women accused of infanticide had recently been pregnant, and examined women in annulment cases where it was alleged that the husband was impotent or that the marriage had not been consummated. Courts were empowered to call a jury of matrons, twelve married women who elected their own forematron, whose job it was to determine whether a woman was pregnant.

Their judgements themselves produced further litigation, particularly in relation to cases of inheritance. Medical uncertainty about the duration of pregnancy caused many problems. Generally, the courts favoured the supposition that a child born to a woman whose husband had died within about ten or eleven months of the child's birth was his child. Edward Andrews died of the plague on 23 March 1610 after only a day's illness and on 5 January 1611 (41 weeks and 2 days later) a daughter was born to his wife. During the last month of her pregnancy she was harassed by her father-in-law, being finally turned out on to the street whence she was rescued by a kindly woman when her labour began. Eleven years later Mrs Andrews and her daughter were prosecuted by her husband's family on the grounds that the child was illegitimate and that they had inherited the husband's estate under false pretences; the husband's family lost.

'Social Crime'

This apparently tautological term is used to describe contraventions of the law where the law breaker had some motive other than simple greed. There is an implication that such crimes were committed by normally law-abiding people who had been forced to crime by some external circumstance. There was certainly an association made in the early modern period between property crime, poverty and social dislocation. Such crimes were most commonly associated with men, and in particular men who had moved into the towns, lost their occupations or left the army. In several counties in the late sixteenth century, increases in property crime largely coincided with periods of scarcity and an increase in food prices. In 1650 the Earl of Leicester observed that he found 'some of these felons to be very civil men and say that if they could have had any reasonable subsistence by friends or otherwise they should never have taken such necessitous courses for support of their wives and families'.[1] Longer-term data indicate that rises in prices are associated with an increase in the number of property crimes.

The rise in vagrancy and in the awareness of vagrancy in the late sixteenth century affected women. In 1572 two women were sentenced at the Middlesex sessions to be hanged as incorrigible vagrants; one was reprieved because she was pregnant, but the other was executed. A third woman was executed in 1582. These women had presumably cut adrift from their families and were able to scrape by on casual prostitution conducted from alehouses.

This kind of crime was an essentially individualistic activity, but there were larger-scale demonstrations against food shortages and high prices in which women played a noticeable part, and which were treated with some severity by the authorities lest public order get out of hand. It is possible to argue that demonstrations such as grain riots were essentially political actions, and that this is another example of women expressing political views by subversive means. However, there are certain features to many of these riots which suggest that this is not a sufficient explanation and that, while women's participation is important, it was more a measure of the severity of the situation and the desperate need for a remedy than an explicitly political demonstration.

The study of demonstrations in the early modern period has been much influenced by E. P. Thompson's work on the moral economy of the eighteenth-century crowd, which draws attention to the political action of the disenfranchised. He argued that the riots which took place in the eighteenth century, chiefly provoked by economic hardship and rising grain prices, were not simply spontaneous combustions of anger, but were a form of popular political action motivated by a strong sense that the rioters were defending traditional rights or customs. Where violence was directed against individuals or property, it was aimed at people or things implicated in the violation of rights: for example, corn merchants, ships or corn waggons. He noticed that riots were commonly initiated by women, and that the leaders were usually in

---

[1] Historical Manuscripts Commission, De L'Isle and Dudley MSS, VI, 590.

trades which worked in groups, like colliers and road menders, rather than agricultural labourers: the labourers were participants rather than leaders. Among the Gloucestershire food rioters in 1766, it was mainly men who were indicted for creating a disturbance, while women were charged with theft afterwards. In Ruscombe, Gloucestershire, in 1766 the servant of a Stroud baker was attacked by a crowd of women and the sixteen dozen loaves she was carrying were seized. Most of those charged with the theft of 6 tons of cheese from an Alderley farmer and cheese factor were women in the same disturbances.

The prominence of women is ascribed by Thompson to two factors: firstly, that women, both as customers and as small-scale retailers, were more sensitive than men to food shortages and price rises; and second, that they were less afraid of the law and its repercussions thanks to the widespread belief that women could not be held responsible in law for their actions. Women might lead the rioters, as they did in Northampton in 1693 when they advanced on the market with knives in their belts, or at Stockton, Co. Durham in 1740 when the mob was raised by a woman with a stick and a horn. The years 1739 and 1740 experienced particularly widespread food riots because of the very high price of grain. Thompson suggests that women most frequently initiated spontaneous demonstrations, and that those which were organized and advertised beforehand were prepared by men.

Other historians, influenced by Thompson, have carried his thesis back into the sixteenth and seventeenth centuries. They highlight the local character of demonstrations and the fact that they were a response to local and immediate conditions un-enlightened by any grand theory.

In the late sixteenth and early seventeenth centuries, there were a number of food riots, mainly in cloth-manufacturing areas suffering from recession. Attacks were often directed against the carriers of grain at ports and markets. In 1605 there was a series of small disturbances in the Medway ports in Kent; all except one involved no more than fifteen people. The riot at Chatham, led by women, involved over a hundred people. In 1608 a grain ship at Southampton was boarded and unloaded by a party of women.

The riots of the sixteenth and seventeenth centuries were similar to those of the eighteenth century in having a common target, those whose trade was in grain. But they differed in that sixteenth-century assaults were most often against the carriers of grain. The eighteenth-century crowd had become more sophisticated and, seeing that middlemen might use any increase in grain prices as an opportunity for profiteering, most often attacked middlemen like millers and bakers, who bought grain and passed on the increased price to their customers. Certainly the eighteenth-century Oxfordshire crowd conforms to this pattern. In 1693 poor women in Oxford market clamoured at the price of corn, and pelted millers, mealmen and bakers with stones. In 1713 at Burford in Oxfordshire, five loads of wheat were stolen from a maltster, and five men and two women were charged with the theft. In the 1757 riots at Bicester, Oxfordshire, four women and five men were charged, two with robbing a waggon. In 1766 men, women and children raided Holywell mill, near Oxford, removed 120 sacks of flour and distributed it at Carfax.

Land and its disposition could provoke furious demonstrations. Both enclosure of common land and the drainage of the fens prompted riots, some of them involving large numbers of people. Like grain riots these were demonstrations about something that immediately affected the livelihoods of the local populace. Enclosure riots contained an element of challenge to the gentry, who were the chief enclosers. In a number of sixteenth-century riots, women were the principal participants: at Giggleswick, Yorkshire, in 1537 400 people, mainly women and children, took part in three riots against the Earl of Cumberland's enclosures of common land.

Women were prominent in the riots against the drainage and enclosure of the fens in the seventeenth century, though the gentry played an important part in opposing as well as proposing fen drainage schemes. At Soham, Cambridgeshire, in 1632–3, women took part in demonstrations against Sir Robert Heath's attempt to enclose part of the common land in exchange for turning over a larger area of poorer land to common use. Anne Dobbs, one of the rioters, was held in Cambridge gaol until she agreed to give information about the instigators of the riot. Fenland protestors were not only from the lesser sort: Lady Dymock lent her support to an attack on fenland drainers in Parliament. The dowager Countess of Exeter was, by contrast, a landlord enthusiastic about fen drainage schemes. Women were to be found on both sides when, in 1685, Mrs Sarah Reading and two other wives pelted objectors to her husband's enclosures with stones while a number of women took part in an attack on the Readings' house. Other demonstrations took place against cutting down trees and mining, on the grounds that these jeopardized ancient common rights. In the early seventeenth century, Stephen Proctor's Nidderdale miners were stoned by women carrying knives and led by 'Captain Dorothy'.

The prominence of women owed something to the continued and widespread belief that women could not be held responsible for their actions, despite the court of Star Chamber's judgement of 1605 to the contrary. In 1642 five women were indicted at the Salisbury assizes for riot in breaking and entering the close of John Marvin at Knoyle, Wiltshire, and tearing down hedges and levelling ditches. They were bound over to good behaviour until the next assize. The women who in 1608 broke down hedges and fences at Waddingham, Lincolnshire, were prosecuted for assault, and they and their husbands for riot. This suggests that the lawyers' view was that women were responsible, and so were their husbands even if they had not actively participated themselves. The fifteen women who dug up fences and hedges by night at Dunchurch, Warwickshire, in 1659 were prosecuted with their husbands, fathers and masters, despite the women's assertion that their menfolk had not put them up to it. An important reason for joining husbands, fathers and masters in the action was to ensure that fines and damages could be exacted. Husbands were liable for the payment of fines and recognizances (sums of money paid into court to guarantee the accused's appearance at a future date).

Punishment

During the earlier part of the period there were still a good many ancient manorial courts which dealt with minor public order offences. The kinds of sentence they were able to impose upon women were the cucking and ducking stools, stocks, the pillory and the tumbrel. Church courts might use other methods of shame, such as public admissions of fault. The secular courts might impose sentences of whipping, walking behind a cart, or cutting off a woman's hair. The intention of these punishments was deterrent and retributive. Despite the wide variety of punishments open to the courts to use, there is little evidence of many of them actually being used. Whipping and branding were quite commonly used in the seventeenth century, and the use of brutal public punishments increased in the eighteenth century.

The classification of crimes as capital was enlarged in both the sixteenth and the eighteenth centuries. In 1689 fifty offences were classed as capital crimes, and there were more than two hundred by the end of the eighteenth century. However, the use of legal discretion in the application of punishments, especially for felonies, was very great. Many property crimes were capital crimes, but few resulted in the execution of a person found guilty. When offences like pickpocketing and shoplifting were removed from benefit of clergy (a means by which convicted felons might be exempted from the death penalty), there was significant under-reporting.

Men might claim benefit of clergy to escape hanging, but it was unusual for a woman to do so; what was much more usual was for women to claim that they were pregnant. It was a requirement that a woman sentenced to death but adjudged pregnant by a jury of matrons must have her sentence deferred until the child was born; in fact it is doubtful that many of these women were subsequently executed. The figures for the home circuit, the most populous judicial region of England, for 1559–1625 show that of 1,624 women accused of felony, 44 per cent were convicted and a third of those convicted claimed pregnancy and a third were executed. In 1550 Alice Cowland of Tottenham in Middlesex was pardoned after pleading pregnancy, having pleaded guilty to the theft of goods worth about £2. In the period 1663–94 at the Surrey assizes, thirty women were sentenced to death, twenty-two were pardoned and eleven women pleaded pregnancy. Spinsters were more likely than married women to be charged with felonies, but were also more likely to receive a sympathetic sentence. It was unusual for a spinster to be executed at all except for the crime of infanticide. So not only was there a low conviction rate for capital crimes, but there was also a low rate of executions being carried out.

Punishments were also affected by the persistence with which the offender had offended and the need of the culprit. The crime was mitigated if something was stolen for use rather than resale, especially if it was food. Women's thefts were generally of articles of small value; the courts would give them the arbitrary value of less than a shilling, making the offence petty larceny, which did not carry a death penalty, rather than grand larceny, which did. There seems to have been some distaste, too, for brutal public deaths of women. Women found guilty of murdering their husbands were actually guilty of a species of treason which carried the penalty of being burned at the stake, but it was very unusual for this actually to be carried out. The pressing to death of Margaret Clitherow in 1586 for aiding Catholic priests was considered to have been politically inept because of the brutality of the punishment.

Transportation began to be used in the late seventeenth century. By the early eighteenth century, more people were being transported than executed and capital sentences were often commuted to transportation. However, there were increasingly strong protests from America against transportation and it was unpopular among convicts. Women at Newgate were famous for smashing up their cells before they were taken away. A smaller proportion of women was transported than of men.

For much of the period 1500–1760, people were not sentenced to terms in prison. Prisons were chiefly used for detaining people awaiting criminal trial, for debtors, and occasionally for people who were too dangerous to let out. Trials usually took place within a few weeks, and capital sentences were carried out within a few days. Prisoners were allowed to wander about during the day and had some access to visitors. Gaolers might admit prostitutes for a fee. In smaller prisons women and men were not segregated, though at Newgate some attempts were made to keep them apart. There were about 200–300 women at Newgate in the mid-eighteenth century, about half of the number of men. The reforms of the eighteenth century introduced separate quarters and work for prisoners; women might be set to work on laundry while men picked oakum. The prison population of women rose towards the end of the eighteenth century. Prisons were run as private enterprises and more than one was actually run by a woman.

Bridewells, or houses of correction, were established in the sixteenth century to deal with the vagrancy problem; the first one was in London and others soon followed in various provincial towns. Inmates might be released by expressing penitence and a desire to enter service, but they were required to find someone who would employ them. Bridewells were intended for the destitute and tended to be used for people who were seen as a social problem, like unmarried mothers and persistent drunks, rather than for criminals, though they were increasingly used in the eighteenth century for people who had committed mis-demeanours. The prison population of women was small, but it was common for women to be sentenced to short terms in the Bridewell, the usual term being between one and fifteen days. On 7 December 1655 Goody Pywell was released from the Coventry Bridewell, where she had been sent on 30 November for 'living idly', because her legs had so swelled up that she could not work.

Two acts which were progressively decriminalized between the sixteenth and the eighteenth centuries were infanticide and suicide. Infanticide was a felony carrying the death penalty, but it became increasingly unusual for women to be found guilty. The number of prosecutions declined after the requirement from the early eighteenth century that evidence be produced that the baby had been born alive. Juries were more likely to be lenient to unmarried women charged with infanticide than to married women, though married women made up a much smaller number of the accused. The plea of insanity was more readily accepted too; there was an increasing recognition that a newly delivered women might be in an altered psychological state. Suicide was technically a felony, but it became increasingly usual for coroners' courts to find that the person took her own life while insane. In sixteenth-century Nottinghamshire most suicides were declared felonies, but in north Wiltshire in the mid-eighteenth century for every verdict that a suicide was a *felo de se*, there were eight of lunacy. There seems to have been a real transformation in sensibility, treating behaviour which could result in such unnatural deaths as madness rather than crime. How this squares with the increase in brutal public punishments is difficult to say, unless we see both as manifestations of a belief that individuals, where they are responsible for their own actions, are fully responsible, which required an enlargement of the definition of 'not responsible'.

For some years the orthodoxy among historians of crime has been that the early modern period saw a transition from a society in which violence most preoccupied the law enforcement officers to one in which property crime was their major concern, and that this epitomized the transition from medieval to modern society. Recent work, notably by J. A. Sharpe and J. M. Beattie, has shown that in sixteenth- and seventeenth-century England violence and interpersonal relations remained very important. What we now await is an historian who can interpret these developments in the light of the obvious gender differences in criminality.

CHAPTER EIGHTEEN

Women in 1500, Women in 1760

My concerns in this book have been to show how women led their lives in the period 1500–1760 and what changes took place over that period. In contrast to a history of men over the same period, we see a reduction in the opportunities for women to work in different trades and a dimunition of their rights to hold office. Nevertheless, there were many ways in which women were able to exercise power. There were also many ways in which they were at the mercy of forces whose *raison d'être* was to protect the power of high-ranking men. There is a tension between, on the one hand, the view that women understood the system and resourcefully worked behind it to secure their own advantage and, on the other, the view that all women were simply part of a silent proletariat, the majority, oppressed, regardless of their class, by patriarchy. Until recently, women, with very few exceptions, were regarded as faceless and passive, the subjects of historical developments unleashed by men.

The historical developments unleashed by men which deserve particular consideration are the Reformation, the English Civil War and the start of industrialization. All of these are perceived, in conventional historiography, as developments which have fundamentally advanced the economic and social development of English society, often with the implication that this advance marked beneficial progress. It is no longer sufficient to argue that what was true for men was true for everyone. As we have seen, what benefited men did not universally improve women's circumstances. The developments which were a consequence of the Reformation, the Civil War and industrialization contributed in different ways to raising the status of the individual at the expense of the community.

Readers may feel that there has been inadequate discussion of patriarchy and the oppression of women by men and male-dominated institutions. The purpose of this book has been to explore what women were able to do, not what they were prevented from doing. Early modern England was not a golden age for women, though their position deteriorated as their opportunities to win self-respect by their own actions declined. The community of late medieval society was patriarchal, but it was a community in which women were as much participants as men, though in different terms from men. The replacement of the community by the family and the individual made patriarchal authority much more immediate. To be a good wife became the apogee of feminine achievement. The process of breaking down the old community was not painless: the rise and decline of witchcraft prosecutions, largely a female offence, may be seen in this context. The elevation of individual values above community values might have liberated men, but it certainly restricted women.

Better-off women were increasingly confined to the home. The great freedom of the merchant wives of London in the sixteenth century was a matter for comment by foreign visitors. By the eighteenth century, public activity was much frowned upon except in the performing arts. Women's social contacts were limited and their economic activities restricted as the locus of trade and manufacture moved away from the household.

Urban work became less varied for women, as they came to be excluded from trades outside victualling and clothing; and the proletarianization of rural labour, by the increased specialization of agricultural work, meant that the lot of the rural poor was increasingly deprived and dreary. Agriculture during the seventeenth and eighteenth centuries came to depend on male wage labour, which became more specialized, while women's work, where it continued to exist, became more precarious. The increasing use of putting-out, industrial work which was done at home, made households more dependent upon the suppliers of the raw materials and the purchasers of the goods they manufactured (usually the same person). Demand for men's labour might keep them in the market place as freely negotiating individuals. For the majority of women, it simply increased their dependence on other people. They regulated their own time, but their lives were increasingly unaffected by the seasons. They had cash to buy food, but they could only afford the most monotonous of diets and were unable by the rhythm of their work to supplement their supplies by their own efforts in growing food or keeping livestock. Little wonder that work in the towns seemed attractive.

Likewise the development of individualism in personal relations did not necessarily benefit women. The economic necessity of marrying – that is, the lack of opportunity not to marry and the evident problems faced by women who did not marry – is surely as important as the freedom to choose a partner. But at least poor men and women in both town and country had a free choice, whereas parental influence remained strong in noble marriages because a large amount of property was at stake. For the growing number of people in between, freedom to choose a marriage partner may have increased, but this may have been the consequence of there simply being more people in the gentry and middling groups. For the majority of the population, family relationships were determined by proximity and mortality. It is hard to imagine how complete the break must have been when the only contact between relations was visits or oral messages because no one could read or write letters. Even among the literate, distance could make contact between parents and their adult sons and daughters infrequent, so that whole families were rarely present for the major rites of passage. People had the expectation that their spouses and close relations might die at any time, but this did not (in twentieth-century terms) diminish the affection they had for their close relations. What it did do was to equip them with a quality of resignation to accommodate loss.

Individualism is one of those concepts which did not seem to exist at the time, but which serves to describe a clutch of observable developments. These developments are generally perceived as beneficial because they favoured modernization, a process which was of much greater advantage to men than to women. Similarly, the greatest exponents of individualism as a useful historical concept have been men. I find it difficult to escape the conclusion that individualism is a concept devised by men to describe a process which freed men from ancient constraints, but which was of much less advantage to women. It liberated men from the restraints of the community and gave them the whole market place in which to operate; it deprived women of the support of the community while not substantially increasing their opportunities for personal choice and action.

It is fair to make the point that many of the women who appear on these pages do so only because their untypicality was remarked upon and that is why we know they existed. This is certainly the case with women like Mary Frith, the model for the Roaring Girl, or Mary Beale, the painter, or the Duchess of Portland and her collection, or Mrs Coade and her artificial stone works. But the lives of the women who worked as servants or retailers, or who took on apprentices after their husbands' death, or whose health and old age we are able to examine are not unusual. It is only by painstaking work in archives, looking at thousands of individual cases, that it is possible to develop a sense of what is typical. We are only at the beginning of that process now, and it is quite likely that within the next decade our view of what is typical will have discernibly shifted. This book is an account of progress so far.

Finally, what about the attitudes of men to women? I have deliberately said little about this because it is a field well covered in other books. It is also a subject which spawned a vast array of jokes, chiefly of the mother-in-law type, portraying women as quarrelsome, bossy, lascivious and deceitful, and marriage as a trap for men. The riddle form was much used in joke books, and such riddles as these could have come from virtually any century:

Question: What kind of garment do women most love to wear?
Answer: The breeches.
Question: What kind of water is the most deceitful?
Answer: A woman's tears.
Question: Why is the worst woman in the world good?
Answer: Because she's good for something, or good for nothing.

And the woman's reply:

> How wretched is a woman's fate,
> No happy change her fortune knows;
> Subject to man in every state,
> How can she then be free from woes?

Anon., *Woman's Hard Fate* (1733)[1]

---

[1] From *Eighteenth Century Women Poets*, ed. R. Lonsdale, Oxford University Press, 1989, p. 136.

Guide to Further Reading

Many of the works mentioned are informative on many subjects to do with women; in the interests of space, I have usually only mentioned works once.

Chapter 1   Introduction: Women and the Historians

There are a number of excellent and readily available books on early modern English social history: Joyce Youings, *Sixteenth Century England* (Penguin, 1984); Roy Porter, *English Society in the Eighteenth Century* (Penguin, 1982; revised edition, 1990); J. A. Sharpe, *Early Modern England: A Social History 1550–1760* (Edward Arnold, 1988); and Keith Wrightson, *English Society 1580–1680* (Hutchinson, 1982).

General works on the history of women are being produced in considerable numbers at the moment. In particular, Bonnie S. Anderson and Judith P. Zinsser, *A History of their Own: Women in Europe from Prehistory to the Present* (Penguin, 1989) is a thought-provoking work. Antonia Fraser, *The Weaker Vessel* (Weidenfeld and Nicolson, 1984) has details of the lives of many seventeenth-century English women.

Much of the recent work on women, not always explicitly on women but on more general and social and economic subjects, has appeared in articles in historical journals. Journals such as *Signs* and *The Feminist Review* which concentrate on women's studies carry little material about women in the early modern period. Women's history journals, such as the *Journal of Women's History* (Indiana University Press), *Women and Work: An Annual Review* (Sage) and *Women's History Review* (Triangle), contain more, but they are not always easy to obtain. Journals particularly useful for the discussion of broader historical subjects are the *Economic History Review*, *Social History*, *Continuity and Change* and the *Journal of Interdisciplinary History*. For the discussion of specific examples, *Local Population Studies*, *The Local Historian*, *Northern History*, *Southern History*, *Midland History* and *Family History* are useful. The myriad of county historical, archaeological and record society publications are invaluable.

See also the forthcoming guide to sources for the history of women by

Mary Prior, and on seventeenth-century women see the forthcoming book by Patricia Crawford and Sara Heller Mendelson.

Chapter 2 Gender, Class and Race

On social status, see Lawrence Stone, *The Crisis of the Aristocracy 1558–1641* (Oxford University Press, 1967), *The Family, Sex and Marriage 1500–1800* (Pelican, 1979) and, with Jeanne C. Fawtier Stone, *An Open Elite? England 1540–1880* (Oxford University Press, 1986), all abridged editions of longer scholarly works. On domestic servants, see D. A. Kent, 'Ubiquitous but invisible: female domestic servants in mid-eighteenth century London', *History Workshop Journal*, 28 (1989); on farm servants, see Ann Kussmaul, *Servants in Husbandry in Early Modern England* (Cambridge University Press, 1981).

There are many books which deal with attitudes to foreign peoples, but attitudes to foreign women have not so far attracted much attention; however, see Anne Laurence, 'The cradle to the grave: English observation of Irish social customs in the seventeenth century', *The Seventeenth Century*, 3 (1988) and Nicholas Canny, 'The permissive frontier: the problem of social control in English settlements in Ireland and Virginia 1550–1650' in K. Andrews, N. Canny and P. Hair (eds), *The Westward Enterprise* (Wayne State University Press, 1979). On blacks in England, see Peter Fryer, *Staying Power: The History of Black People in Britain* (Pluto Press, 1984); J. Walvin, *Black and White: The Negro and English Society 1555–1945* (Allen Lane, 1975); and *The Black Presence: A Documentary History of the Negro in England 1555–1860* (Orbach and Chambers, 1971). On Jews, see V. Lipman, 'Sephardi and other Jewish immigrants in England in the eighteenth century' in *Migration and Settlement. Proceedings of the Anglo-Jewish Historical Conference 1970*, Jewish Historical Society of England (1971). The admirable publications of the Huguenot Society of London are a rich mine of material, in particular, see Irene Scouloudi (ed.), *Huguenots in Britain and their French Background 1550–1800: Contributions to the Historical Conference of the Huguenot Society of London* (Macmillan, 1987) and Robin D. Gwynn (ed.), *A Calendar of the Letterbooks of the French Church of London 1643–1659*, Huguenot Society of London, Quarto Series 54 (1979).

Chapter 3 Women in the Population

E. A. Wrigley and R. S. Schofield, *The Population History of England 1541–1871* (Edward Arnold, 1981; new edition Cambridge University Press, 1989) has set the bench marks for the study of historical demography in the early modern period.

On the effect of food shortages on the population, see Andrew Appleby, *Famine in Tudor and Stuart England* (Liverpool University Press, 1978) and R. B. Outhwaite, 'Dearth and government intervention in English grain markets 1590–1700', *Economic History Review*, 2nd Series, 34 (1981). On ageing, see M. Pelling and R. M. Smith (eds), *Life, Death and the Elderly*

(Routledge, 1991) and P. Laslett, *A Fresh Map of Life: The Emergence of the Third Age* (Weidenfeld and Nicolson, 1989). On infant mortality, see R. Wall, 'Inferring differential neglect of females from mortality data' and Roger Finlay, 'Differential child mortality in pre-industrial England: the example of Cartmel, Cumbria 1600–1750', both in *Annales de Démographie Historique* (1981).

On marriage statistics, see Jack Goody, *The Development of the Family and Marriage in Europe* (Cambridge University Press, 1983). On bastardy, see P. Laslett, *Family Life and Illicit Love* (Cambridge University Press, 1977). Pamela Sharpe, 'Literally spinsters: a new interpretation of local economy and demography in Colyton in the seventeenth and eighteenth centuries', *Economic History Review*, 44 (1991) sets spinsters in a social context; see also the *Journal of Family History*, 9 (1984), which is devoted to spinsters.

On households and their composition, see P. Laslett (ed.), *Household and Family in Past Time* (Cambridge University Press, 1972) and Michael Anderson, 'The emergence of the modern life cycle in Britain', *Social History*, 10 (1985), and Marjorie McIntosh, 'Servants and the household unit in an Elizabethan English community', *Journal of Family History*, 9 (1984).

On migration, see especially P. Clark and D. Souden (eds), *Migration and Society in Early Modern England* (Hutchinson, 1987); Peter Earle, 'The female labour market in London in the late seventeenth and early eighteenth centuries', *Economic History Review*, 2nd series, 42 (1989), and Ann Kussmaul, 'The ambiguous mobility of farm servants', *Economic History Review*, 2nd series, 34 (1981). On vagrants, see A. L. Beier, *Masterless Men* (Methuen, 1985).

Chapter 4   Marriage

On marriage in general, see J. R. Gillis, *For Better, for Worse* (Oxford University Press, 1985) and Lawrence Stone, *The Family, Sex and Marriage 1500–1800* (Pelican, 1979). On the reform of marriage, see Eric Josef Carlson, 'Marriage reform and the Elizabethan High Commission', *Sixteenth Century Journal*, 21 (1990) and C. Durston, ' "Unhallowed wedlocks": the regulation of marriage during the English Revolution', *Historical Journal*, 31 (1988).

On courtship and popular marriage customs, see Martin Ingram, *Church Courts, Sex and Marriage in England 1570–1640* (Cambridge University Press, 1987); J. A. Sharpe, 'Plebeian marriage in Stuart England' *Transactions of the Royal Historical Society* 5th series, 36 (1986); and G. R. Quaife, *Wanton Wenches and Wayward Wives: Peasants and Illicit Sex in Seventeenth Century England* (Croom Helm, 1977). On seasonality of marriage, see Ann Kussmaul, 'Time and space, hoof and grain: the seasonality of marriage in England', *Journal of Interdisciplinary History*, 15 (1984) and David Cressy, 'The seasonality of marriage in Old and New England', *Journal of Interdisciplinary History*, 16 (1985).

On marriage breakdown, see Roderick Phillips's sensitive study,

Untying the Knot (Cambridge University Press, 1991), an abridged version of his *Putting Asunder: A History of Divorce in Western Society* (Cambridge University Press, 1988), and Lawrence Stone, *The Road to Divorce: England 1530–1987* (Oxford University Press, 1990) and the succeeding volumes *Uncertain Unions* (Oxford University Press, 1992) and *Broken Lives* (Oxford University Press, 1993). On separation, see D. A. Kent, ' "Gone for a soldier": family breakdown and the demography of desertion in a London parish 1750–91', *Local Population Studies*, 45 (1990) and Pamela Sharpe, 'Marital separation in the eighteenth and early nineteenth centuries', *Local Population Studies*, 45 (1990). On wife-sales, see S. P. Meneffe, *Wives for Sale* (Blackwell, 1981).

On remarriage, see Barbara J. Todd, 'The remarrying widow: a stereotype reconsidered', in Mary Prior (ed.), *Women in English Society 1500–1800* (Methuen, 1985) and Jeremy Boulton, 'London widowhood revisited: the decline of female remarriage in the seventeenth and early eighteenth centuries', *Continuity and Change*, 5 (1990).

On matrimonial offences, see Keith Thomas, 'The double standard', *Journal of the History of Ideas*, 20 (1959) and 'The Puritans and adultery: the Act of 1650 reconsidered', in D. Pennington and K. Thomas (eds), *Puritans and Revolutionaries* (Oxford University Press, 1978).

On marriage and the economic changes of the eighteenth century, see K. D. M. Snell, 'Agricultural seasonal unemployment, the standard of living, and women's work in the south and east 1690–1860', *Economic History Review*, 2nd series, 34 (1981) and David Levine, *Family Formation in an Age of Nascent Capitalism* (Academic Press, 1977).

Chapter 5   Women and Sex

On age of menarche, see P. Laslett, 'Age at menarche in Europe since the eighteenth century', *Journal of Interdisciplinary History*, 2 (1971–2) and P. Crawford, 'Attitudes to menstruation in seventeenth-century England', *Past and Present*, 91 (1981). On the nature of fertility, see Angus McLaren, *Reproductive Rituals: The Perception of Fertility in England from the Sixteenth to the Nineteenth Century* (Methuen, 1984). For the demographer's approach, see E. A. Wrigley, 'Family limitation in pre-industrial England', *Economic History Review*, 2nd series, 19 (1966); and R. B. Morrow, 'Family limitation in pre-industrial England: a reappraisal' and E. A. Wrigley, 'Marital fertility in seventeenth century Colyton: a note', both in *Economic History Review*, 2nd series 31 (1978). See also, Dorothy McLaren, 'Marital fertility and lactation 1570–1720', in Mary Prior (ed.), *Women in English Society 1500–1800* (Methuen, 1985) and Linda Campbell, 'Wetnurses in early modern England: some evidence from the Townshend archive', *Medical History*, 33 (1989).

On attitudes to sex, see Margaret Spufford, *Small Books and Pleasant Histories* (Cambridge University Press, 1981); J. A. Sharpe, *Defamation and Sexual Slander in Early Modern England: the Church Courts at York*, Borthwick Papers, 58 (1980); R. Davenport-Hines, *Sex, Death and Punishment* (Collins,

1990); and Paul-Gabriel Boucé (ed.), *Sexuality in Eighteenth Century Britain* (Manchester University Press, 1982). On same-sex relations, see A. Bray, *Homosexuality in Renaissance England*, 2nd edn (Gay Men's Press, 1988) and Martin Bauml Duberman, Martha Vicinus and George Chauncey, Jr (eds), *Hidden from History: Reclaiming the Gay and Lesbian Past* (Penguin, 1991). On prostitution, see O. Hufton, 'Women without men: widows and spinsters in Britain and France in the eighteenth century', *Journal of Family History*, 9 (1984).

Chapter 6   Motherhood, Family and Friends

On pregnancy and childbirth in general, see Audrey Eccles, *Obstetrics and Gynaecology in Tudor and Stuart England* (Croom Helm, 1982) and the many good essays in Valerie Fildes (ed.), *Women as Mothers in Pre-Industrial England* (Routledge, 1990). On attitudes to motherhood, see P. Crawford, 'Attitudes to pregnancy from a woman's spiritual diary 1687–8', *Local Population Studies*, 21 (1978) and Cynthia Huff, 'Chronicles of confinement: reactions to childbirth in British women's diaries', *Women's Studies International Forum*, 10 (1987). On churching, see William Coster, 'Purity, profanity and Puritanism: the churching of women 1500–1700', in W. Sheils and D. Wood (eds), *Women in the Church*, Studies in Church History, 27 (1990).

On risks to the mother, see R. Schofield, 'Did the mothers really die?', in L. Bonfield, R. Smith and K. Wrightson (eds), *The World We Have Gained* (Blackwell, 1986) and Alain Bideau, 'Accouchement "naturel" et accouchement à "haut risque" ', *Annales de Démographie Historique* (1981). On psychological disorders, see M. Macdonald, *Mystical Bedlam: Madness, Anxiety and Healing in Seventeenth Century England* (Cambridge University Press, 1981); A. Laurence, 'Women's psychological disorders in seventeenth-century Britain', in A. Angerman, G. Binnema *et al.* (eds), *Current Issues in Women's History* (Routledge, 1989); and Phyllis R. Freeman, Carley Rees Bogard and Diane E. Sholomskas, 'Margery Kempe, a new theory: the inadequacy of hysteria and post-partum psychosis as diagnostic categories', *History of Psychiatry*, 1 (1990).

On illegitimacy, see P. Laslett, K. Oosterveen and R. M. Smith, *Bastardy and Its Comparative History* (Edward Arnold, 1980). On abandonment, see John Boswell, *The Kindness of Strangers: The Abandonment of Children from Late Antiquity to the Renaissance* (Penguin, 1991) and Otto Ulbricht, 'The debate about foundling hospitals: infanticide, illegitimacy and infant mortality rates', *Central European History*, 18 (1985). On infanticide, see P. Hoffer and N. Hull, *Murdering Mothers: Infanticide in England and New England 1558–1803* (New York University Press, 1981) and Keith Wrightson, 'Infanticide in earlier seventeenth century England', *Local Population Studies*, 15 (1975).

On care of the newborn, see P. Crawford, ' "The suckling child": adult attitudes to child care in the first years of life in seventeenth century England', *Continuity and Change*, 1 (1986)) and Valerie Fildes, 'The age of weaning in Britain 1500–1800', *Journal of Biosocial Science*, 14 (1982) and *Wet Nursing: A History from Antiquity to the Present* (Blackwell, 1988).

On family relationships, see Ralph Houlbrooke, *The English Family 1450–1700* (Longman, 1984) and Linda Pollock, *Forgotten Children: Parent–Child Relations from 1500 to 1900* (Cambridge University Press, 1983); see also their useful collections of documents about family life: Ralph Houlbrooke, *English Family Life 1576–1716* (Blackwell, 1988) and Linda Pollock, *Lasting Relationships: Parents and Children over Three Centuries* (Fourth Estate, 1987); and C. Durston, *The Family in the English Revolution* (Blackwell, 1989).

On affection, see Lawrence Stone's various works, especially *The Family, Sex and Marriage 1500–1800* (Pelican, 1979), and critiques such as Lois G. Schwoerer, 'Seventeenth-century Englishwomen engraved in stone', *Albion*, 16 (1984). See also Alan Macfarlane, *Marriage and Love in England 1300–1840* (Blackwell, 1986) and A. Laurence, 'Godly grief: individual responses to death in seventeenth-century Britain', in R. Houlbrooke (ed.), *Death, Ritual, and Bereavement* (Routledge, 1989). For the correspondence between a grandmother and her granddaughter, see Gladys Scott Thomson (ed.), *Letters of a Grandmother 1732–1735* (Cape, 1946).

Chapter 7   Health and Strength

On plague, see A. Appleby, 'The disappearance of plague: a continuing puzzle', *Economic History Review*, 2nd series, 33 (1980); and P. Slack, 'The disappearance of plague: an alternative view', *Economic History Review*, 2nd series, 34 (1981) and *The Impact of Plague in Tudor and Stuart England* (Routledge and Kegan Paul, 1985). On various diseases, see John H. Bayliss, 'Epidemiological considerations of the history of indigenous malaria in Britain', *Endeavour*, 9 (1986); Anne Hardy, 'Diagnosis, death and diet: the case of London 1750–1909', *Journal of Interdisciplinary History*, 18 (1988); and Alan Dyer, 'Epidemics of measles in a seventeenth century English town', *Local Population Studies*, 34 (1985).

On doctors and their patients, see F. Poynter and W. Bishop, 'A seventeenth century doctor and his patients: John Symcotts (1594–1662)', *Bedfordshire Historical Record Society*, 31 (1951); William G. Hall, 'A country general practitioner at work in Somerset, 1686–1706: John Westover of Wedmore', *The Local Historian*, 20 (1990); and L. M. Beier, *Sufferers and Healers: The Experience of Illness in Seventeenth Century England* (Routledge and Kegan Paul, 1987).

On psychological disorders, see H. C. Erik Midelfort, 'Madness and the problems of psychological history in the sixteenth century', *Sixteenth Century Journal*, 12 (1981) and Katherine E. Williams, 'Hysteria in seventeenth century case records and unpublished manuscripts', *History of Psychiatry*, 1 (1990). On suicide, see Michael Zell, 'Suicide in pre-industrial England', *Social History*, 11 (1986) and M. Macdonald and T. Murphy, *Sleepless Souls: Suicide in Early Modern England* (Clarendon Press, 1990).

On health and nutrition, see John Walter and R. Schofield (eds), *Famine, Disease and the Social Order* (Cambridge University Press, 1989) and the special issue of the *Journal of Interdisciplinary History* 14 (1983) on nutrition and history.

Chapters 8 and 9   Women's Livelihoods and Varieties of Work

On women's work in general, see the classic by Alice Clark, *Working Life of Women in the Seventeenth Century* (Routledge, 1919; new edition, Routledge and Kegan Paul, 1982). For a useful summary of the position of the debate, see Harriet Bradley, *Men's Work, Women's Work: A Sociological History of the Sexual Division of Labour* (Polity Press, 1989) and K. Honeyman and J. Goodman, 'Women's work, gender conflict and labour markets in Europe, 1500–1900', *Economic History Review*, 44 (1991); see also Lindsey Charles and Lorna Duffin (eds), *Women and Work in Pre-industrial England* (Croom Helm, 1985) and Bridget Hill, *Women, Work and Sexual Politics in Eighteenth Century England* (Blackwell, 1989).

On the structure of women's daily lives, see Barbara Hanawalt (ed.), *Women and Work in Pre-industrial Europe* (Indiana University Press, 1986) and *The Ties that Bound* (Oxford University Press, 1986). On starting work, see J. Dunlop and R. Denman, *English Apprenticeship and Child Labour: A History* (London, 1912) and K. D. M. Snell, *Annals of the Labouring Poor* (Cambridge University Press, 1985). On parish apprentices, see E. M. Hampson, *The Treatment of Poverty in Cambridgeshire 1597–1834* (Cambridge University Press, 1934). On apprentices in general, see Ilana Krausman Ben-Amos, 'Women apprentices in the trades and crafts of early modern Bristol'; Graham Mayhew, 'Life cycle service and the family unit in early modern Rye'; and Pamela Sharpe, 'Poor children as apprentices in Colyton 1598–1830', all in *Continuity and Change*, 6 (1991).

On tradeswomen in London, see S. Rappaport, *Worlds within Worlds: Structures of Life in Sixteenth Century London* (Cambridge University Press, 1989); J. Boulton, *Neighbourhood and Society: A London Suburb in the Seventeenth Century* (Cambridge University Press, 1987); and Peter Earle, *The Making of the English Middle Class: Business, Society and Family Life in London 1660–1730* (Methuen, 1989) and 'The female labour market in London in the late seventeenth and early eighteenth centuries', *Economic History Review*, 2nd series, 42 (1989). On provincial traders, see Mary Prior, 'Women and the urban economy', in Mary Prior (ed.), *Women in English Society 1500–1800* (Methuen, 1985); Diane Willen, 'Women in the public sphere in early modern England: the case of the urban working poor', *Sixteenth Century Journal*, 19 (1988); W. Thwaites, 'Women in the market place: Oxfordshire c.1690–1800', *Midland History*, 9 (1984) and Susan Wright, ' "Holding up half the sky": women and their occupations in eighteenth century Ludlow', *Midland History*, 14 (1989).

On agricultural work, see Ann Kussmaul, *Servants in Husbandry in Early Modern England* (Cambridge University Press, 1981) and *A General View of the Rural Economy of England 1538–1840* (Cambridge University Press, 1990). On the sexual division of labour in agriculture, see Michael Roberts, 'Sickles and scythes: women's work and men's work at harvest time',

History Workshop, 7 (1979); Peter King, 'Customary rights and women's earnings: the importance of gleaning to the labouring poor 1750–1850', Economic History Review, 44 (1991); and Gregory Clark, 'Yields per acre in English agriculture 1250–1860', Economic History Review, 44 (1991).

On manufacture and proto-industrialization, see Maxine Berg, The Age of Manufactures (Fontana, 1985). For particular instances, see R. Millward, 'The emergence of wage labour in early modern England', Explorations in Economic History, 18 (1981) and Pat Hudson, 'Proto-industrialisation: the case of the West Riding', History Workshop, 12 (1981). For the sceptic's view, see D. C. Coleman, 'Proto-industrialisation: a concept too many?', Economic History Review, 2nd series, 36 (1983).

On goldsmiths, see Ann Bennett, 'The goldsmiths of Church Lane, Hull, 1527–1784', Yorkshire Archaeological Journal, 60 (1988); Ann Bennett, 'The Mangies of Hull: a family of provincial goldsmiths', Yorkshire Archaeological Journal, 57 (1985); and Philippa Glanville and Jennifer Faulds Goldsborough, Women Silversmiths 1685–1845 (Thames and Hudson, 1990).

On retailing, see C. Dyer, 'The consumer and the market in the later middle ages', Economic History Review, 2nd series, 42 (1989). On credit, see B.A. Holderness, 'Credit in a rural community 1660–1800', Midland History, 3 (1975) and 'Credit in English rural society before the nineteenth century', Agricultural History Review, 24 (1976); see also Norman Jones, God and the Moneylenders: Usury and Law in Early Modern England (Blackwell, 1989). On domestic service, see J. Hecht, The Domestic Servant in Eighteenth Century England (Routledge and Kegan Paul, 1956; reprinted, 1980). On nursing, see Robert Dingwall, Anne Marie Rafferty and Charles Webster, An Introduction to the Social History of Nursing (Routledge, 1988). On wet-nurses, see Valerie Fildes, Wet Nursing (Blackwell, 1988) and Linda Campbell, 'Wetnurses in early modern England: some evidence from the Townshend archive', Medical History, 33 (1989). On women in the performing arts, see E. Howe, The First English Actresses: Women and Drama 1660–1700 (Cambridge University Press, 1992) and Jacqueline Pearson, The Prostituted Muse: Images of Women and Women Dramatists 1642–1737 (Harvester Wheatsheaf, 1988).

Chapter 10   Women and Material Culture

On women and their possessions, see Joan Thirsk, Economic Policy and Projects (Oxford University Press, 1978); Lorna Weatherill, 'A possession of one's own: women and consumer behaviour in England 1660–1740', Journal of British Studies, 25 (1986) and Consumer Behaviour and Material Culture in Britain 1660–1760 (Routledge, 1988); and Carol Shammas, The Pre-industrial Consumer in England and America (Clarendon Press, 1990). On clothing, see Margaret Spufford, The Great Reclothing of Rural England (Hambledon Press, 1984); Madeleine Ginsburg, 'The tailoring and dressmaking trades 1700–1850', Costume, 6 (1972); and Beverly Lemire,

'Developing consumerism and the ready-made trade in Britain 1750–1800', *Textile History*, 15 (1984).

On the second-hand market, see Madeleine Ginsburg, 'Rags to riches: the second-hand clothes trade 1700–1978', *Costume*, 40 (1980); and Beverly Lemire, 'Consumerism in pre-industrial and early industrial England: the trade in second-hand clothes', *Journal of British Studies*, 27 (1988) and 'The theft of clothes and popular consumerism in early modern England', *Journal of Social History*, 24 (1990).

On food, see S. Mennell, *All Kinds of Food* (Blackwell, 1985); Reay Tannahill, *Food in History* (Penguin, new ed, 1988); Peter Clark, 'The alehouse and the alternative society', in D. Pennington and K. Thomas, *Puritans and Revolutionaries* (Oxford University Press, 1978) and *The English Alehouse: A Social History* (Longman, 1983); and Lois W. Banner, 'Why women have not been great chefs', *South Atlantic Quarterly*, 72 (1973).

On buildings, see J. H. Bettey, 'Seventeenth century squatters' dwellings: some documentary evidence', *Vernacular Architecture*, 13 (1982) and Trevor Lummis and Jan Marsh, *The Woman's Domain* (Viking, 1990). An exciting work on how women used buildings is Alice T. Friedman, *House and Household in Elizabethan England: Wollaton Hall and the Willoughby Family* (University of Chicago Press, 1989); see also Mark Girouard, *Life in the English Country House* (Yale University Press, 1978) and Kate Mertes, *The English Noble Household 1260–1600* (Blackwell, 1988).

On women painters, see Germaine Greer, *The Obstacle Race* (Picador, 1981) and Iain Pears, *The Discovery of Painting* (Yale University Press, 1988). On Mrs Coade, see Alison Kelly, *Mrs Coade's Stone* (Self-Publishing Association and the Georgian Group, 1990).

Chapter 11 Literacy and Learning

On literacy, see David Cressy, *Literacy and the Social Order* (Cambridge University Press, 1980); Frank Davies, *Teaching Reading in Early England* (Pitman, 1973); and W. B. Stephens, 'Literacy in England, Scotland and Wales 1500–1900', *History of Education Quarterly*, 30 (1990); Margaret Spufford, 'First steps in literacy: the reading, and writing experiences of the humblest seventeenth-century autobiographers', *Social History*, 4 (1979).

On schools and women's education, see Dorothy Gardiner, *English Girlhood at School* (Oxford University Press, 1929) and *The Bedfordshire Schoolchild: Elementary Education before 1902*, ed. David Busby, Bedfordshire Historical Record Society, 67 (1988).

On women's reading matter, see Susan Hull, *Chaste, Silent and Obedient: English Books for Women 1475–1640* (Huntingdon Library, 1982); Kathryn Shevelow, *Women and Print Culture: The Construction of Femininity in the Early Periodical* (Routledge, 1989); and I. Rivers, *Books and their Readers in Eighteenth Century England* (Leicester University Press, 1982). On a woman printer, see Susan M. Allen, 'Jane Yetsweirt (1541–?): claiming her place', *Printing History*, 9 (1987).

There are many good anthologies of women's writing in the early modern period, though the seventeenth and eighteenth centuries are rather better served than the sixteenth century. See, for example, *Her Own Life: Autobiographical Writings by Seventeenth Century Englishwomen*, ed. E. Graham, H. Hinds, E. Hobby and H. Wilcox (Routledge, 1989).

On women and scholarship, see Myra Reynolds, *The Learned Lady in England 1650–1760* (Houghton Mifflin, 1920); J. Sowards, 'Erasmus and the education of women', *Sixteenth Century Journal*, 13 (1982); and Sylvia Harcstark Myers, *The Bluestocking Circle: Women, Friendship, and the Life of the Mind in Eighteenth Century England* (Oxford University Press, 1990).

Chapter 12   *Women's Religious Communities*

On pre-Reformation nuns, see Eileen Power, *Mediaeval English Nunneries c.1275–1535* (Cambridge University Press, 1922). On the process of the dissolution, see G. Baskerville, *English Monks and the Suppression of the Monasteries* (J. Cape, 1937). On what became of the nuns, see particularly the fascinating G. A. J. Hodgett (ed.), *The State of the Ex-Religious and Former Chantry Priests in the Diocese of Lincoln 1547–74: From the Returns in the Exchequer*, Lincolnshire Record Society, 53 (1959) and G. Baskerville, 'Married religious and pensioned religious in Norwich diocese 1555', *English Historical Review*, 48 (1933) and 55 (1940).

On the exiled English convents, see the many publications of the Catholic Record Society. On the Institute of the Blessed Virgin Mary, see Susan O'Brien, 'Women of the "English Catholic community": nuns and pupils at the Bar Convent, York, 1680–1790', *Monastic Studies*, I, Headstart History (n.d.).

On Protestant communities, see Bridget Hill, 'A refuge from men: the idea of a Protestant nunnery', *Past and Present*, 117 (1987).

Chapter 13   *The Practice of Christianity*

On women and religion in general, see W. Sheils and D. Wood (eds), *Women in the Church*, Studies in Church History, 27 (1990); Patricia Crawford, *Women and Religion in England 1500–1720* (Routledge, 1993); and R. L. Greaves (ed.), *Triumph over Silence: Women in Protestant History*, Contributions to the Study of Religion, 15 (Greenwood Press, 1985).

On women in the Reformation, see Susan C. Karant-Nunn, 'Continuity and change: some effects of the Reformation on the women of Zwickau', *Sixteenth Century Journal* (1982); R. Whiting, *The Blind Devotion of the People: Popular Religion and the English Reformation* (Cambridge University Press, 1989); P. Collinson, *The Birthpangs of Protestantism: Religion and Cultural Change in the Sixteenth and Seventeenth Centuries* (Macmillan, 1988); and C. Cross, 'Priests into ministers: the establishment of Protestant practice in the city of York 1530–1630', in P. N. Brooks (ed.), *Reformation Principle and Practice* (Scolar Press, 1980).

On Roman Catholics, see J. C. H. Aveling, *Catholic Recusancy in the Diocese of York 1558–1791*, Catholic Record Society (1970); Marie Rowlands, 'Recusant women 1560–1640', in Mary Prior (ed.), *Women in English Society 1500–1800* (Methuen, 1985); and E. S. Worral (ed.), *The Returns of Papists 1767*, 2 vols, Catholic Record Society (1980 and 1989).

On the established church, see Mary Prior, 'Reviled and crucified marriage: the position of Tudor bishops' wives', in Mary Prior (ed.), *Women in English Society 1500–1800* (Methuen, 1985); Patrick Collinson, *Godly People* (Hambledon Press, 1983); and S. J. Wright (ed.), *Parish, Church and People: Local Studies in Lay Religion 1350–1750* (Hutchinson, 1988). On lay patronage, see D. Hirschberg, 'The government and church patronage in England 1660–1760', *Journal of British Studies*, 20 (1980).

On women in the Civil War sects, see Claire Cross, ' "He-goats before the flocks": a note on the part played by women in the founding of some civil war churches', in G. J. Cumming and D. Baker (eds), *Popular Belief and Practice*, Studies in Church History, 8 (1972); Anne Laurence, 'A priesthood of she-believers: women and congregations in mid seventeenth century England', in W. Sheils and D. Wood (eds), *Women in the Church*, Studies in Church History, 27 (1990); Patricia Crawford, 'Historians, women and the civil war sects, 1640–1660', *Parergon*, new series, 8 (1988); and P. Mack, *Visionary Women* (University of California Press, 1992).

On Quaker women, see Elisabeth Potts Brown and Susan Mosher Stuard (eds), *Witnesses for Change: Quaker Women over Three Centuries* (Rutgers University Press, 1989). On women in early Methodism, see John Walsh, 'Methodism and the mob in the eighteenth century', in G. J. Cumming and D. Baker (eds), *Popular Belief and Practice*, Studies in Church History, 8 (1972); Wesley F. Smith, 'The women itinerant preachers of early Methodism', *Proceedings of the Wesley Historical Society*, 28 (1951); Deborah M. Valenze, *Prophetic Sons and Daughters: Female Preaching and Popular Religion in Industrial England* (Princeton University Press, 1985); and Earl Kent Brown, 'Women of Mr Wesley's Methodism', *Studies in Women and Religion*, 11 (Edward Mellen Press, 1983).

Chapter 14   Custom, Belief and Popular Culture

On popular culture, see Charles Phythian-Adams, 'Ceremony and the citizen: the communal year at Coventry 1450–1550', in P. Clark and P. Slack (eds), *Crisis and Order in English Towns 1500–1700* (Routledge and Kegan Paul, 1972); Barry Reay (ed.), *Popular Culture in Seventeenth Century England* (Croom Helm, 1985); M. Spufford, *Contrasting Communities: English Villagers in the Sixteenth and Seventeenth Centuries* (Cambridge University Press, 1974); D. Underdown, 'The taming of the scold: the enforcement of patriarchal authority in early modern England', in A. Fletcher and J. Stevenson (eds), *Order and Disorder in Early Modern England* (Cambridge University Press, 1985); and Joan R. Kent, ' "Folk justice" and royal justice in early seventeenth century England: a charivari in the Midlands', *Midland History*, 8 (1983).

There is a large literature dealing with different aspects of witchcraft, much of it inspired by H. Trevor-Roper's essay, *The European Witch-Craze of the Sixteenth and Seventeenth Centuries* (first published 1967; republished Penguin, 1969). Keith Thomas, *Religion and the Decline of Magic* (Weidenfeld and Nicolson, 1971; Penguin, 1973) and Alan Macfarlane, *Witchcraft in Tudor and Stuart England* (Routledge, 1970) are important contributions to the subject. For various parts of the country, see P. Rushton, 'Women, witchcraft and slander in early modern England: cases from the church courts of Durham 1580–1675', *Northern History*, 18 (1982); Annabel Gregory, 'Witchcraft, politics and good neighbourhood in early seventeent century Rye', *Past and Present*, 133 (1991); and J. A. Sharpe, *Witchcraft in Seventeenth Century Yorkshire: Accusations and Counter Measures*, Borthwick Papers, 81 (1992), his particularly helpful article, 'Witchcraft and women in seventeenth century England: some northern evidence', *Continuity and Change*, 6 (1991) and his forthcoming book on witchcraft. For a feminist view which adds little to the history, see Marianne Hester, 'The dynamics of male domination using the witch craze in the sixteenth and seventeenth century England as a case study', *Women's Studies International Forum*, 13 (1990) and *Lewd Women and Wicked Witches: A Study of the Dynamics of Male Domination* (Routledge, 1992.)

Chapter 15   Women, the Law and Property

The best recent article is Amy Louise Erickson, 'Common law versus common practice: the use of marriage settlements in early modern England', *Economic History Review*, 2nd series, 43 (1990). Strict settlement has generated a large literature, much of which has appeared in the *Economic History Review*. See, for example, Eileen Spring, 'Law and the theory of the affective family', *Albion*, 16 (1984); Lloyd Bonfield, 'Affective families, open elites and strict family settlement in early modern England', *Economic History Review*, 2nd series, 39 (1986); and Eileen Spring, 'The strict settlement: its role in family history', *Economic History Review*, 2nd series, 41 (1988).

On other aspects of women's property, see J. Broad, 'Gentry finances in the civil war: the case of the Buckinghamshire Verneys', *Economic History Review*, 2nd series, 32 (1979); Lawrence Stone and Jeanne C. Fawtier Stone, *An Open Elite? England 1540–1880* (Oxford University Press, 1986); E. A. Wrigley, 'Fertility strategy for the individual and the group', in C. Tilly (ed.), *Historical Studies of Changing Fertility* (Princeton University Press, 1978); S. J. Payling, 'Social mobility, demographic change, and landed society in late medieval England, *Economic History Review*, 45 (1992); and S. Staves, *Married Women's Separate Property in England 1660–1833* (Harvard University Press, 1990).

On women's wills, see Claire Cross, 'Northern women in the early modern period: the female testators of Hull and Leeds 1520–1650', *Yorkshire Archaeological Journal*, 59 (1987) and Mary Prior, 'Wives and wills

1558–1700', in J. Chartres and D. Hey (eds), *English Rural Society 1500–1800: Essays in Honour of Joan Thirsk* (Cambridge University Press, 1990).

Chapter 16   Women in Men's Worlds

On the general issues, see Susan Dwyer Amussen, *An Ordered Society: Gender and Class in Early Modern England* (Blackwell, 1988). On the family in political theory, see Gordon J. Schochet, *The Authoritarian Family and Political Attitudes in Seventeenth Century England* (Transaction Books, 1988).

On women's political action in the seventeenth century, see Patricia Higgins, 'The reactions of women with special reference to women petitioners', in B. Manning (ed.), *Politics, Religion and the English Civil War* (Edward Arnold, 1973); P. Crawford, 'The challenge to patriarchalism: how did the revolution affect women?', in J. Morrill (ed.), *Revolution and Restoration: England in the 1650s* (Collins and Brown, 1992); and T. Harris, *London Crowds in the Age of Charles II* (Cambridge University Press, 1987). On the later seventeenth century, see Charles Chenevix Trench, *The Western Rising: An Account of Monmouth's Rebellion* (Longman, 1969); Lois G. Schwoerer, 'Women and the Glorious Revolution', *Albion*, 18 (1986); and Lois G. Schwoerer (ed.), *The Revolution of 1688–1689: Changing Perspectives* (Cambridge University Press, 1992).

On women living as men, see Julie Wheelwright, *Amazons and Military Maids* (Pandora, 1989); and Dianne Dugaw, *Warrior Women and Popular Balladry 1650–1850* (Cambridge University Press, 1989) and *The Female Soldier; or, the Surprising Life and Adventures of Hannah Snell* (London, 1750), Augustan Reprint Society Publication, 257 (1989).

Chapter 17   Women and Crime

The best detailed study on crime is J. M. Beattie, *Crime and the Courts in England 1660–1800* (Clarendon Press, 1986). A good, more general work is J. A. Sharpe, *Crime in Early Modern England 1550–1750* (Longman, 1984). See also J. Cockburn (ed.), *Crime in England 1550–1800* (Methuen, 1977); R. Shoemaker, *Prosecution and Punishment: Petty Crime and the Law in London and Rural Middlesex* (Cambridge University Press, 1991); Cynthia B. Herrup, *The Common Peace* (Cambridge University Press, 1989); and Carol Z. Weiner, 'Sex-roles and crime in late Elizabethan Hertfordshire' and J. M. Beattie, 'Criminality of women in eighteenth century England', both in *Journal of Social History*, 8 (1975). On specific subjects in the history of crime, see J. A. Sharpe, 'Quantification and the history of crime in early modern England: problems and results', *Historical Social Research*, 15 (1990) and his *Defamation and Sexual Slander in Early Modern England: The Church Courts at York*, Borthwick Papers, 58 (1980); Thomas R. Forbes 'A jury of matrons', *Medical History*, 32 (1988); and P. Hair, 'Notes and queries: homicide, infanticide and child assault in late Tudor Middlesex', *Local Population Studies*, 9 (1972).

On 'social crime', see E. P. Thompson, 'The moral economy of the English crowd in the eighteenth century', *Past and Present*, 50 (1971); Adrian J. Randall, 'The Gloucestershire food riots of 1766', *Midland History*, 10 (1985); W. Thwaites, 'Women in the market place: Oxfordshire c.1690–1800', *Midland History*, 9 (1984); Roger B. Manning, *Village Revolts: Social Protest and Popular Disturbances in England 1509–1640* (Oxford University Press, 1988); Buchanan Sharp, *In Contempt of All Authority: Rural Artisans and Riot in the West of England 1586–1660* (University of California Press, 1980); and Keith Lindley, *Fenland Riots and the English Revolution* (Heinemann, 1982).

On punishment, see Margaret de Lacy, *Prison Reform in Lancashire 1700–1850: A Study in Local Administration*, Chetham Society (1986); C. Harding, Bill Hines, Richard Ireland and Philip Rawlings, *Imprisonment in England and Wales* (Croom Helm, 1985); and J. A. Sharpe, *Judicial Punishment in England* (Faber, 1990).

Index